Insane
and
Unseemly

John Saville

Insane
and
Unseemly

"Is it desirable to allow these insane and unseemly spectacles to continue?"
(Emmanuel Shinwell MP, June 1941)

Matador
9 De Montfort Mews
Leicester LE1 7FW, UK
Tel: (+44) 116 255 9311 / 9312
Email: books@troubador.co.uk
Web: www.troubador.co.uk/matador

ISBN 978 1848760 349

A Cataloguing-in-Publication (CIP) catalogue record for this book is available
from the British Library.

Mixed Sources
Product group from well-managed
forests and other controlled sources
www.fsc.org Cert no. TT-COC-2082
© 1996 Forest Stewardship Council

Typeset in 11.5pt Bembo by Troubador Publishing Ltd, Leicester, UK
Printed in the UK by The Cromwell Press Ltd, Trowbridge, Wilts, UK

Matador is an imprint of Troubador Publishing Ltd

CONTENTS

INTRODUCTION

Just after two minutes past five on Saturday, 1st September 1945 Bats Wing passed the post at Stockton, thirteenth and last in the Farndale Maiden Stakes, Division 2. Wartime racing was over at last. Early the following morning Japanese delegates would sign formal surrender documents aboard *USS Missouri*. Two days later there would be racing at York for the first time since August 1939, with the St Leger returning to Yorkshire. It would be the first midweek meeting away from Newmarket for more than four years. In the following weeks the cracks that had started to appear in the familiar pattern of World War Two racing would rapidly widen, with the whole structure crumbling as fixtures became more frequent and course after course reopened.

This would hardly have troubled the Stockton customers as they headed for the gates through the usual detritus of an afternoon's racing. Their thoughts would have been on the crowded bus or train home, tea, and then, perhaps, an evening at the cinema, the pub or listening to the radio. For most people the war was already over. It had finally ended on VJ Day, though the main prize had been the defeat of Germany three months earlier. If they were aware of it at all, the ceremony on the *Missouri* was only the last punctuation mark in a long and grim story.

It was different at Manchester on the same day of 1939. Racing had gone ahead for a last afternoon of unreal normality, though the

Germans were rampaging into Poland, the reserve and territorial forces had been called up, the Cabinet was in continuous session, children were being evacuated from cities in their tens of thousands and barrage balloons were starting to float skywards. As they left in the stifling heat of impending thunder, many in the crowd must have wondered when they would go racing again. Some perhaps wondered whether they would see another Saturday afternoon.

This book describes racing in Great Britain during the six years between those two first Saturdays of September. More than any other sport it had opponents who wanted to stop it. Some were sincere patriots who believed it was an unaffordable drain on resources, whilst others were puritan opportunists who hated racing on principle. It also had friends, sometimes in unexpected quarters, and there were neutrals determined to be fair and objective. There were slices of good luck and bad, defenders scored own goals and enemies overplayed their hands, but racing managed to carry on and survive until peace returned.

What follows is not offered as a work of profound scholarship, though it has been conscientiously researched and cross-checked where possible, but a story worth telling that has not been told before. It is hoped it will interest racing enthusiasts and entertain more general readers, and that the former will put up with explanations of things they may feel are blindingly obvious. The subject is explicitly racing in Britain, rather than breeding, betting or Irish racing, though all are mentioned in passing, and it does not attempt to give systematic information about such things as owners', trainers' or jockeys' championships. Also, strict accuracy has been sacrificed to brevity by referring to the Home Office on many occasions when the reference should technically be to the Ministry of Home Security, a parallel department reporting to the same minister.

Many people generously helped with information or advice, for which the author is exceedingly grateful. Ron Blake, Gerry Blum,

Doug Jemmeson and Sidney Outen kindly gave long interviews about their experiences, and Ann Hemming, Bill Parrish and Cyril Whiterow also provided wartime recollections. Jane Godfrey, Alan Clarke and Alan Medlock helped with obtaining access to Jockey Club minutes. Others who helped in various ways were Alan Brunton, Alastair Campbell, Jane Clarke, Jeannie Chantler, East Lothian Council (Craig Statham), Alice Everett, Kate Hills, Ron Hogston, David Hunter, James Hutchinson, Karen Jones, Barry Maltby, Peter Nevett, Newport Museum and Art Gallery (Rachael Anderton), North Ayrshire Council (Hazel Menzies), The Royal Archives (Pamela Clark), Dede Scott Brown, Peter Willett and Geoff Wragg. Chris Pitt and Anton Rippon gave practical advice and Tim Cox not only gave access to his unique library but was an invaluable source of encouragement and helpful suggestions. Above all, the author's wife, Ann, was very patient with him throughout the long period of researching and writing.

The diagram in Appendix 6 was produced by Jonathan S.H. Saville.

CHAPTER 1

IN ARCADIA – THE 1930s

"Line up, jockeys: triers in front, the rest behind!"

This order from the starter of a fifty-runner maiden race is probably apocryphal, but says a lot about racing between the wars: no starting stalls, no division of races with large numbers of entries, unlimited fields regardless of safety, and a tacit assumption that some of the contestants would not be particularly anxious to win. In short, a racing world very different from the present one. A racegoer who travelled back seventy years from the early twenty-first century would probably be bewildered and horrified at first, but later perhaps a little envious too.

The most obvious paradox is that despite there being far less racing, meetings were held at many more places and the sport was more deeply embedded in national consciousness. Compared with the 2008 allocation of 1,504 days' racing between 60 courses, the fixture lists for the last complete flat and jumping seasons before the war look very strange. A paltry 588 days were spread between ninety-two courses, twenty-three of which had only one meeting. In sixteen cases it was only a single day.

All racing was on turf and it had long been axiomatic that, apart from the exceptionally wide Rowley Mile at Newmarket, no course could stand more than about eight days a season. It was also common for fixtures to last two or more days, so meetings at any particular course tended to be few and far between, making them more of a special event locally. They were unofficial holidays at places such as Lincoln and Chester, and for the Northumberland Plate at Newcastle. The solitary annual meetings at Ascot and Goodwood were important in the London social calendar, while the likes of Bungay, Rothbury and Much Wenlock were eagerly anticipated days out. People would know that race week was coming, whether or not they personally were interested in it or approved of it.

Many did not approve. At Derby, for instance, some of the churches and chapels, far from being innocently unaware of the approach of the August meeting, used to put on alternative entertainment for working men who might otherwise find the races attractive. Such anxiety was justified. Crowds at the more popular meetings could be enormous by present standards. The Grand National, though held on a Friday, attracted a quarter of a million, and mundane bank holiday flat racing at Birmingham and Wolverhampton produced up to 30,000. Northumberland Plate day (a Wednesday in June) would find 40,000 packed into Gosforth Park. Big races, such as the Derby and St.Leger, were national events and Gordon Richards was a sporting superstar on a par with giants like Stanley Matthews and Don Bradman.

There seems, however, to have been something deeper than simple, factual awareness of racing. Although a less powerful or distinct influence than in Irish life, it held a position in the national collective consciousness that has been almost lost because of social change and wider choices, but which could then trigger cultural responses we might not expect. For example, in *The Man of Property*, John Galsworthy mentions that the grand stand at Epsom (as distinct from, say, the line of the downs) can be seen in the distance from the house at Robin Hill. When Old Jolyon dies peacefully in the garden on a perfect summer afternoon, Galsworthy includes the distant view of the grand stand with the grazing cattle, the scent of the flowers and the hum of the bees in the idyllic scene. He must have known that his readers would recognise it as iconic.

The Man of Property dates from 1906, but Galsworthy relied again on an underlying awareness of racing in *Swan Song* in 1928. The staid and elderly Soames Forsyte goes racing for the first time and we follow his puzzled responses as he begins to grasp what is happening. The message is clear – Soames may be at sea, but the rest of us understand racing, don't we?

The classic documentary film of 1936, *The Night Mail*, targeted a wider audience than Galsworthy's literate middle class. Early in the film a farm worker is seen stabling a heavy horse, both clearly standing as archetypes of traditional England, as the train approaches through the twilight, and an evening paper is thrown out as it races past. The labourer picks it up, eagerly scanning not the lead story but the stop-press racing results, and calls to an unseen friend that he has had a winner. Again, the director must have been sure that the audience would relate to this as authentically English.

Later still, in *The Lion and the Unicorn* (1941) George Orwell refers to people in left wing circles feeling it "a duty to snigger at every English institution, from horse racing to suet puddings".

None of this meant that the public at large had any say in how racing was run. That was for a small, self-selecting and self-referential oligarchy of peers and baronets, with a sprinkling of retired army officers and some exceedingly wealthy also-rans. They were the Jockey Club, rulers of flat racing since the late eighteenth century, and the more squirearchical National Hunt Committee, which had taken responsibility for jump racing in the 1860s but was still seen as a poor and slightly common relation and junior partner. Left wing politicians might characterise them as the Privileged Few or the Idle Rich but, advantaged and rich though most undoubtedly were, they were rarely idle and often led busy lives of public service. Even those who did not sit in the House of Lords were the kind of men who were Lords Lieutenant, chairmen of county councils or hospital boards, or constituency Conservative association presidents and had been brought up to run things their way without being argued with. Though their justice was generally fair and they did not set out to be oppressively autocratic, punishments meted out to offenders were sometimes harsh and men could lose their livelihoods overnight with no appeal. In that more deferential age, however, people were mostly content to accept this as part of the natural order.

Racing was, therefore, run largely in the interests of big owners and owner/breeders and, to some extent, commercial breeders. Crucial to the whole enterprise was defending the British thoroughbred and the export markets for it against all comers, particularly the ever more threatening Americans and annoyingly successful French, whose bloodstock had now recovered from the First World War. Possessing intimate knowledge of what had gone before and taking a long view ahead were crucial. Short-termism could be fatal and new ideas were treated with great circumspection.

An example of this mindset was the early closing of entries for some of the most important races. As now, entries for the Classics were made when horses were yearlings, many months before they saw a racecourse, with the stakes falling due by stages on dates when entries could be withdrawn by forfeiting only the earlier instalments. At that time, however, no entries could be made later for horses that proved unexpectedly promising. This had the effect both of adding to the sale value of horses holding entries and of creating a bigger pot of prize money from forfeited stakes from the many original entries which inevitably fell by the wayside. The same system applied to some other races besides the Classics, the extreme example being produce races, for which the unborn foals of specified mares were entered to run as two-year-olds or even three-year-olds. By this device prize money for the National Breeders Produce Stakes and Imperial Produce Stakes, run at the relatively upstart Sandown and Kempton Parks, far exceeded that of the prestigious Ascot and Newmarket two-year-old races.

Others to benefit from the provider-driven set up were racecourse company shareholders. Only five courses were run on a non-dividend basis: Ascot and Newmarket, which were owned by the Crown and the Jockey Club respectively, Salisbury, Stockton and municipally owned York. A few more were owned (though not necessarily operated) by local authorities, but the great majority were limited companies which were in business to make money. With no subsidies from the betting industry (except the recently created Tote) for improving facilities or holding meetings on less attractive days, they were exposed to the full commercial risk of everything they did: in other words, all meetings were similar to what would now be classified as "enterprise" fixtures. Those finding themselves operating on an unintentionally non-dividend basis for any length of time joined the steady trickle of closures which had always existed, although the casualty list for the 1930s was only seven minor jumping courses. Unfortunately, many made their profits by low investment and providing patrons with the minimum they could get away with. The spectator often got little more than the opportunity to watch six races (and only rarely more) in a degree of discomfort which varied only according to the enclosure he or, occasionally, she could afford. Admission charges were higher than now in real terms, Tattersalls ring typically costing fifteen shillings – equivalent to around £30. It was not always possible to get into the club enclosure by simply paying for day membership: one sometimes had to be introduced by an annual member and fill in a form about such matters as one's club and regiment. At the other end of the scale, the cheap ring might have no shelter, no raised viewing areas, primitive toilets and minimal refreshment facilities. However, as people still turned up in droves for the more popular meetings racecourse executives understandably felt under no pressure to do better.

Overall, there was an odd but striking resemblance between racing and the Church of England. Both were national institutions driven by strict calendars with fixed high points; everyone and anyone was welcome to come, and those in charge were delighted when they did come, but nothing was explained and nothing was changed – the punters simply had to take what they found and nobody dreamed that it could be otherwise.

Day-to-day activities were sustained by a modestly paid army of people, particularly those who worked in training stables, stable lad being a job for life for men who had taken a long time to acquire the skills, knew nothing else and had few other opportunities. Stables rarely contained more than fifty horses and the traditional practice of a lad looking after only two still held good. High standards were expected, not only of horsemanship and stable craft but often personal appearance, and always of discipline, loyalty and trustworthiness. The notion that the betting public has some kind of right to know what is going on in stables would have seemed absurd and many trainers went to great lengths to prevent information getting out, seeing it as the private and valuable property of their owners and themselves. At Newmarket there were men whose job was to try to penetrate this secrecy - the "touts" who spent the early mornings watching dozens of trainers' strings on the many training grounds. Between them they could recognise any of the hundreds of horses trained in the town and passed on the information they gleaned to the press and others willing to pay for it. Sometimes they were able to get inside information, but a lad giving it risked his job in a sport where the rules prohibited trainers from engaging anyone without a satisfactory written reference from his former employer.

The normal way into this career was apprenticeship, usually on leaving school at fourteen and lasting up to seven years. Many boys came from poor homes in cities and had no previous contact with horses. They were educated slowly, starting with menial tasks, then learning to ride a pony kept for the purpose before graduating to racehorses, which could take a year or more. There were none of the apprentices' training schools that now exist and every trainer had his boys taught in his own way. They were always strictly disciplined and occasionally harshly treated, badly housed and poorly fed, but many were given a start in life they would not otherwise have had. As now, a tiny minority made the grade as jockeys but most ended up "doing their two" for the rest of their working lives.

If men and boys had it hard, women were hardly visible. They could own and breed horses, ride in ladies' races at point-to-points (they had been banned from riding against men in 1929) and get into Tattersalls' ring at a discount, but that was about the limit. A few worked in stables, but apprenticeships were explicitly for boys, there was a sufficient supply of time-served lads, and girls were thought not to be strong enough to ride racehorses properly. Nor did anyone think for a moment that they could be jockeys, starters, local stewards or members of the Jockey Club. Neither Jockey Club nor NHC would license them as trainers, though they did acquiesce in a few cases where a woman was de facto trainer, provided that the actual licence was held by someone with more acceptable genitalia. Among these few were Norah Wilmot who took over her father's substantial Binfield Grove stable when he died, the licence being held by the head lad, and Louie Dingwall who trained a few horses on the beach at Sandbanks. The licence was held by her motor mechanic husband who helped run the independent bus company that provided their main income. In the days of unrestricted competition the Hants and Dorset company tried to put her out of business by exhorting the public to "Patronise the Green Buses", to which she responded by painting her own fleet green overnight. Only that kind of woman could survive in pre-war racing.

National Hunt racing in the thirties was beginning a slow transition. It had been looked down upon as a rather seedy activity mainly for the benefit of participants who were hard-riding foxhunters, dim cavalry officers and sundry others with more courage than sense. In spring and autumn it took place at obscure country places but in winter, between flat seasons, it was staged at many of the bigger courses. Prize money for mundane races was about the same as now in real terms: the difference was that practically all the races were mundane – not so much bread and butter racing as bread and thinly spread margarine. The few highlights mostly came close together in the early spring. For aficionados there was the National Hunt Steeplechase, a four mile amateur maiden race that had originally been held on a different course each year, but settled at the embryonic Cheltenham festival in the 1900s. For everyone else there was the Grand National. This was the only jump race that everyone knew about and it completely dominated the season, with prize money greater than the total for all the races run everywhere in a normal week. The supporting jump races at the Grand National meeting were also worth winning, as was the Scottish Grand National at Bogside a few weeks later and the Grand Sefton at the Aintree November meeting. Significantly, all these were run at mixed meetings at which most races were on the flat. Apart from the National Hunt Steeplechase the only important races at all-jumping meetings were the Lancashire Steeplechase, Manchester's Easter Monday highlight, and the Imperial Cup handicap hurdle at Sandown Park in March.

Things started to change in the mid-1920s with the inauguration of the Cheltenham Gold Cup and Champion Hurdle, which were not handicaps but true, weight for age championships. Admittedly, the Gold Cup was originally seen as just another Grand National trial but it started to take on a life of its own in the 1930s when Golden Miller caught the public imagination by winning it five times. Kempton Park's King George VI Chase was first run in 1937 but was abandoned in 1938 and did not become a Boxing Day "classic" until the early fifties. The Champion Hurdle also established itself as being what it said on the tin and a further step forward was the first running of the Triumph Hurdle, a championship for four-year-olds, at Hurst Park in March 1939. Jumping was on the long climb towards something like equality with flat racing; the flat might still sometimes be called "racing proper" but journalists no longer referred to jumping as "the illegitimate sport".

It was a decade of change for point-to-pointing too. Once unregulated, cross-country racing fun for hunting people, it had gradually moved towards greater formality and away from natural courses, making traditionalists complain that point-to-points were becoming "nothing but bastard race meetings" in which genuine hunting people had no chance. There was enough truth in this for the NHC to feel it should become more involved. After some friction with the Masters of Fox Hounds Association Point-to-Point Committee, joint liaison arrangements were set up in 1934, with revised rules under an appendix of the NH code, vetting of courses by inspectors and a tighter definition of who had "ridden for hire" and, therefore, could not take part. There were still complaints that the sport was becoming too professional but, in reality, it was still overwhelmingly local, amateur, firmly linked to hunting and a long way short of today's semi-professionalism.

Sitting between point-to-pointing and NH racing proper were bona fide hunt and military steeplechases. Like point-to-points, these were for hunters and took place between February and May but were held under full NH rules, appeared in the fixture list and form books and were occasionally held on licensed racecourses. The military meetings were a startling example of how much horses still featured in army life even in the thirties, but the hunt meetings were little more than a device to allow charging of spectators by getting round the rule that only parking charges could be made at point-to-points.

The thirties were also the heyday of Pony Turf Club racing, which burgeoned before the war almost as quickly as it collapsed afterwards. Formed in 1923, the PTC astutely wooed the Jockey Club and achieved recognised turf authority status within two years, after which its activities grew quickly. The ponies were not the kind ridden by children in gymkhanas but thoroughbreds that had not grown above fifteen hands, and were professionally trained and ridden by people whose careers had often started in normal racing. The advantage was that the cost of keeping a pony in training, about £150 a year, was a fraction of that at Newmarket or the big southern training centres, opening ownership to many for whom it would have been unaffordable. At first the meetings were held at West Country places such as Bovey Tracey and Lamberts Castle, but in the late twenties there was a bold move towards centralisation on purpose-built courses at Portsmouth and Northolt Park. The latter put other courses to shame with state of the art stands, a paddock visible from all enclosures, electric timing of races on a large clock which could be seen by the crowd and, from 1937, race commentaries over the loudspeakers. Orthodox racing men thought this sort of thing was unspeakably vulgar, but the public loved it. Unfortunately, they did not love it quite enough: although the Northolt Derby attracted five figure crowds, average attendance was only 3,500 and by the time war broke out Northolt Park was being run by a receiver.

Last in the pecking order was unlicensed racing, or flapping, which the Jockey Club had been trying to suppress since the mid nineteenth century. Held under whatever conditions individual promoters thought fit, it was unregulated, sometimes dangerous, always a paradise for the unscrupulous, but often a lot of fun. At one time there had been some well known meetings, particularly those on the formerly licensed courses at Blaydon and Chesterfield. Blaydon's popularity almost compared with the Northumberland Plate, but meetings there ended ignominiously in 1916 after riots followed a disqualification. Chesterfield succumbed in the mid twenties and flapping receded towards its traditional strongholds in Wales, northern England and southern Scotland, but defiantly refused to go away. It has still not quite done so, although some of its vitality has been sapped by the increased opportunities for moderate horses at all-weather meetings under rules.

★ ★ ★ ★

In the final analysis, the thirties should be remembered as a golden age of flat racing, with outstanding horses, jockeys and trainers and some formidable owners.

Hero of the early thirties was Brown Jack, a juvenile hurdler before going on to excel in stayers' flat races. He won the longest in the calendar, the Queen Alexandra Stakes at Ascot, six times and attracted the same dewy-eyed public adulation as Desert Orchid much later.

There were some outstanding Classic winners. It would be untrue to say that horses then were not bred for speed, since racing is always about the quickest horse between two points, but it is certainly true that breeding for stamina was important. The ideal three-year-old would have the speed to win a Guineas race in early May, the conformation for the Derby or Oaks on the testing Epsom course a few weeks later and stamina for the St. Leger in September – the Triple Crown. Only Bahram achieved this in the 1930s, but four other colts and three fillies won two Classics. Among them, the diminutive Hyperion, Windsor Lad and Blue Peter were outstanding by any standards, and the filly Rockfel was as good as most.

The ideal Classic horse traditionally progressed to Cup races over extreme distances and this was still happening. Singapore and the filly Quashed successfully did so, with Quashed winning three in addition to big staying handicaps and proving herself among the gamest ever of her gender.

Present-day followers of racing seem not to understand how good the leading jockeys of the time were. Among others, Harry Wragg, Charlie Smirke, Freddy Fox, Dick Perryman, Eph and Doug Smith and Tommy Weston would have reached the top in any generation, and yet they were utterly dominated by Gordon Richards. Champion 26 times from 1925, he was defeated only once (in 1930 when Freddy Fox beat him by one) in any season when he was not ill or injured. The first since Fred Archer to ride 200 winners a season regularly, his highest score remains a record for a flat jockey.

Furthermore, he was a thoroughly normal and decent human being, without the personality flaws that marred the lives or reputations of those with whom he is usually compared. No wonder the entire public took him to their hearts.

They were a tough lot, many having grown up in the school of hard knocks, and photographed in their street clothes some of them looked alarmingly like B-movie gangsters. There were some bitter enmities, notably that of Smirke towards Richards. The need for common safety ensured that there was an unwritten code as to what kind of riding was acceptable, but the absence of patrol cameras meant that they could get away with more in races than is now possible. Disciplinary action depended on what the stewards had spotted at the time and the evidence of other riders.

Among the hundreds of trainers, perhaps the closest to genius was Fred Darling, the master of Beckhampton. A cold-eyed martinet and ruthless to the point of cruelty, but admired by loyal staff who could meet his demands, he had trained eleven Classic winners and won two championships by 1938. However, racing was still a sport as well as a business, so there was room for amusing eccentrics like the fiery and secretive Major Beatty, who fought an unending battle of wits with the Newmarket touts. Amputation of a leg in 1936 neither stopped him riding nor dented his reputation for entertaining a lady friend in the back row of the cinema.

Owners came in all shapes and sizes, few of them odder in shape, size and behaviour than Dorothy Paget, a pathologically shy perfectionist who had been hopelessly spoilt as a child before inheriting a vast fortune from her American grandfather. She was as well known for her steeplechasers as her flat horses and with her unflattering clothes and female entourage she was a familiar sight on the racecourse.

The owners who really counted were big breeders, notably the Third Aga Khan, who won seven Classics in the thirties and was leading owner five times, and Lords Derby, Rosebery and Astor. The

17th Earl of Derby was leading owner twice in the decade despite having cut his racing interests during the depression, and as a long standing member of the Jockey Club, former Lord Mayor of Liverpool, cabinet minister and ambassador to France there can have been little he did not know about running racing or the country. The physically formidable and mentally sharp 6th Earl of Rosebery, another Jockey Club veteran, had been a Liberal MP in the 1900s and one of General Allenby's staff officers in the Great War but, though he owned the powerful Mentmore stud, 1939 was the only year he led the owners list, thanks to Blue Peter. The leading owner in 1936, Waldorf, 2nd Viscount Astor, had been elected to the Jockey Club in 1929. Though born in America, he was Eton and Oxford educated and had been a Conservative MP until inheriting the title. He raced only horses he had bred himself and, despite enormous wealth, never bet on them.

This was the racing world of the 1930s. Despite its oddities and shortcomings those who knew it have written of it with great affection. We should accept their testimony at face value.

CHAPTER 2

IN FEAR (MARCH TO OCTOBER 1939)

The 1939 Cheltenham festival meeting took place during the last week in which belief that the Munich agreement had averted war with Germany was still reasonable. There had always been doubts and few people really trusted Hitler, but the hope was that his expansionist ambitions had been contained and, so far, he had done nothing to disappoint the optimists. In the months after his coup at Munich, Chamberlain had managed to convince much of the press, including the editor of the highly influential Times, that all was going to be well. This may not have been difficult, as most papers were telling their readers what they desperately wanted to hear: the Daily Express headline *There Will Be No War This Year* may have been ridiculed ever since but it went down well then. Nevertheless, there was a minority convinced that this was all wishful thinking and that war was near, and so, alongside the hopes for peace, rearmament went on with increasing urgency. By January 1939 the RAF was receiving 400 new aircraft a month and the government asked employers to release volunteer and reserve pilots for six months' full time training. The following month it announced plans for producing thousands of air raid shelters and an increase of £175 million in the defence budget. It was as if the country knew the old steeplechasing maxim "hope for the best but sit for the worst".

Accordingly, whilst those who gathered at Cheltenham on 7th March may have been apprehensive about the future, there was no feeling of immanent dread.

The National Hunt Meeting, as it was then always known, was mainly a gathering of racing and hunting people and smaller, less hyped and more for the initiated than it has since become. Most of the crowd were from rural parts of the south and midlands, though there would be some from the north, a few from Ireland and a London contingent whisked there at nearly a mile a minute by special restaurant car express from Paddington to the racecourse station. The prevailing impression was of tweeds, heavy overcoats, bowler hats, well polished brown shoes and neatly trimmed moustaches.

Lord Rosebery leads in Blue Peter and Eph Smith
after winning the last pre-war Derby.

The 1939 meeting was the first without Golden Miller since almost the start of the decade. He had put the Gold Cup on the map by winning it five times in succession from 1932 to 1936 and might well have won again in 1937 had not the race, unthinkably now, been abandoned because of the weather. He returned in 1938 aged eleven and received another hero's welcome despite just failing to catch Morse Code, but when he reappeared at Newbury in February 1939 he finished a distant seventh and it was clear that his time had passed.

Despite a winner's prize of £1,000 for the first time, there was a feeble five runner field for the Gold Cup, for which Morse Code looked a certainty but ran appallingly and was beaten by Brendan's Cottage. In contrast, the Champion Hurdle was a competitive and dramatic race, with Solford and Bahuddin falling independently while disputing the lead at the last flight, impeding the pursuing group and letting African Sister dash past and become the first mare to win the race. Ridden by Keith Piggott, Lester's father, she was trained near the course by his uncle Charlie. There was only one Irish-trained runner at the meeting, Bally Hopeful, who finished third in the Seven Springs Handicap Chase.

The week ended with two days at Hurst Park, where the French-trained Grey Talk won the first running of the Triumph Hurdle, and army bona fide meetings at Windmill Hill. And then the blow fell.

On March 13th Hitler advised the fascist leaders in Slovakia to declare independence and two days later the Germans occupied the parts of Bohemia and Moravia they had not taken the previous autumn. With the Hungarians simultaneously moving into Ruthenia, Czechoslovakia had been torn apart. Hitler was back to his old ways and Chamberlain had been made to look a fool for trusting him. The press now started to turn against the Prime Minister, with the Daily Mail, once seen as almost sympathetic to the fascists, urging him to prepare for war, reflecting the feeling of the country better than his convoluted arguments that the latest events did not really break the Munich agreement. The question was where Hitler would strike next, and the obvious answer was Poland, where his dispute over Danzig now looked like an opportunity for aggression.

The next few weeks saw a frightening skid towards war. By the end of March plans to double the size of the Territorial Army were announced and Britain and France had guaranteed Poland's borders. In April the government produced plans to evacuate two and a half million children from cities in the event of war, for the country to be run by twelve regional commissioners if their regions were cut off, and for a stupendous increase in the defence budget. 80,000 air raid shelters were being delivered each week. In late April, following menacing military parades to celebrate his birthday, Hitler abrogated the 1935 Naval Agreement and the non-aggression treaty between Germany and Poland and demanded the return of Danzig. Chamberlain warned him that use of force there would mean war, and by the end of May Parliament had voted for conscription for men of 20 and 21.

But in late spring the pace of the rush to destruction seemed to slacken. Although nothing had been solved and warlike preparations continued, no new crisis erupted. The royal tour of Canada began, Northamptonshire won a county cricket championship match for the first time in four years and 99 attempts, and people started to enjoy the usual summer activities, sometimes with a special intensity from knowing it might be their last opportunity for a long time.

The Football Association had responded to the expansion of the TA with a circular urging players to join and players from most Football League clubs did so. Liverpool, for example, joined as a club and the whole team found themselves in camp within weeks of the end of the season. Racing did no such thing but trundled inexorably on as though nothing out of the ordinary were happening, which was strange, considering how many members of the Jockey Club understood politics and international affairs from personal experience. Perhaps racing was such a closed and inward looking world that nobody believed in their hearts that a passing event such as an international crisis could affect it. Whatever the reason, it was business as usual with no apparent thought, let alone contingency plans, for possible disruption.

The Grand National and the early flat fixtures had come and gone and jumping was winding down at the usual country meetings. The hero of May was Sawfish, ridden by Mr Geoffrey Scudamore, the next three generations of whose family would produce outstanding professional jockeys. The pair had already won two hunter chases in six starts, but now they dashed round the country rattling up successes in similar events at Devon & Exeter, Woore, Wye, Colwall Park and finally, on Whit Monday, Buckfastleigh. The total prize money of £567 for the seven wins probably delighted the horse's connections, as it was a lot more than they would have got from winning one of the big Cheltenham or Aintree hunters' races.

That year's Derby, on 24th May, was unusually early. As expected, it went to Lord Rosebery's Blue Peter, a strong, handsome colt with a flawless action. Spotted as an exceptional prospect for the Classics as an immature juvenile the previous autumn, he returned to prove he could act on the tricky Epsom course by winning the Blue Riband Trial Stakes and followed up with a narrow but easy success in the Two Thousand Guineas. In the Derby he murdered them, taking the lead half way down the straight and sweeping clear from Fox Cub and the Chester Vase winner, Heliopolis, to become one of the most impressive winners of the century.

The One Thousand Guineas winner, the French-bred and American-owned Galatea II, likewise went on to win the Oaks, but only just. Having scored comfortably at Newmarket she was odds-on and took the lead early in the straight but her rider, Bobby Jones, started easing her too soon and she held on by only a head from the fast finishing White Fox. Another odds-on favourite to win at the meeting was Tant Mieux, who made all the running under Gordon Richards to win the Woodcote Stakes, traditionally the first six-furlong two-year-old race of the season. Richards also won the Coronation Cup, in which he supplanted Brownie Carslake on Scottish Union, the 1938 St.Leger winner.

After the popular Whit week meeting at Manchester the next major milestone was Ascot in mid June, where Scottish Union and Galatea failed expensively as favourites for the Gold Cup and Coronation Stakes, but Heliopolis comfortably won the Prince of Wales's Stakes. Among the two-year-olds Tant Mieux again led all the way in the New Stakes, Prince Aly Khan's Turkhan was highly impressive in the Coventry and, in a huge field of fillies for the Queen Mary, Gordon Richards got Snowberry back up in the last stride after being headed. However, the main talking point was the failure of an astronomical plunge by Dorothy Paget on Colonel Payne in the Cork and Orrery. He had not run for nearly two years but so impressed Fred Darling at home that he told Miss Paget to put her maximum on him at Ascot. Her first bet was £10,000, and that was only the start. He started as odds-on favourite but failed to see out the trip and finished seventh. Another major punt, this time by the public at large, that went painfully wrong was on Portobello in the King's Stand Stakes, the final race of the meeting. He had whipped round at the start when favourite for the Granville Stakes the day before but, with Gordon Richards now riding, he was reckoned a good thing. He went clear at half way, only to be caught and passed by Mickey the Greek and Rue de la Paix, and they were sadder but wiser punters who left the last Royal Ascot for seven years.

Unusually, the King and Queen were not at Ascot, because their tour of Canada was still going on. The King had two unplaced runners, Licence and Great Truth, which had been favourite for the Queen Mary. The usual royal jockey, Jack Crouch, rode Great Truth but within a week he had been killed in a plane crash on the way to Newcastle. This left William Jarvis, who trained for His Majesty and a select few others at Egerton House, Newmarket, with a problem over who should ride Mr Esmond Harmsworth's two-year-old Godiva at the Newmarket First July meeting. She was as temperamental as she was brilliant and after winning at the first attempt had refused to race next time. Snowy Outen, then an Egerton House apprentice, recalled in 2006 "She was a right madam. She needed a crack round the hocks to go down and another to start, every time. You could do that sort of thing in those days because there was no TV".

One of the few who could ride her was Doug Marks, the stable's senior apprentice, and Jarvis courageously decided that, rather than book a fashionable jockey, Marks should ride her on the racecourse. He was immediately justified when she won the Stud Produce Stakes from Snowberry, a red hot favourite after her Ascot success.

In France a serious challenger to Blue Peter had emerged. This was Pharis II, who impressively won the French Derby and the Grand Prix de Paris within a fortnight. He was owned by Marcel Boussac, a textiles millionaire who had built up a powerful stud and was carrying all before him in France, besides keeping a few horses in Britain. Pharis was not only entered for the St.Leger but likely to meet the engagement. The fascinating prospect of this challenge to Blue Peter on home territory by the impudent French generated ever-increasing speculation, heightened when Blue Peter won the Eclipse Stakes easily but only narrowly.

It was now high summer and still Hitler had made no move, but the nagging tension beneath the surface of everyday life did not ease. Not only were the first conscripts now training but the RAF had received another 750 new aircraft in June, and early in July the King approved the formation of the Womens' Auxiliary Air Force. Announcement of plans for a Ministry of Information was another sign that the government was preparing to put the country on a war footing, but people still hoped for the best. It was the first summer of the Holidays With Pay Act 1938, which pushed many more employers towards giving workers a week's paid holiday each year. Annual factory closures had been feared as weeks without money to make ends meet, but from 1939 many more workers could afford at least days out, or perhaps even a week at one of the holiday camps that were starting to spring up. On 10th August The Sporting Life observed that Derby races had seen "a large attendance of Birmingham folk" who were having holidays with pay for the first time. The weather might stop their days at the seaside, the races or hiking in the country, but fear of a war that might not happen was not going to get in the way. The middle classes likewise took the train to resorts that catered for the better sort of person and the really wealthy headed for France or, a bit later, the grouse moors.

Just as Cheltenham had preceded the dashing of hopes for lasting peace, so Glorious Goodwood proved to be the prelude to the final convulsion. Mickey the Greek was one of four Ascot winners to score again there. So too was Olein, who won both the Sussex Stakes and the Nassau Stakes, and also the Rose of England colt, both of them owned by Lord Glanely. Sometimes known as Old Guts and Gaiters, Glanely was not an aristocrat but a former merchant seaman and office boy who had become a shipping magnate by his own efforts. Though a member of the Jockey Club, he tended to appear at all but the most formal summer meetings in white flannels and a panama hat. His Ashford Bend also won, making him leading owner at what was to be his last Goodwood.

In the same week, however, the Germans in Danzig had started putting pressure on Polish interests there and by early August there was a full scale dispute between Poland and the Danzig senate, now openly supported by Germany. The Nazis began a propaganda offensive accusing the Polish government of persecuting ethnic Germans, a re-run of their campaign against Czechoslovakia the year before, and from then onwards the situation deteriorated ever faster. On 21st August even The Sporting Life recognised that not everything was quite as it should be. Reporting the defeat of Britain by Germany in an athletics match in Cologne it noted that "International crises seemed far away when the teams came onto the track, the crowd of 40,000 giving the British athletes a terrific ovation as they marched round". This was the paper's first reference to the spectre that had been haunting the country for months.

The government repeatedly warned that an attack on Poland would mean war, but on 22nd August a completely unexpected non-aggression pact between Germany and the USSR was announced. The one potential adversary that might have made Hitler think again had been taken out of the equation and war, despite frenzied efforts to avoid it, was inevitable. After a final week of excruciating tension the Germans invaded Poland at dawn on Friday, 1st September. Hitler had, in fact, ordered his commanders to prepare to launch an attack on that date as long ago as April.

By then the country was already in a strange, twilight world between peace and war. On the preceding Monday 104 Defence Regulations under the hastily-approved Emergency Powers Defence Act had been published and on the Wednesday army and RAF reservists were called up, the navy mobilised and plans for mass evacuation of children from cities activated, all placing enormous strain on the railways, the most important means of mass transport. The effect on sport was patchy. On Thursday there was racing as planned at Brighton, Haydock Park and Devon & Exeter and the lead story in The Sporting Life assured readers that Pharis was definitely coming over from France the following day for the long-awaited clash with Blue Peter in the next week's St. Leger. Friday's edition, which was being delivered to newsagents as German tanks crossed the Polish frontier, announced that the Folkestone meeting on that day and Saturday had been abandoned because of curtailed rail facilities, as had Northolt's PTC fixture on Saturday and Monday, but Manchester would go ahead: reports that the military had taken over the course were untrue. And go ahead it did, despite everything, as did the Football League programme.

When Joe Taylor and Larchfield won the closing St.Denis Plate on the Saturday Chamberlain was still prevaricating, trying to resist cabinet pressure to send an ultimatum to Germany. He still hoped Hitler might agree to halt his advance but, in truth, everyone knew the game was up. As the racegoers trooped off the course at Manchester towards an unknown future the weather seemed to be imitating life, an uncomfortably hot, sticky afternoon turning relentlessly into a night of widespread heavy thunderstorms.

Even as the Manchester meeting was going on the RAF was requisitioning the Rowley Mile racecourse at Newmarket by the highly effective means of landing Wellingtons of 99 Squadron on it without warning. Mr Mariott, the Jockey Club's dictatorial manager of Newmarket heath and racecourses, was seen coming out of his house waving his walking stick in protest, but for once he did not get his way: he soon even had to give up the house for the C.O. of what was now RAF Newmarket Heath. Other airmen were less fortunate and had to bed down in the stands.

Soon after eleven next morning the bruised and deflated prime minister told the nation by radio that the ultimatum he had finally been compelled to send had received no response and he regretted that a state of war now existed between Great Britain and Germany. Listeners reacted in different ways. Some were irritated by Chamberlain's moralising tone, which made Hitler sound like some feckless tenant who had failed to pay his rent after promising to do so, some were gripped by icy fear, but others were glad that the shame of Munich had not been repeated. Gordon Richards, as usual on Sunday mornings, had gone to Ogbourne to ride work for Martin Hartigan, who had served in the 10th Hussars. It was when he saw a tear roll down Hartigan's cheek during the broadcast that he realised the enormity of the disaster. On the other hand, professional footballer Jack Wheeler heard the news on his way home from playing snooker and was not much concerned – he was young, single and sure it would not last long.

One immediate result of the declaration of war was cancellation until further notice of all spectator sport and other public entertainments, including not only the St.Leger meeting and the showdown between Blue Peter and Pharis but also the Doncaster yearling sales that went with it. The main reason was fear of air raids. Ever since Stanley Baldwin, the former prime minister, had gloomily warned Parliament that "the bomber will always get through" there had been anxiety about what modern air warfare would bring. It was widely assumed that the sky would be black with German bombers within hours of war starting and the government's worst case scenario foresaw 5,000 tons of bombs falling in a day, causing 175,000 casualties and mass panic. There was also the great unknown of poison gas. The calculation of casualties per ton of bombs was extrapolated from figures from the Spanish Civil War and Great War Zeppelin raids and turned out to be about three times the actual rate. The Luftwaffe was also incapable of dropping anything like the feared tonnage, because it had been equipped with medium bombers, few of which could carry more than 2,000 pounds of bombs. What the government could not know was that Hitler had no intention of attacking civilian areas, calculating that, left unscathed, Britain and France might be ready for peace once the hapless Poles had been battered into submission.

Racecourses make ideal emergency camping grounds, with acres of space and large scale catering and toilet facilities, and a number were taken over for territorial units to mobilise, notably Hurst Park and Aintree. These were soon released again, but others stayed in military hands for the duration. Among them Sandown Park accommodated various guards regiments at different times, Kempton Park was first occupied by the Scots Guards and later became a prisoner of war camp, and Yarmouth was a forward defensive position. With East Anglia a likely invasion area, some Newmarket stables were requisitioned by the army, particularly Lagrange, where Basil Jarvis trained for Lord Glanely, and half the yard at Egerton House.

Bookmakers were hit, too, with nothing to bet on but three or four Irish meetings a week. Future magnate Joe Coral closed his Stoke Newington business and moved to Biggleswade, but continued to stand at Walthamstow greyhound meetings when they resumed. The Tote's business was all on-course and its operator, the Racecourse Betting Control Board, decided on 6th September to cease business immediately, though keeping a skeleton staff for a possible resumption if circumstances allowed.

Racehorse owners and trainers were in a quandary and their immediate responses varied according to how they thought the war might go. Some owners cut down or disposed of their interests, but many decided to wait and see whether racing resumed. Trainers who were military reservists (and many were, training having always attracted retired officers) had no choice but to close their stables and return to duty and others, like Geoffrey Barling, closed down and volunteered. A few went to Ireland, including Capt. D.T.D. Rogers who had been struggling at Cranborne but prospered when he returned to The Curragh. The size of the remaining trainers' strings was reduced everywhere so, at first, many of them were not unhappy to see the younger paid lads disappear into the forces. Some of the better bred and more valuable horses were taken to Ireland or exported; others were taken home by their owners or given away. Most of the rest were destroyed. At Egerton House, where William Jarvis was under particular pressure to reduce his string because of the army takeover, Snowy Outen, still only fourteen, had to hold about ten horses steady as they were shot. He was given sixpence or a shilling a time. "I was sorry and upset" he said "but it didn't worry me. I didn't really understand what was going on". Child abuse was clearly not an issue in 1939.

Air raid precautions began to affect stable routines. Defence Regulations had extended British Summer Time but they had also introduced the blackout, which soon caused evening stables to be brought forward from the traditional 4.30 so that the work could be finished before dark. There was also the question of shelter from bombing. Nothing could be done for the horses, but at Egerton House, which was at particular risk because of its proximity to the newly created aerodrome, slit trenches were dug for staff caught in the open, who otherwise took refuge under the stairs of the massive stone house. At Stanley House, the other side of Newmarket, where Walter Earl had recently taken over as private trainer for Lord Derby, a shelter was constructed inside the building. The only other air raid precautions remembered by Gerry Blum, an apprentice of Earl's since the previous year, consisted of a demonstration by the head lad of how to use a stirrup pump.

After a few days it began to dawn on everyone that the bombers were not coming – at least, not yet – and life was going to be very dull without entertainment of any kind: if The Sun had existed it would probably have carried headlines about *The Bore War*. Soon there was pressure for the restrictions to be eased, and the second Saturday of the war saw 31 professional football friendlies. That day's Sporting Life reported the retirement of Blue Peter to stud but also ran a prominent editorial which, though professing to understand the government's position, claimed that restrictions on sport in general and racing in particular were causing an unaffordable loss of tax revenue and should be lifted forthwith. The racing press harked back to 1914, when meetings had resumed after about three weeks and soon returned to something close to normal. This was, of course, a false comparison which disregarded the fact that autumn 1914 was a time of naïve confidence that the war would last only months. The country was now back to total war and a better paradigm would have been the latest similar year, 1918, remembered for victory but mostly a time of bleak and desperate struggle, with flat racing confined to Newmarket from the end of May and jumping banned at last after a short and thin season.

Behind the scenes the Jockey Club was at work. Lord Harewood visited the Home Office and the Ministry of Transport on 12th

September and reported to meetings of the Club and the NHC next day. At the Home Office he appears to have seen the Home Secretary, Sir John Anderson, in person and was pleased to hear that there was nothing in defence regulations as such to prevent racing. Although local chief constables could ban gatherings on public safety grounds, it was felt unlikely this would affect race meetings away from major cities. On the other hand, it was emphasised that only a very small amount of racing could take place in wartime. This warning was inexplicably left out of the Permanent Secretary's letter of confirmation, an omission the Jockey Club was later to exploit. Harewood was received less cordially at the Ministry of Transport where they had more urgent matters to deal with and told him it was useless even to ask before 1st October. Given the time needed to organise a meeting and entries this meant there was no prospect of racing before 15th October.

There was genuine urgency behind these enquiries. The war could not have come at a worse time for commercial breeders, who had been expecting to sell their yearlings at Doncaster or at Newmarket in October. The former had already been cancelled and, even if Newmarket sales went ahead, with no racing and no prospect of any, who would buy? Instead of turning a profit on their investments they found their capital tied up in animals with no current value, the continued feeding and accommodation of which would involve further, unplanned costs. And there was more: the 1941 Classics were due to close on 31st October, when entry fees would become due. In a normal year these would be paid by the horses' new owners, but now the breeders risked incurring liability themselves for those not sold. Some faced ruin unless confidence in the future of racing could quickly be restored.

After hearing Harewood's news the Jockey Club decided there was no alternative but to abandon the rest of the 1939 fixtures and return all entry fees, with a limited programme of replacement meetings being arranged where and when they could from mid-

October. They also decided to extend the closing date for the 1941 Guineas races until 5th December and ask the Epsom authorities to do the same for the Derby and Oaks in the hope that "people might regain a little confidence in the stability of the country, with the idea that racing might go on in 1941 or 1942 in something like the same way as it had in the past".

On 19th September the government agreed to allow greyhound racing and professional football to resume subject to stringent limits on crowds, which varied according to whether a fixture was in an evacuation, reception or neutral area and the proviso that all dog racing must be held in daylight. Racing was not included because the Home Office believed the Jockey Club, through Harewood, had recognised that it would be severely limited. On the day before this announcement the Home Office had sanctioned meetings at Newmarket, Newbury and Thirsk, and the next week's Racing Calendar announced two two-day meetings at Newmarket, starting on 18th October and 1st November. These were to be on the July Course, the Rowley Mile being officially described as unavailable, but there would be substitute versions of the Cambridgeshire, Cesarewitch and Middle Park Stakes, and also a bloodstock sale. Details of two-day meetings at Newbury and Thirsk, starting on 25th and 27th October soon followed and Newbury's clerk of the course circulated local trainers to find out what horses they had and what sort of races they wanted. At last people could plan. There were only about half the usual number of horses in training, but a few of the empty boxes now began to fill, trainers started winding up horses that were nearly ready to run and yearlings were spruced up for the sales.

In the real world Poland had surrendered, split in two after a Russian invasion in mid-September, but though Hitler's subsequent peace offensive had been spurned, there were still no air raids. On the home front, income tax had been increased and legislation introduced to stop profiteering on food, which was not yet rationed (although petrol rationing had started on 15th September), and a new series of the comfortingly cheerful ITMA had begun on the radio. There was still a feeling of apprehension, but mixed with relief that the worst had not happened. The British Expeditionary Force was safely in France, even Hitler would not be mad enough to attack the Maginot Line in winter and, by the time he did, we would be ready to give him a bloody nose.

Even before the first meetings took place there were moves to arrange further racing. On 11th October the NHC rushed in where angels feared to tread, writing to the Minister of Transport, whom they had not even tried to meet, to say that they were planning to organise some meetings in areas not prohibited by the Home Office and asking if he had any comments. Anticipating a favourable reply, they produced a fixture list with 20 days' racing on eight courses between 20th November and 30th December, an average of nearly four days a week, and proceeded to publish it in the Racing Calendar. This tactlessness nearly queered the pitch for the Jockey Club. An earlier meeting with Captain Wallace, the Minister of Transport, had gone well, with a helpful official attitude towards both getting yearlings to the sales and a request for twelve more flat meetings, provided they made no demands on transport. Thanks to the NHC, Wallace had got the wind up by the next meeting but fortunately Harewood, representing the Jockey Club, was able to exploit its responsible attitude to date. Minutes of the Club's meeting to which he reported said that "the Club was given an extremely good mark. They were told they had played the game and kept in close touch with the Minister". They got the meetings they wanted and, surprisingly, so did the NHC.

All was ready for the resumption on 18th October, but there was actually one earlier race, the Newmarket Town Plate, the unique 3 mile 6 furlong event founded in 1665 by Charles II "to be rid yearly, the seconde Thursday in October, for euer". Being neither under Rules nor a flapping meeting, women could ride and nobody risked punishment for taking part. The winner by a head was Contrevent, the 1938 Cesarewitch winner, ridden by Miss V. Bullock, from Miss Angela Earl on Lord Derby's Roanoke, another serious horse. The only male rider was last.

Though entries for the early meetings were massive, how many spectators would come was anybody's guess and courses were taking a chance by racing at all, which was reflected in the prize money. Officers in uniform could get into Tattersalls at Newbury at a discount, as could other ranks into the cheap ring. At Newmarket and Newbury bookmakers were, as an unusual concession, to be admitted at the same price as the public, but the magisterial Sir Loftus Bates was having none of that at Thirsk. Pointing out that in the absence of the Tote they would have a monopoly he emphasised

On the first day of wartime racing there is plenty of room in the stands as Gyroscope (R.Lacey) just holds off the grey His Highness (Paddy Maher) to win Class 1 of the Cambridgeshire.

that "racecourses risk losing a considerable amount and I think it only fair that bookmakers should help us out".

Nobody need have worried. There were good crowds, including a fair sprinkling in uniform, on both days at Newmarket, with car parks well filled and special trains from London, racing beginning at the unearthly hour of 12.00 to allow the spectators to get back in daylight. Although everything except the uniforms and the absence of the Tote was reassuringly normal, those watching the 25 runners cantering down for the opening Isleham Plate probably felt as if years rather than a few weeks had passed since they last went racing. The main race of the meeting was a shortened Cambridgeshire, run over the Bunbury Mile rather than, as might have been expected, the last nine furlongs of the Ellesmere Course. Presumably this was to avoid racing round a bend. Despite division of races being almost unknown at the time, there was no alternative but to run it in two "classes" because of the enormous entry, and the same happened in both nursery handicaps at the meeting. Class 1 of the Cambridgeshire, in which the better horses ran, was won by Gyroscope, and Orichalque took Class 2 for Major Beatty, mildly fancied at 25 to 1 despite his decidedly inconspicuous earlier efforts. The combined prize money for both classes was barely a third of normal for the race. The accompanying sales did not seem at the time to be particularly successful, but Lord Rosebery told the Jockey Club a fortnight later that they had saved some breeders from bankruptcy.

It was a similar story at Newbury a week later, when 274 horses ran in 13 races over the two days, though only one division was needed. The total prize money was only £1,704, compared with £4,330 at the corresponding meeting in 1938, but 39 runners chased £100 in the Russley Handicap, which turned out to be the largest field for any wartime race. Again, the meeting was well attended, with the Great Western Railway running the usual special trains from Paddington and the added reassurance of a police-operated portable air raid siren. Over the next two days there were plenty of runners at Thirsk also, and crowds with which Sir Loftus Bates pronounced himself "satisfied", Yorkshire dialect for thrilled to bits.

CHAPTER 3

IN DENIAL (NOVEMBER 1939 TO MAY 1940)

Wartime life in autumn 1939 was unlike anything that had been imagined, with no massive land battles on the western front (in fact, no western front at all), no air attacks on civilian or economic targets and no poison gas, though everyone dutifully carried their gas masks with them. So far, only petrol was rationed and, while some prices rose, there were few shortages of food or consumer goods. Many of the younger men were in the forces or awaiting call-up, but few of them were actually fighting the Germans. Wartime was rather like a disjointed and inconvenient version of peacetime but people gradually became used to this new kind of everyday life, which the American press was calling the Phoney War or Sitzkrieg.

After the tentative resumption in October the flat racing season ran on to its conclusion with more confidence, and big fields trying to make the best of limited opportunities regardless of the poor prize money. On 1st November, the first day of the final Newmarket meeting the Middle Park Stakes, the only survivor of the big autumn two-year-old races, was run for £776 – about a quarter of usual. Nevertheless, Marcel Boussac thought it worth sending Djebel from France and the horse staked his claim for the 1940 classics by beating Tant Mieux by an easy two lengths. A close third despite a poor start was Godiva, again ridden by Doug Marks. In a normal year she would probably have run in the Cheveley Park Stakes to avoid taking on the colts. The main race of the second day was the Cesarewitch, shortened to the two miles of the Summer Course, with a massive field of 35 and won by Cantatrice, the favourite, ridden by Doug Smith. In an unbroken series of 101 renewals of the race, this was the first not run over the traditional course.

Meetings at Stockton and Thirsk followed in the next two weeks, after which southern flat racing ended with a mundane but well supported programme at Newbury. This time things were less comfortable for the crowd, the permanent buildings being unavailable and tables protected by canvas awnings having to suffice. No explanation was given, but it was probably connected with partial army occupation of the course. The season ended, as usual, at Manchester, where the meeting on 18th November was arranged with some difficulty as a morale booster at the request of the Regional Commissioner. The Manchester November Handicap went to Lord Rosebery's Tutor and Eph Smith, and the season faded into the November murk with Lord Glanely's Holy Terror winning the Final Plate. The last day of the season also saw The Sporting Chronicle cease publication indefinitely, but the Tote resumed business, eventually finishing the year with a turnover of £4.6 million, a fall of 26% on 1938.

The campaign to resume racing had achieved its objective: owners had supported the meetings, the public had turned up but the Luftwaffe had not, and there seemed to be a future for breeders. This led to successful Newmarket December Sales at which the Aga Khan's yearlings alone fetched 36,000 guineas.

November had started with a tirade in The Sporting Life against the pony racing authorities by Leonard Jayne, the sport's staunchest supporter and long-standing chief advocate. He berated them for doing nothing when the rest of racing was managing to re-start, suggesting that the PTC should lease a Jockey Club course if

Northolt were unavailable because the company was in receivership. The course had, in fact, been requisitioned at the outbreak of war but was about to be released as unsuitable for its intended use, and on 14th November the receiver approached the Home Office as to whether racing might be allowed. The press was soon reporting rumours of possible meetings in 1940.

The Jockey Club too was starting to look towards 1940 when it met at the beginning of the month. The Minister of Transport had warned them not to "blazon a great programme abroad", but they decided to put forward a Newmarket programme on the express understanding that it would be cancelled if not feasible in the circumstances or if the government objected, also making clear that it might be run on either course. Lord Hamilton of Dalzell, the King's representative at Ascot, told them it was hoped to hold the meeting there "on something like the ordinary scale". The atmosphere seems to have been no more than cautiously hopeful, but the next day's Sporting Life reported rumours, which must have come from an insider, that the Jockey Club was optimistic about 1940 and contemplating a near-normal programme.

A fortnight later the NHC met and decided, in its bull-at-a-gate fashion, to tell the Minister of Transport that four days' racing a week was the minimum acceptable and to send him a fixture list on that basis for January and February. This had already been leaked to the press, as had offers from Newbury and Gatwick to stage the Grand National if it could not be run at Aintree. The Committee accepted the Newbury offer despite Gatwick's experience of running substitute Nationals from 1916 to 1918. They also refused licences to Tommy Carey, the PTC champion jockey (not to be confused with T.F.Carey, an established NH rider) and two PTC trainers, which seems harsh in view of the fact that they soon afterwards granted a licence to Charlie Smirke. Another decision which was to cause ill-feeling was not to sanction point-to-points in 1940, despite the fact that many hunts were managing to carry on.

The extended British Summer Time ended on 19ᵗʰ November and the following day "the winter game", as journalists liked to call jump racing, resumed at Leicester with what, in other circumstances, would have been a humdrum card. Charlie Smirke lost no time in making use of his new licence, winning the selling hurdle on Speed Trap. There were plenty of runners, except in the concluding Paddock Chase, in which the long odds-on favourite Rightun finished alone after one of his two rivals pulled up and the other dropped dead. The Sporting Life produced one of its effusive but faintly condescending reports that conveyed the impression that NH racing was an activity carried on by an alien species, observing that "the thoroughly sporting folk associated with the cross-country sport were really glad to be active again and it was pleasing to see that some had managed to get leave from their military duties to take a hand".

The paper's correspondence columns were enlivened by a spat over the point-to-point ban. An Old Un, from Somewhere in Leicestershire, noted that hunts were finding things hard and had been looking forward to the financial benefit of their point-to-point. The ban was unjustified, because there would be no extra petrol consumption: it was rationed, so what was used for one thing could not be used for another. There was some support for this, though WWC (obviously a traditionalist) thought the answer was less elaborate meetings over natural courses. However, Another Old Un from Melton Mowbray asserted that the meetings could not be viable, so the ban was saving would-be organisers from themselves.

In early December the Chief Constable of West Sussex wrote to the Home Office asking for advice about forthcoming meetings at Fontwell Park, where he felt large crowds should not be allowed because it was only two miles from RAF Tangmere. When told it was government policy to allow racing where possible, he wrote again to say he would allow the meetings but wondered (probably tongue in cheek) whether the same would apply to Goodwood.

Racing continued, prosaically but well supported, until the middle of December for the four days per week that had been wrung out of Captain Wallace and then took a break until Boxing Day. The heroics of the Battle of the River Plate lifted public morale, but Christmas was a time of mixed emotions. It was the only wartime Christmas with no significant shortages; there was enough food, enough to drink, enough coal, some luxuries, and presents and cards available to buy. The shortages were not material but human. Many thousands of families sat down to dinner feeling the absence of someone who was trying to make the best of the day in a forces canteen, possibly "somewhere in France", or, perhaps, as a guest of some kindly family in a distant part of Britain.

With Kempton Park in military hands, Boxing Day racing moved to Windsor where, according to The Times correspondent "there was a very large attendance of visitors, one of the largest, if indeed not quite the largest I have seen at a Windsor jumping meeting. Runners were plentiful and the racing was most interesting and enjoyable in spite of a cold and damp afternoon". The second day was also cold and damp, but frost was coming and it was to be the last racing for eight weeks. The next morning's race special had just left Paddington for Cheltenham when news came that the meeting had been abandoned. Incredibly by present standards, the Great Western stopped the train at Slough, hauled it promptly back to London and refunded all the fares. A two day meeting at Newbury was due to follow but had to be abandoned when the weather failed to improve, knocking out the Sefton Handicap Chase which had been intended as a replacement for the Grand Sefton, normally the only valuable race early in the season, but lost that year with the rest of the Aintree November meeting.

In the new year the weather simply worsened. Meeting after meeting was abandoned and on 17th January the Thames froze in London for the first time since 1888. Three days later the Red Cross Handicap Chase was due to take place at Leopardstown in connection with a sweepstake for the Irish Red Cross Society, authorised by a special Act of the Irish Parliament. To be run over 4 miles 250 yards, the race had attracted continuous interest ever since it was announced, which was hardly surprising in view of the stratospheric first prize of £2,610 – more than three times that for the Irish Grand National and within hailing distance of the total winners' prize money for the Punchestown meeting, the pinnacle of the Irish season. The course was frozen solid on the long awaited day but the race had to take place somehow, so the meeting was put off for a week. A large contingent of British spectators braved a tempestuous Irish Sea and there were even four British-trained runners, but conditions were truly dreadful: the course was a bog and rain and mist made it impossible to see the far side. There is a tale, unfortunately impossible to verify, that the BBC radio commentator, Raymond Glendenning, found himself unable to see parts of the race because of the conditions and so, forbidden by defence regulations from mentioning the weather, made up what was happening until he could see the runners again. In the end only six of the 22 finished, with Jack Chaucer, the favourite, taking nine minutes 35 seconds to plough his way to victory.

The enforced break was filled by news and argument about the coming year's programme. Between mid-January and early February the cancellations were announced first of Chester, then of both Epsom meetings, and then of Ascot. The loss of Epsom meant that entries for the Derby and Oaks were void, raising the question of how substitute races were to be organised.

It is worth considering the status of substitute races, as references to them have sometimes implied that they were not the real thing but a sub-standard alternative. In terms of the sense of occasion this was usually true: a Derby at Newmarket would never be like one at Epsom, though it is harder to say why a Guineas race on the Bunbury Mile should be inherently worse than one just the other side of the Ditch. That, however, is not the issue; it is crucial to concentrate on the races themselves, not their surroundings, and decide whether they were intended to fulfil the same role as the normal ones for which they were substitutes, whether they succeeded in this, and whether people at the time saw them as doing so. If a race was called a Derby, was intended as the main test of three-year-olds over the Derby distance, was contested by the best of that generation, was recognised as such at the time, and was later trusted by breeders as a true test, then it should be accepted as a real Derby. Whether or not it was a "substitute" for the original version is unimportant, and the same applies to most other big races that took place away from their peacetime home. A question only really arises when there was a fundamental difference between the normal race and the substitute, such as some handicaps later in the war that were limited to horses from a particular region.

Just before the cancellations were announced the Home Office started to worry about what the Jockey Club might be planning. "My letter to Lord Harewood [of 21st September] may have led to some misconception" explained a file note by Sir Alexander Maxwell, the Permanent Secretary. The idea had been to confirm that three particular meetings could be held, and the Club had "recognised that there could be very little racing". The department would need to think very carefully before allowing Goodwood, Ascot or Epsom, and should try to get an arrangement for comparatively small meetings to be held. There was, therefore, consternation when Col. W.B. Vince of the Air Raid Protection Department saw the draft fixture list for the flat season to the end of May, which arrived on 2nd February. This proposed 67 days' racing on 24 courses, compared with 90 days on 36 courses which had been allocated for that period in the abortive list published in August 1939. Apart from a couple of two-day slots where it was helpfully indicated that the NHC wanted to race at Cheltenham and Gatwick, there were only five blank days. Within a day Vince had analysed the programme alongside typical attendance figures for the corresponding peacetime meetings and produced a damning report.

An anti-aircraft gun inside the home bend at Derby racecourse early in 1940. The straight mile crosses the low ground in the middle distance and disappears over a slight ridge.

Referring to Maxwell's September letter as to the type of meetings allowable, he said "The list now drawn up is by no means of that kind, and appears to approximate to a normal racing programme". Although the Ministry of Transport was not prepared to object from a railway point of view and had told the railway companies they could run special trains if there was no interference with normal traffic, "it appears to us that this programme goes far beyond what is permissible in war time". In view of the cutbacks in football, he suggested that the Jockey Club should be asked to restrict racing to Saturdays and bank holidays and hold meetings either at "country places" where large crowds were unlikely or near large population centres to avoid strain on transport. In a comically naïve conclusion he wondered whether it would be possible for attendances to be reduced by making meetings less interesting than usual!

The report went to Maxwell with a manuscript note from F.C.Johnson, a principal civil servant, who agreed that it looked like a peacetime programme and went beyond "what may be necessary to keep up the people's spirits". He would have expected a stiffer line from the Ministry of Transport. Maxwell, noting that the proposal was inconsistent with the football situation, passed it on to the Home Secretary, who felt there should be a substantial reduction. He made it clear, though, that they should "give special consideration to individual race meetings which might be regarded as having a certain national significance". The outcome was a letter to Mr Francis Weatherby at the Jockey Club Registry, telling him that the Home Secretary had thought the Club recognised that there could be very little racing and now felt that the proposed programme "goes much beyond what could properly be permitted in war time". They were asked to confine racing, like football, to Saturdays and bank holidays, the letter ending with a not particularly veiled threat to restrict crowd numbers severely at meetings near large towns.

On 7th February the Home Secretary asked the Cabinet Civil Defence Committee (CDC) to back this hard line before he spelled it out to Harewood, but was humiliatingly rebuffed. The Minister of Health was concerned about curtailing outdoor recreation and wanted to see racing restored "if only for the keen interest taken by hundreds of thousands of workers who seldom see an actual race". Quite how reading the Daily Mirror's racing page constituted outdoor recreation was not explained, but he was strongly supported by the Minister of Pensions and Sir John Reith, the Minister of Information. The Ministry of Agriculture wanted fewer restrictions on greyhound racing and thought horse racing was small beer anyhow. Only the Treasury supported the Home Secretary, thinking Lord Haw Haw would have a field day if restrictions were relaxed and that the French and Poles would be upset (though one might think the defeated Poles would have had more pressing concerns than the British racing programme). The Minister of Transport rather lamely hoped that Harewood would be told that restrictions would have to be reimposed if extensive bombing started. Anderson was authorised to confer with Harewood but, by now, with practically no cards in his hand. By the end of the day Reith had consulted the French and confirmed that near-normal racing would not worry them, disposing of the one argument advanced in Anderson's favour.

Next day Anderson had a letter from the Secretary of State for India, Lord Zetland, a member of the Jockey Club. He naturally supported the majority line, but on the grounds that owners and breeders would be unable to carry on without sufficient racing. Admitting his interest as a breeder, he reassured the Home Secretary that "a fairly regular programme could be carried on without undue ostentation".

Anderson had been a top civil servant and knew a lost cause when he saw one: he was not going to waste any more time on this issue. When he met Harewood and Ilchester he merely explained why his department had been worried and left Sir Thomas Gardner, Home Security Permanent Secretary, to agree a fixture list with Mr. Weatherby. They settled on 51 days at 23 courses (later changed to 52 days on 26 courses), with the Derby and the Oaks to be run at Newbury on the 12th and 13th June.

The affair was a small example of the Chamberlain administration's lack of focus and inclination to dodge issues rather than address them with proper rigour, which enabled the Jockey Club to play off one minister against another. Did the Club double-cross the Home Office by saying they accepted that only minimal racing could be allowed but then plotting a much bigger programme? Perhaps they were not that cynical. The Home Office was not yet really recognised as the leading department for restriction of sport, so the Jockey Club may have assumed that the Ministry of Transport was the key player, as its predecessor had been in the Great War. Having found they could push Wallace around more or less at will, perhaps they felt that all bets with Anderson were off.

The Home Office had agreed in January to the idea of holding a few PTC meetings at Northolt, despite opposition from the Commissioner of the Metropolitan Police for public safety reasons and because "it would create an awkward precedent", and they had told CDC that "it is not proposed to interfere with the holding of National Hunt, point-to-point and other similar local meetings held in country districts". Consequently, Northolt fixtures from Easter to the end of April were soon announced and there was a NHC request to discuss meetings to replace those lost in the big freeze, now into its second month. Pressure for this had started in early January with a Sporting Life article by J.L.Taylor criticising the decision to end the season at Easter, which was exceptionally early that year, and accusing the authorities of doing too little to prevent jumping being treated as a poor relation and expendable in the interests of flat racing. After some letters of support the paper published a pious editorial saying that, whilst replacement fixtures would be welcome, flat racing was of primary concern and jumping "may have to be sacrificed after Easter in the interests of the more important code". However, by mid-February the situation had become desperate. It was left to Gardner to meet Rosebery and Fred Withington, the Grand Old Man of jump racing, and they told him that their suggested programme from Easter Monday to the end of May was only a tenth of usual, there would be very few spectators and that jumping was small, insignificant and no threat to the transport system.This was how Col. Garratt had inveigled the Board of Trade into allowing some NH racing in the winter of 1915/16 at a time of draconian restriction of flat racing, and it worked again. The 22 days agreed actually represented nearly a quarter of the 1939 equivalent after excluding bona fide meetings and Easter Saturday, which had been in April that year. Gardner agreed because of the supposedly small crowds and remoteness of the venues, on condition that there should be "no large publicity", another example of senior civil servants' odd belief that racecourse companies would put on meetings but keep quiet about them or deliberately make them boring to discourage patrons.

Two days earlier the Home Office had agreed to allow the Grand National to be run at Aintree. The decision had been put off pending settlement of the flat programme and was taken despite a letter from Capt. A. F. Hordern, the Chief Constable of Lancashire, strongly opposing the idea. Although the crowd would probably be less than the normal 250,000 there were practically no shelters and in an air raid the stands and enclosures would be excellent targets and "veritable death traps". Should spectator numbers be limited, as in the case of football? The reply was that the government did not want to stop racing altogether and that "fixtures of national significance, such as the Grand National, merit special consideration; in short, the view taken here is that the Grand National should be held if at all possible".

On 24th February the Home Office sent a circular to all chief constables, listing the agreed fixtures and emphasising that "it is not desired that, generally speaking, any restriction should be placed on the number of persons attending these race meetings". The Department must be consulted where special risks made it desirable to limit numbers. This stimulated some lateral thinking by the Chief Constables of Shrewsbury and Shropshire. The latter, Major H. A. Golden, wrote to ask whether the absence from the list of a flapping meeting they had wanted to suppress for years meant it could and must be prohibited. The Home Office solemnly replied that they could not say that meetings not on the list should automatically be barred, though it was open to chief constables to use their powers under the Public Entertainments (Restriction) Order 1939, Paragraph 1(b), if they thought circumstances warranted it, whereupon Major Golden threw in the towel.

The government's surprisingly liberal attitude was in tune with the mood of the country, which had changed from fearful to relieved and then to almost cocky. Cartoons depicted the Germans as comically inept, like Funf, the ITMA character; everyone sang "We're gonna hang out our washing on the Siegfried Line", and on film George Formby, complete with ukelele, humiliated Hitler single handed. Later the LMS Railway produced Holidays by LMS, a 684 page guide with 100 pages of photographs. Unfortunately, none of this was justified. As Mark Connelly points out, it betrayed a sense of sang froid built not on knowing the odds and accepting them stoically, but upon ignorance and fantasy.

The weather changed at last and racing resumed at Newbury on 21st February with a fairly good attendance, given that nobody knew the meeting was definitely on until the morning papers appeared. Gowran Ranger, ridden by Tom Hanbury, was first past the post in the United Services Handicap Chase but an hour or so later the connections of the favourite, which had finished fourth, noticed that Hanbury was in trooper's uniform. They objected on the grounds that he was not qualified to ride *because he was not an officer,* and must have got all of £10 for third place when the winner was disqualified and the race awarded to Tetray. Ironically, Tetray was ridden by Mr.I.K. (Kim) Muir, who normally rode Gowran Ranger. Muir was a subaltern in the 10th Hussars, a fearless amateur rider and rather a favourite with the racing press.

The following Sunday Greenwich Mean Time gave way to British Summer Time and would not return until October 1945. With the approach of spring, thoughts started turning to flat racing, particularly the fillies' classics and the respective merits of Golden Penny and Godiva. Early in March the Doncaster executive announced that they were planning to race but the Jockey Club conceded that the Newmarket Craven and First Spring meetings would have to be on the July Course.

The Cheltenham festival was down to two days, with the Spa

Hurdle and the Cotswold Maiden and Swindon Selling Chases deleted as well as the three amateurs' races on the National Hunt course. The Gold Cup, worth only £495, was shortened to three miles because part of the course was under plough. On the first day Dorothy Paget's Solford caught African Sister close home to win the Champion Hurdle comfortably, Golden Knight was disqualified for impeding Iceberg II in the Broadway Novices Chase and G.Legge became one of the more unlikely trainers of a festival winner when Bachelor's Gown took the Grand Annual: Legge was equestrian all-rounder Harry Llewellyn's stud groom, but held the licence for his employer while he was in the army. Overnight snow prevented racing on the scheduled second day but the importance of the meeting was such that a week's postponement was sanctioned. Gold Cup favourite Roman Hackle, another of Dorothy Paget's many entries, had the benefit of a successful run at Windsor on the intervening Saturday and never looked like being beaten in a depleted field.

Easter fell the next weekend and saw the biggest racing programme of the entire war, starting with jumping at Newbury, Manchester, Plumpton and (for the last time) Loughborough on the Saturday. Newbury's feature, the Great Berkshire Chase, a one-off event worth £830 to the winner and second only to the Grand National in value, was won by Rockquilla, ridden by T.F.Carey and trained by George Beeby. On Easter Monday the flat season opened at Birmingham and Hurst Park, where there were huge fields. PTC racing resumed at Northolt Park and drew big crowds despite competition from Hurst Park. There was jumping at Manchester, where Roman Hackle could manage only third in the Lancashire Chase, Hereford, Huntingdon, Wetherby, Taunton (in place of army-occupied Wincanton and with specially extended car parks) and Torquay, where it also turned out to be the last meeting ever.

April began with a two-day version of the Lincoln meeting, displaced from opening the flat season but with a London contingent, as usual, among a reasonably good crowd. The Sporting Life predicted that the new flat season would be a great success. The rest of the week was taken up by the Grand National meeting, where the value of some races had severely reduced, particularly the jumping ones other than the National. Despite the value of the Grand National itself falling from £7,285 in 1939 to £4,225 it was still by far the most valuable jump race of the year. The winner was Lord Stalbridge's Bogskar, ridden by Mervyn Jones, who survived a last fence mistake to outpace MacMoffat. On the final day the Champion Chase was replaced by a Becher Chase with different conditions from the one normally run in November, narrowly won by Sawfish, now ridden by F.Poole. The Stanley Chase went to Mr David Sherbrooke, a vet, on his own Poet Prince.

There was no royalty at Aintree, though Lord Derby was in his box and Lord Sefton was also present. Mr Chamberlain was not there either: he was telling the House of Commons that although he could not explain why Hitler had not attacked while he had the advantage "one thing is certain: he missed the bus". Saturday's Daily Express carried an assurance from General Ironside, the CIGS, that "we are ready for anything they may start". The very next day it became clear that the Germans were about to launch an invasion of Norway and Denmark for which British forces were not prepared. They rushed to help the Norwegians but were soon defeated by the more numerous, more experienced and better equipped Germans. Before the end of April they had been driven from the south of the country and it was only a matter of time before the rest succumbed. The Phoney War was over.

Even before this, rumours began circulating that no more racing would be allowed when the current fixture list expired at the end of May, which led to the Home Office receiving an incandescent letter from a senior government officer, Sir Warren Fisher of Civil Defence HQ in Manchester. After fulminating against a supposed government line that amusement was not consistent with the implications of war he listed the usual arguments for continuing racing and finished with a demand that if the government's policy was to stop entertainment they should jolly well make it clear. A file note by Johnson dismissed this as "just nonsense", and Johnson was best placed to know because that very day he had agreed the programme from June to August – not even Gardner was involved now. There were to be 101 days, nearly three quarters of 1939 level, including a two-day substitute Ascot meeting at Newmarket in late June, the Bibury Club at Salisbury, the Carlisle meeting and the Northumberland Plate, but no Goodwood. When Lord Ilchester described this at the Jockey Club meeting the following week as a good list he was not exaggerating. He went on to explain that matters generally were not easy. The stewards wanted to hearten owners and trainers, but had to persuade the government that they were not trying to race too much, which was what had been thought when they first saw the programme. The stewards had had hopes for Epsom and Goodwood, but the army would not release the courses, and the Rowley Mile. The Air Ministry and Air Marshal Baldwin, the area commander, had been very kind and helpful about the latter, but it would not have been possible for the RAF to vacate the buildings for race meetings and there would have been a risk of abandonments at short notice in bad weather because they might need to use Newmarket Heath if the "going" on the grass runways there was better than at Mildenhall. The real problem, though, had been the police, who insisted that RAF sites had "technical points" that must be guarded against the IRA. If it were not recorded in Jockey Club minutes, the idea of suspending wartime operations at a front line base for race meetings to be held there would seem completely surreal.

Racing itself was now going great guns, with interest centring on Classic trials. Djebel had already won in France, but Tant Mieux had beaten Stardust in the Greenham Stakes at Newbury and Lord Derby's Lighthouse II won the Column Stakes, which was a three-year-old produce race in peacetime. Lord Glanely's Rose of England colt, now named British Empire, was favourite for the Craven but finished a disastrous last and was soon exported to Argentina. Among the fillies, Golden Penny had won the Severals Stakes, but Godiva was waiting for the One Thousand Guineas itself. At Alexandra Park the veteran Brownie Carslake collapsed in the weighing room after winning on Ipswich in a desperate finish. It looked bad, and was: serious heart disease was diagnosed, compelling immediate retirement. He died the following year. Meanwhile, April jumping produced a record 149 runners in nine races at Worcester, and a military race open to other ranks at Bangor-on-Dee which was won, appropriately, by Tom Hanbury on Paladin.

When the Two Thousand Guineas took place on 1st May Djebel and Charlie Elliott swept through in the last furlong to beat Stardust and Tant Mieux comfortably, with Lighthouse only sixth. Two days later came the One Thousand Guineas, for which Golden Penny was odds on. Gordon Richards got her away smartly, but Godiva and Marks also got a good start for once and they had the race between them until the final furlong, where Godiva drew away to win by a stunning five lengths.

Events in the wider world suddenly started moving with bewildering speed. The Norway disaster had discredited Chamberlain's judgement once again and people began to feel the war was not going to be won with a prime minister who looked and sounded like an Edwardian bank manager. The crisis came on 7th May with a House of Commons adjournment debate on Norway that turned out to be one of the most important Parliamentary events of the century, partly because Britain was still a pre-eminent world power and partly because Parliament had not yet been entirely taken over by professional party politicians. Jeremy Paxman points out that apart from the passion, the other striking aspect was how many of the contributors seemed to know what they were talking about. The government, with a nominal majority of 213,

Godiva (Doug Marks) at Hurst Park in May 1940.
William Jarvis is behind her (left).

won the vote by only 81 after numerous Conservatives supported the opposition or abstained. Chamberlain's resignation was inevitable and he was succeeded on 10th May by Churchill, despite the misgivings of some who thought him a maverick opportunist whose own judgement had sometimes been questionable. That same day the Germans invaded Holland and Belgium (and racegoers grumbled because there were no special trains to Newbury).

The new coalition government grabbed the tiller firmly. The Whitsun bank holiday was cancelled, as was all racing until further notice, and on 14th May Anthony Eden made a radio appeal for Local Defence Volunteers as the military situation rapidly deteriorated. A week later, with the BEF retreating towards the Channel ports, Parliament passed the Emergency Powers Act, giving the government almost unlimited control over people and property. The Dunkirk evacuation was ordered on 26th May with Churchill in a power struggle with some of his own cabinet, led by Lord Halifax, who wanted to make peace overtures to Hitler through still-neutral Italy.

Despite the impending catastrophe the Home Office not only gave permission for racing to re-start, which it did at Manchester on 18th May, but then proceeded to beat off all attempts to stop it again. This was distinctly controversial and was taken up in The Times, which had switched from supporting appeasement to hawkish patriotism and ran an article entitled *Are We At War?* criticising various activities and occupations perceived not to assist prosecution of the war. Writers to The Times joined in with gusto. R.A.Hayes of Trinity Hall, Cambridge, asserted that broadcasting racing results gave the wrong message to our allies. F.Harrison-Baker from Cheshire agreed, and said that racing personnel could be put to better use. George A.Bonner (Oxford and Cambridge Club, Pall Mall) wanted to add dog racing and pools to the list of useless jobs, and Clive Bell of Lewes thought the government would not be taken seriously until it stopped all racing. Later, Norman Mackinnon and E.B.Wilbraham were concerned about a possible air raid on the Derby. It was not one way traffic, as there were pro-racing letters from R.C.Lyle (who omitted to mention that he was the Times racing correspondent) and the editor of The Sporting Life, A.B.Clements, who criticised the "virtuous wrath" of "Olympians": the war was not to be used as "an excuse by the unco' guid for prohibiting those things of which they do not approve". Finally, the Hon. George Lambton quoted a Times editorial commending the courage to go on quietly doing one's job: his job was training racehorses and he would do it as long as the Minister of Labour approved.

On the day the Times correspondence began the Home Office received a letter querying the wisdom of continuing to race. This came from the Chief Constable of East Sussex, who asked them, because of the international situation, to consider cancelling the forthcoming meeting at Lewes, which was within sight of Newhaven and vulnerable. He also felt his men should not be taken from their normal duties to police the races. By the time the reply was sent the Dunkirk operation was in full swing and the Sussex coast effectively in the front line, but despite this it said that "it is the policy of the government that racing should, for the present, continue to the extent to which it has hitherto been permitted" and the meeting should go ahead "though circumstances might arise which would require its cancellation at very short notice". The Mayor of Salisbury, too, was slapped down with no more than an assurance that the situation was under constant review when he asked for cancellation of the meeting there. The Jockey Club had announced that no general alteration of fixtures was contemplated, although meetings might be cancelled at the shortest notice. And so racing went ahead at Bath, and at Salisbury, and at Hurst Park and at Lewes, while rail travel in the south was being massively disrupted by movements of the 186 special trains taking troops away from the coast as fast as the rescue fleet could land them, and while BEF soldiers, among them Lieut.I.K.Muir, were being killed only a few score miles away. It is difficult to understand what the Home Office was thinking. Perhaps they were afraid of the effect of stopping racing on the morale of the public, which had not yet been told the magnitude of the military disaster, but their file papers give no indication of this. One can only assume that they truly felt the situation was still not grave enough for more than a warning that current policy might have to change at short notice, but whether that was through cool realism or lack of any realism at all is impossible to judge.

Besides Kim Muir, Gerry Duncanson, another good amateur, had been killed but a third, John Hislop, was evacuated unhurt, and among the last rescued was Major Leslie Petch of the Green Howards, one of the Jockey Club judges. Hector Christie and Roger Mortimer were among the racing men captured, and at sea the

Aston Tirrold trainer Jack Bisgood had been wounded. The Duke of Norfolk, a member of the Jockey Club, returned with his battalion of the Royal Sussex Regiment and arrived home on the evening of 2nd June. Next day he was at Lewes to see his wife's Midas Touch run in the Berwick Plate, which was doubtless his way of coping with the appalling experience he had been through. Today he would probably be offered counselling.

CHAPTER 4

IN PERIL (JUNE TO DECEMBER 1940)

One result of the German offensive and change of government was
a reversal of policy on interning enemy aliens. In October 1939
Chamberlain's administration decided to intern only those who
individually posed a security risk, but now, with a Fifth Column
scare by the Daily Mail and the real possibility of invasion,
everything changed and orders were given to round up all German
and Austrian nationals aged sixteen upwards. Asked if this included
those who had fled here from Nazi persecution Churchill replied
"Collar the lot!", so bewildered Jewish refugees found themselves
whisked off to the local police station and then a holding camp.
Many internees from the London area were taken to Lingfield Park,
then still "Leafy Lingfield", completely enclosed by trees and a
delightful spot in May if one happened not to be in custody.
Impromptu entertainments devised by the prisoners included
concerts and betting on the numbers shown by the automatic
counters when the turnstile gates were given a brisk twirl. Over
several weeks of uneasy coexistence between the refugees and some
of the less anti-Nazi inmates they were gradually dispersed. The
unlucky were put aboard the Arandora Star, which was sunk en
route to Canada, whilst others were sent to long-term internment
camps in such places as Huyton and the Isle of Man. One transit

stop was Ascot racecourse, guarded by defeated BEF troops whom the refugees found uninterested in differentiating between one sort of German and another. Most of the innocent managed to obtain release during the next year or so. Lingfield received a second wave in mid-June when Italian nationals were arrested in the wake of Mussolini's mistaken decision that it was now safe to declare war on Britain and defeated France. Some spent the rest of the war at Lingfield, but several hundred were lost with the Arandora Star.

In the face of unease about the continuance of horse and greyhound racing Anderson told the Commons on 30th May that "experience has proved that if workers are to maintain their efficiency for more than a limited period some measure of relaxation is essential. For that reason the government has been anxious not to interfere unduly with facilities for sport and recreation. The whole position is being kept constantly under review and I will not hesitate, if circumstances demand it, to impose such further restrictions on public entertainment as may be necessary".

The same day news broke that not only had Doncaster's June meeting been cancelled but the race committee chairman was pessimistic about holding the St. Leger there, the course having been taken over as the Royal Army Veterinary Corps headquarters (though that could not be made public). It also transpired that Djebel would not be coming from Chantilly for the Derby which, in the circumstances, was not a surprise. As a result, Lighthouse became favourite. The final opportunities for winding up horses for the Newbury classics were the Derby and Oaks Trials at Hurst Park. Fred Darling had sent Pont L'Eveque to beat weaker opposition at Salisbury the day before to keep out of the way of his first string, Tant Mieux, which duly beat Hippius and Turkhan without difficulty. Godiva made another of her slow starts in the Oaks Trial but soon led her moderate rivals easily, causing some good judges to believe that only her temperament could beat her at Newbury.

Then, suddenly, it was not to be Newbury. With only nine days to go Weatherbys announced that the meeting had been abandoned and all races transferred to Newmarket. No reason was given and there is nothing on the files of the Home Office, though they must have authorised the change. Ante-post bets were unaffected because the conditions of the races stipulated that they could be run at Newbury or the July Course. There was mild surprise next day when Djebel was among the final acceptors for the Derby, but it was assumed that the scratching notification had failed to get through because of the chaos in France and he was treated as a non-runner in the betting.

On the eve of the Derby, with France collapsing, the government got cold feet about allowing it. Strong representations that "an unfortunate impression might be created if the arrangements for the substitute Derby were allowed to stand" were made to Anderson from someone unidentified but influential enough to make him consult the Foreign Secretary. They agreed it was too late to stop the meeting but thought steps should be taken to discourage publicity about it and the results.

Independently, the BBC prissily cancelled the commentary and substituted a documentary entitled *A Visit to an Arms Factory*, saving no petrol and penalising only those who had responsibly decided not to travel to Newmarket. CDC thought the decision "unfortunate" despite its having unintentionally fulfilled ministers' wishes about publicity.

Derby Day was 12th June and crowds flocked to Newmarket by every means available. Two special trains from Kings Cross brought 1,400 but most came in coaches and traffic jams grew as the military checked identity cards, causing some spectators to miss the big race. Many hundreds walked from the town centre and the stands were uncomfortably packed with an estimated 10,000 people and probably the largest crowd seen at the July Course, but greatly exaggerated by the popular press. They were described as "gay, well dressed and with plenty of money to spend". Racecards sold out before racing and were offered by enterprising profiteers at five shillings each. Servicemen in uniform were fairly well represented but it did not feel particularly like wartime, let alone the middle of the most serious crisis the country had ever faced.

In the Derby itself, Stardust and Tant Mieux failed to stay when Sam Wragg went for home more than a quarter of a mile out on Pont L'Eveque, a moment captured in one of the best known of all wartime racing photographs. Charlie Smirke challenged persistently but to no avail on Turkhan, and Lighthouse barely got home in third. The press verdict was that the best stayer had won convincingly.

The crowd was smaller for the following day's Oaks, for which Godiva was favourite at a generous 7 to 4 because of a rumour that she was, as The Sporting Life delicately put it, "sexually amiss". Again she fooled around at the start and was tailed off in the early stages but two furlongs out, in the words of Bloodstock Breeders' Review, "D.Marks on Godiva shot past the senior jockeys with an exceedingly saucy epithet" and it was all over. Her time equalled the course record and only Silverlace got anywhere near her. There was "a deal of hand clapping" as she came into the winner's enclosure, which was no more than her due as one of the best Classic fillies of the century.

Reactions to the success of the meeting varied widely. A particularly myopic article in The Sporting Life claimed it had been good propaganda and an answer to the "doleful prohibitionists" which celebrated "the cheeriness of the British character at times of stress", but others were not remotely amused. As Roger Mortimer later wrote, the events of Derby day aroused a suspicion in some minds that the nation as a whole was not treating the war with the seriousness it unfortunately deserved. One such suspicious mind was that of Mr Higgs, MP for Birmingham West, who asked the Home Secretary in the Commons next day whether racing should be allowed to continue. Anderson parried this by referring to his earlier explanation of government policy but pointed out that there had just been further cuts in the programme. These appeared in that day's Racing Calendar and, as well as cancellation of the Northumberland Plate meeting which had already been announced, included Aintree's summer meeting and reduction of Newmarket's First July meeting from four days to two.

On 17th June France sought an armistice. Even the most sanguine of Britons could no longer delude themselves about the threat of a German attack, and next day Churchill warned them that "The Battle of France is now over. I expect that the Battle of Britain is about to begin".

At this point it was the Jockey Club that decided enough was enough: though a two-day Wolverhampton meeting went ahead, the stewards announced on 19th June that there would be no more racing until further notice, including cancellation of the substitute Ascot which was about to take place. The announcement referred to consultation with the government, but there is no record of pressure from that quarter and later Home Office papers make it clear that the decision was the Jockey Club's. It was an astute and timely repetition of what had happened in April 1917, when the stewards found that the cabinet was about to ban racing and, realising that if that were to happen they would have no influence over when it started again, asked to be allowed to suspend it themselves. The PTC suspended racing on 20th June and the NHC did the same, though there was no urgency in their case because the season had ended a month earlier. With only Irish and greyhound racing to cover, The Sporting Life announced that it would come out only on Mondays until the ban was relaxed: little did the publishers imagine how long it would be before it appeared daily again.

Racecourses were again used as emergency camping grounds to cope with the unplanned return of troops from France. 30 Field Regiment Royal Artillery was disbanded at Ascot, Cheltenham was briefly home to the 2nd Middlesex, and Aintree and Haydock Park were the first ports of call for French sailors. Nottingham was used for forming the new 7th Leicestershires, who remained there until early 1941 without preventing racing. Bath also went into military occupation that was to last several years, as did Beverley, which became a night fighting training ground.

Racing people were now completely in limbo, with no idea when meetings would resume (or whether they would do so at all). Unlike the previous autumn, when they could hope things would settle down and the war soon started to seem quite distant, the prospect was for an invasion attempt which would have to be resisted before life could be anything like normal again. Faced with not knowing what to do, most carried on with what they were doing already. At Beckhampton Fred Darling told his staff he intended to keep the yard going, with the horses ticking over at a level from which they could quickly be got fully fit if the time came, and much the same happened at other stables. At Egerton House, for example, the string trotted and cantered on alternate days. Nevertheless, a few more owners and trainers decided they could no longer carry on.

One activity to which they could enthusiastically commit themselves was the Home Guard, which had a number of units whose core membership came from the racing world. The Lewes Racecourse platoon is believed to have been the only mounted one in the Home Guard, and Newmarket had had its own unofficial defence company before it was incorporated into the LDV. Its operations included one in which Harry Wragg and the vicar of St. Agnes church found themselves sharing a slit trench on Long Hill awaiting an expected drop of enemy parachutists, which fortunately failed to materialise. At first Harry's shotgun represented a high proportion of the company's firepower, but he was later given a Lewis gun with which it became his ambition to shoot down one of the enemy aircraft that had taken to flying arrogantly low over the town. In the event, whenever one flew close enough something always happened to prevent the gun being brought to bear, to Harry's intense annoyance but to the relief of Mrs Wragg, who felt that shooting at the Germans would only annoy them and make them try to bomb the house next time.

A village platoon was formed at Beckhampton and Fred Darling announced that he would command it. Second in command was Norman Bertie, his travelling head lad, who enjoyed his new status and played Captain Mainwaring to Darling's Napoleon. Some competition might have been expected from the other Beckhampton trainer, the wealthy but odd Herbert Blagrave, who trained a dozen or so horses of his own at The Grange, but he was quite content to be a sergeant. The platoon paraded after stables on Sunday mornings for drill and shooting on a makeshift range and then, on the stroke of noon, marched to the Wagon and Horses, where they fell out and all had a pint on the commanding officer. There was also a weekday evening parade, when there were lectures from NCOs from local camps, and night patrols on the downs. Later in the war one such exercise led to a terrible demonstration of Darling's ruthlessness. During a surprise inspection of the unit by senior officers an observation post under the command of Templeton, the head lad, was found to be unoccupied because the defenders were a few hundred yards away in the pub at Bishops Cannings. This was a grave military offence, but to Darling it was even more, and he summarily sacked Templeton from his job. When Gordon Richards implored him to change his mind, if only to avoid losing one of the best head lads in the business, Darling adamantly refused because "he made me look a bloody fool". The job had been Templeton's whole life and soon afterwards he shot himself.

During 1940 the army suddenly requisitioned the Coronach yard, part of the stables named after the 1926 Derby winner whose success had financed its construction, and a "hush-hush" unit of about 25 men was the first to be stationed there. They were never seen and it became apparent that they were training secretly on the downs at night. One day a soldier went round the houses in Beckhampton asking if a night's accommodation could be provided for wives of the members of the unit, as they were being allowed a short visit. This was arranged, the wives arrived, stayed overnight and returned home, and within a day the soldiers had gone. The villagers later heard that every one of them had been killed in the operation for which they had been training.

The story of the Battle of Britain has been told often enough not to need repeating, but the air war did sometimes affect the racing community. The affair of Harry Wragg's Lewis gun occurred because Newmarket was in the front line, with RAF Newmarket Heath a military target as well as the large amount of army activity that was going on in anticipation of an invasion through the eastern counties. Egerton House was affected by the activities of both sides. Not only was it close to the take-off run of fully laden RAF heavy bombers as they thundered across the Rowley Mile racecourse and staggered into the air, only just clearing the top of The Ditch, which was not good for the highly strung thoroughbreds a few feet below the flight path, but Luftwaffe planes also came over. One evening the siren sounded just after the horses had been mucked out and were about to be brushed over. Going to the door with the head lad, Snowy Outen saw an aircraft coming from the direction of the RAF station and only realised it was hostile when a stick of bombs fell into the grounds of the neighbouring stud. They ran across to help and found that the foaling boxes had been hit, and windows blown out of the stud groom and the stallion man's houses but, fortunately, no casualties. On another occasion the horses were being exercised beside the July Course when an enemy aircraft swooped down towards them but did no more than playfully fire its guns into the ground alongside the string, causing mayhem but nothing worse. Not all German airmen returned safely to base: one shot down over Northamptonshire in September 1940 found himself captured by the Home Guard in the shape of NH jockey and trainer Cliff Beechener, who frog marched him to the police station.

The racing press was keen to emphasise that the suspension was not intended to last for the duration of the war and periodically speculated as to when meetings would resume. This was almost entirely based on rumour and wishful thinking, since the Jockey Club was saying nothing. Bloodstock Breeders Review later criticised the stewards for allowing an atmosphere of depression to build up because of their silence, but this seems unfair in view of the delicacy of the situation. Ironically, the same article deprecated those of the community to whom the realities of the war had still not come home, missing the point that if the racing authorities behaved in a way that seemed to put them in that category they might exasperate the government and lose all sympathy for their aims.

In fact, feelers were put out surprisingly early, given that the desperate military situation was not improving. The first came from Lord Rosebery on behalf of the NHC, of which he was now Senior Steward. In a letter received at the Home Office on 25th July he almost apologetically enquired whether there was any chance of some racing later. He had not intended to raise the question until things were more settled, but was being pressed for advice about whether horses should be kept in training. Jumping people were not well off, and if there were no racing in the coming autumn and winter it would cause unemployment and poverty. A hand-written note at the foot of the letter says that the Minister had seen Rosebery and learned that the stewards hoped to organise a moderate amount of racing from mid-September. A separate note instructed Johnson to speak to Gardner who "does not much like the idea of recommencing racing". The result was a note to Gardner saying, "We should be inclined to say that if they want to race in a small way, we should let them, subject to immediate stoppage when requested. They and the JC stopped of their own accord, not at our request; they made all the announcements; there is now no French opinion to take into account; so long as football and dog racing go on, it is not clear why they should not hold a few jumping or point-to-point meetings if they wish. The newspapers have been referring to Lord Harewood and the JC as wishing to start again, but we have had no approaches that I can trace".

Matters progressed quickly and on 31st July the Minister saw Harewood, representing the Jockey Club and, below stairs, Gardner saw Rosebery for the NHC, and it was agreed that both bodies would announce that they had seen the Minister and hoped it would be possible to arrange a moderate amount of racing from mid-September, subject to stoppage at a moment's notice. Later that day this was reported to CDC, which agreed that unless it became essential to interfere in the interests of national defence, "it would be a mistake to deprive the public of this form of relaxation". They went on to express the hope that officers of the Australian and New Zealand forces would be given an opportunity to participate, which suggests that the issue had been presented to them in terms of jumping as a participants' sport, and that permission for flat racing crept in almost unnoticed. The agreed announcements were published on 5th August, when it was also made known that the Jockey Club was holding a census of horses in training, and the Racing Calendar of 22nd August included a provisional fixture list. This gave great relief and pleasure but, unfortunately, the programme had not been cleared with the Home Office, which hauled in the stewards for a ticking off. Anderson told them that, although there was no objection to their producing a fixture list from the middle of September, there must be no more than three days' racing a week and that meetings other than Newmarket must be limited to single days. Nevertheless, the way was clear for meetings at Hurst Park and Ripon on 14th September, followed by Newmarket, Windsor, Edinburgh, and Leicester, then a return to Hurst Park for a substitute St.Leger on the 28th.

The same day brought the sad news of the death of Godiva from septicaemia shortly after being moved to Ireland, and the next edition of The Sporting Life carried a letter from Doug Marks with a six-line elegy he had written for her. Lycidas it was not, but the racing press has never been a leading publisher of verse and hardly anyone but Marks, who was already becoming one of the sport's more colourful characters, would have attempted it.

The Times had already expressed displeasure at the very idea of racing resuming. The third leader on 23rd August noted that it was to re-start on a small scale, the reasons being understood to be the testing of bloodstock and giving people in the services and the general public a topic of interest besides the war. There was, it claimed, nevertheless a good deal of surprise, not diminished by the prospect of NH racing after the flat season ended. The leader went on elegantly to put the boot in: racing had been suspended because it was inappropriate in critical times and an undesirable expenditure of time, labour, petrol and money when there were so many appeals for economy and concentration of effort on the war. Large attendances at an expensive amusement would give the wrong impression of the spirit that actually prevailed, and it was illogical to encourage people to shelter from air raids but encourage them to gather where they could not shelter. None of these reasons had diminished and "no such case has been made for the resumption of racing as was made for its suspension. There are undoubtedly some who will welcome the concession, but there are very many others who will resent it".

This actually mattered. It is important to appreciate that the views of The Times were then seen not as those of one newspaper among many, but as the considered opinion of the majority of those whose opinions were worth hearing. Incurring the paper's displeasure could be a serious disadvantage. Letters to the editor inevitably followed. J.Holmes, a poultry farmer from Bicester, said that poultry and pig farmers who had been told to cut down by two thirds because of the lack of grain would bitterly resent the resumption of racing, which the government was inconsistently allowing to waste food. Capt.C.Noel Newton of Oakham and lately of the Life Guards had calculated that the annual value of all bloodstock exports would pay for the war for only fifty five minutes. On the other hand, Keith Freeman of the RAVC thought it was worth losing an egg or two a year to save the bloodstock industry. The damage done by a total cessation of racing could not be repaired in a generation, if ever, unlike pig or poultry breeding. Cyril Falls simply thought that racing should be considered in the same way as other entertainments and balanced against its effect on prosecuting the war.

Meanwhile, the Germans had, despite heroic resistance, gradually been getting the upper hand in the Battle of Britain. Their aircraft losses had been greater than British ones, but they were more affordable and the differential was slowly reducing. Three weeks after Eagle Day on 13th August, the start of the all-out effort to break the RAF in preparation for invasion, the critical point was close. Then, a fortnight before the scheduled invasion, Goering lost patience and changed his tactics. Late in the afternoon of 7th September, the last Saturday without racing, South Londoners enjoying the sunshine of a perfect early autumn day became aware of the surging drone of approaching Heinkels and were horrified to see more than a hundred of them heading for the capital in the first mass raid. They came back again that night and many nights for the next eight months, and soon not just over London but most of the country. After fifty three weeks of war the nightmare had come true. But even the Luftwaffe could not attack everywhere at once, and the pressure on airfields and radar stations was relaxed, enabling the RAF to hold out and finally frustrate the invasion plans.

Short of an actual invasion, this was the worst possible backdrop against which to try to re-start racing, because one of the main assumptions on which the decision was predicated – that there was no specific danger to crowds – had been proved false. The Home

Office immediately asked the Jockey Club to cancel the first Hurst Park and Windsor meetings and, at the request of the War Office, Newmarket too. Though the impression was given that avoiding the risk to crowds was the motive in all three cases, the true reason at Newmarket was that the military had judged that the third week of September was a particularly likely period for an invasion: they needed to be on highest alert to resist a landing in Suffolk or Essex. Meetings were still permitted where there seemed to be less risk, starting at Ripon on 14th September, where 97 horses ran in the six races. There was no more racing until the next Saturday, when Edinburgh held a meeting for the Scottish Red Cross Fund, and this was very successful despite hard going keeping the number of runners down. The same day the Home Office considered what to do about the programme for the next couple of weeks, bravely deciding to stick to the existing policy of non-interference where possible, and to judge each meeting on its merits. The second Hurst Park meeting had to go (and with it the substitute St. Leger), as did Windsor again, and the Newmarket First October, but Leicester, Manchester and Thirsk were approved. An incidental casualty was the Newmarket Town Plate, abandoned for the first time ever.

The military were not satisfied with this selective approach and it soon became clear that they wanted a complete ban, the Home Office representative at the Home Defence Executive meeting on 24th September reporting that "Sir Findlater Stewart and the military representatives agreed that both the CIGS and the Commander in Chief are against racing anywhere as a matter of principle and not merely on the grounds of danger to the population. It seems that a paper on this subject is being laid before the cabinet very shortly". Manuscript notes to Norman Brook, Principal Private Secretary, by A.N.Rucker, the civil servant dealing with the issue, said "You will see that the military are opposed to all racing.....My own view is that racing should be permitted unless the military authorities have reasons for objecting to it at particular places. The London area and, if they press it, Newmarket should presumably be ruled out. But I see no reason why Manchester and Scotland should be ruled out if we are prepared to risk chance bombs".

The showdown was set for the War Cabinet meeting on the last day of September, and this was the first real crunch point of the war for racing. Hitherto there had always been an assumption, at first unspoken but later articulated as official policy, that all sports would be allowed at a moderate level unless it became absolutely necessary to suspend them, but racing now seemed about to be singled out for different treatment. It was touch and go. Ongoing racing was no longer the status quo - it was barely ticking over in the north and midlands and not happening at all in the south; there was not much public support for it if the Times correspondence columns were anything to go by; the blitz had brought a new dimension to the public safety questions; the army thought there should be a ban, and who was going to deny them what they wanted when invasion might be imminent?

The paper to cabinet from Anderson, the former civil service mandarin, was an "on the one hand…but on the other hand" masterpiece: reasonable, intellectually sound, apparently balanced, but leaving the reader in no doubt which hand the author preferred. He rehearsed the arguments for both sides but concluded that he saw no reason for changing existing policy. Anthony Eden, Secretary of State for War, concentrated mainly on the difficulties racegoers might cause for army deployment in the event of sudden invasion, a point he would better have kept for an "And Finally" to an argument based on concerns over public safety. Essentially he was asking for racing to stop everywhere and indefinitely because of a hypothetically possible German landing close enough to a meeting for the crowd to hinder army deployment. The cabinet was not impressed and confirmed the policy of allowing limited racing, though the Commander in Chief Home Forces was invited to specify any particular areas where, on military grounds, he felt racing should be banned.

Having won the argument, the Home Office lost no time in

whipping the Jockey Club into line. A note from Brook to Rucker said "I told Lord Sefton that we should be glad if they would continue to take our advice about individual meetings" and went on to tell Rucker to arrange for Vince to see Mr Weatherby at the end of each week about the next week's meetings.

Within a week Anderson had become Lord President of the Council – effectively, general trouble shooter for the cabinet – and Herbert Morrison, the Minister of Supply, had moved to the Home Office. Whereas Anderson was an urbane, clever, establishment figure, Morrison started as an errand boy and worked his way up through the Independent Labour Party to a seat in the Commons and leadership of the London County Council. He was someone unlikely to be instinctively sympathetic to racing, but on his first day in office he was bowled a googly on that very subject by Ernest Bevin, the Minister of Labour. Bevin detested Morrison so much that, overhearing a remark that Morrison was his own worst enemy, he had interjected "Not while I'm alive, he ain't!" Bevin's note said that Harewood had been to see him to propose that the next Newmarket meeting should be replaced by one at Nottingham in early November and that there should be a formal announcement that meetings in the south were cancelled, but that the northern ones would go ahead. This would enable owners to enter horses in the north and act as an inducement for breeders to carry on. Bevin had told Harewood he had no objections and recommended Morrison to adopt the idea. Sir Alexander Maxwell was incensed at this brazen incursion into Home Office territory and attempt to embarrass Morrison, and told Bevin to get lost or, as he explained it to Brook in terms worthy of Sir Humphrey "This letter from Mr Bevin has caused me a little difficulty as we are, as you know, dealing actively with this problem of race meetings ourselves and it would, I think, be a little confusing if another department were to take the matter up. Accordingly, I have spoken to Mr Bevin's Private Secretary and explained the position to him".

This was a pivotal moment. The Home Office had, at last,

established itself firmly in the driving seat for government policy towards racing. It had not only seen off the War Office and the Ministry of Labour and won the support of other departments in cabinet, but had made it clear to the racing authorities that its advocacy for racing to continue depended on their doing as they were asked.

Loss of the substitute St.Leger was a major blow, but a race with the same conditions at the Newmarket Second October meeting was quickly advertised under the unimaginative title of the Substitute Stakes. No sooner arranged than cancelled: when Sefton met Rucker on 8th October the Second October was one of the fixtures they had to agree to abandon, the army still being on high alert in East Anglia. They did agree the proposed Nottingham meeting for the first Saturday of November, when there were to be substitutes for the four most important abandoned Newmarket races. A few days later a brief extension to the season was agreed so that Thirsk could make the fourth and final attempt to hold the St.Leger.

Until the last few days of October there was mundane flat racing, though with large fields, on Saturdays and the odd Monday at five courses from Leicester northwards, and on the 24th jumping resumed with a meeting at Taunton after a planned earlier meeting at Hawthorn Hill had been among those abandoned. By the time it came, Nottingham's big day was almost unnecessary because the army had agreed to allow racing at Newmarket, subject to "operational factors" (later a source of conflicting interpretations), starting with the Houghton meeting. The concession came too late to change the plans for the Middle Park and Cheveley Park Stakes, Jockey Club Cup and Cambridgeshire Handicap, all with fresh entries and prefixed "New", to be run at Nottingham two days after the Houghton. The Cambridgeshire was reduced to a mile, as in 1939, and could be appropriately staged at Nottingham because the course then still had a straight mile. Prize money for these races was

POLICE NOTICE
West Riding Constabulary.

WETHERBY STEEPLECHASES, 28th DECEMBER, 1940

In the event of an Air Raid Warning Message being received, the Wetherby Public Warning Signal will be relayed on the Course by means of the buzzer previously used as the "OFF" signal.

This will be sounded as follows:—

AIR RAID WARNING.

A signal of one minute's duration consisting of a succession of intermittent blasts of about 5 seconds duration separated by a silent period of about 3 seconds.

RAIDERS PASSED.

A continuous signal of one minute's duration at a steady pitch.

RACING WILL NOT BE SUSPENDED ON THE SOUNDING OF THE AIR RAID WARNING

A watcher will be stationed at a prominent place in the paddock, and he will give warning of the approach of suspected enemy aircraft. An announcement will then be made by means of the loud speakers on the course, and racing will be suspended immediately.

If this announcement is made it is advised that everybody should disperse, and not congregate in crowds or groups.

If bombs are dropped in the vicinity it would be safer for people to lie down rather than move about.

You are advised not to take refuge in cars owing to the increased danger from glass, etc.

Motor vehicles will be permitted to leave the Course, but will **NOT** be allowed to turn left at the **York Road Entrance** after the buzzer has sounded the "Air Raid Warning," as this would cause congestion in Wetherby.

Remember that if an Air Raid Warning is received it does not mean that an air raid will take place. Wait for the announcement on the course loud speakers.

G. C. VAUGHAN,
Chief Constable.

County Chief Constable's Office,
WAKEFIELD.

Most courses planned to suspend racing as soon as an air raid warning sounded, but the racecard for Wetherby's Christmas 1940 meeting shows that the gritty Yorkshire jumping folk carried on until the enemy was in sight.

a fraction of normal, though the total for the day was more than Nottingham usually offered at its biggest meeting. The Jockey Club had guaranteed any loss in exchange for a 25% share of any profit, and a crowd that the Nottingham Evening Post thought was the biggest for twenty years ensured a small profit on the day. Fred Darling had been expected to take both two-year-old races. The Rosetta filly (later named Keystone) duly took the Cheveley Park Stakes but Morogoro, unbeaten in four earlier starts, just failed to hold the challenge of Hyacynthus in the Middle Park. Darling sent out Hunters Moon to finish second in the Jockey Club Cup despite having won the Cesarewitch only three days earlier, but the winner's prize still went to Beckhampton via Mr. Blagrave's Atout Maitre. This ended a mixed week for Darling, who had won the Dewhurst Stakes at Newmarket with Fettes but had seen his odds-on chances Owen Tudor and Pont L'Eveque beaten in the Criterion Stakes and Champion Stakes. The Aga Khan's Stardust had finished easily first in the latter, only to be disqualified for crossing Lord Rosebery's Hippius.

The Commander in Chief, General Alan Brooke, soon took up the invitation to specify places where he felt there should be no racing. In a letter to Cabinet, classified as Secret, he explained his reasons for objecting to holding race meetings in general and said he particularly objected to holding them anywhere in the Eastern, Southern and Aldershot Commands or London District (that is, the whole of England south of a line from The Wash to Wyre Forest), within ten miles of the coast in Northern Command, or at Newcastle, Stockton, York, Doncaster, Lincoln, Uttoxeter, Warwick or Chepstow. He concluded "I appreciate these restrictions are considerable but the military situation fully justifies them in my view, and I consider the Cabinet's present policy of allowing only a limited number of meetings is as far as we can possibly go in meeting the wishes of the Jockey Club".

It briefly looked as if the whole issue would return to Cabinet, but the Cabinet Secretary, Sir Edward Bridges, pressed the parties to reach agreement and Anderson was brought in to resolve the policy issues. This he did with the CIGS, now Sir John Dill, whose views were less hard-line than those of Brooke. By this time the NH programme for December and January had become part of the problem, though a handful of November meetings had already been sanctioned by the Home Office, but on 15th November Anderson and Dill met and agreed the list. That a top cabinet minister and the wartime commander of an army of millions should solemnly sit down and discuss a few weeks' jump racing fixtures seems absurd, but somehow characteristic of Britain at the time. Was it an example of such misguided priorities that we should wonder how Britain avoided defeat, or of a flexibility of approach that explains why we avoided it? Either way, the belated publication of the programme, albeit thinner than hoped, came as a great relief to the jumping community.

There was not much public interest in racing in November, a grim and sombre month that saw the death of Chamberlain only weeks after leaving the government, and devastating air raids not only on London but Coventry, Liverpool and Southampton. People had more to worry about than the result of the 1.30 at Newmarket, where bread and butter racing at the two mid-November meetings attracted many runners but few spectators. There was one, final flourish at Thirsk on 23rd November, with the Yorkshire St.Leger. This was effectively the real thing at last, even though the winner's prize was a pathetic £980 despite a grant from the Ascot Authority. Turkhan just held the strong challenges of Hippius and his stable companion Stardust. The Sporting Life (now only obtainable by order from a newsagent), which covered northern racing with the same, slightly patronising tone as jumping, reported that "every enclosure was packed with enthusiastic north country sportsmen, and the cheers that greeted the success of Gordon Richards on Turkhan were more than a pale imitation of the famous Yorkshire Roar".

It was immediately announced that Turkhan and Stardust were to be retired to stud by the Aga Khan, who was living in Switzerland as a result of the fall of France. He had already infuriated British breeders by selling Bahram and Mahmoud to American syndicates, and it now appeared that in 1941 his only horse in this country would be the stayer Winterhalter. He saw racing strictly as business and these disposals were taken as a sign of his belief that Britain would lose the war.

There was now some movement in the bloodstock market after disastrous Newmarket October sales. Facilities for exporting horses had become available again after a three month lapse, with 29 horses being immediately sent to America and 28 to India, and although the December sales started quietly they were well attended and business soon brightened up. This was despite a doom laden speech by Rosebery, who told the Thoroughbred Breeders' Association that "little I can say is not exceedingly gloomy". Emphasising that home trials were "useless" and that the racecourse test was vital, he urged his audience to do all they could to keep racing going, provided nothing was done to hinder the war effort. The one bright note was that he thought those in authority recognised that a little relaxation helped people to work harder.

The Jockey Club's December meeting was devoted to making pragmatic arrangements for 1941 without causing alarm and despondency. The stewards had cancelled the normal fixtures for the year and abandoned races already advertised or closed, feeling it better than courses preparing for an expensive programme that might be impossible to carry out, but Lord Hamilton of Dalzell wanted to advertise a continuous programme for the year with an indication that it might have to be altered. He could not see why the government should object, demonstrating that not everyone yet understood who was now in charge. There was also a spirited argument when J.A.de Rothschild opposed Rosebery's motion that entries for the New Derby should be restricted to horses which had been entered for the abandoned original race, the proposal eventually being withdrawn.

Yearlings were arriving at training stables as usual despite the menacing outlook, if on a smaller scale than normally. In those days they came unbroken, so breaking-in was the first step in their progress towards racing. One arrival at Fred Darling's yard from the National Stud was a filly by Hyperion out of Clarence, who introduced some mutuality into the breaking process – she broke Norman Bertie's wrist, Jack Blake's ankle and Tom Blake's thumb. At the time they probably thought she was not worth it.

NH meetings before Christmas were few and far between, resulting in very large fields. There were 119 runners at Cheltenham in early November, to the surprise of Sporting Life veteran Meyrick Good, who noted that winners had been ridden by an army officer, "Tommies on leave" and a night shift munitions worker. Running the last race at 2.30 was well received, allowing visitors from London and elsewhere to get home before blackout, but not everything was rosy at Cheltenham. There was an increasingly vociferous anti-racing faction in the town, and they had the ear of the MP, Daniel Lipson. A popular councillor and former mayor, he had been the obvious choice for Conservative candidate at a by-election in 1937 but had been passed over, apparently because he was Jewish. Adopting the Louie Dingwall approach to problem solving, Lipson's response was to stand as an Independent Conservative and defeat the official party candidate, after which he energetically fought in Parliament for the town's interests as he saw them. He was a good man for the protestors to have on their side.

When Birmingham and Leicester suddenly became unavailable for racing the NHC simply told the Home Office they had substituted Cheltenham and Nottingham, to be sharply reminded that they must seek approval not only for the total numbers of meetings but the venues also. They quickly learned the lesson and before applying to add meetings at Plumpton and Fontwell Park, the first southern meetings since June, to the fixture list for January, Rosebery sought Dill's views first. He received a positively affable reply from the CIGS, saying there would be no military objection "unless something quite unforeseen happens".

Christmas was less comfortable than in 1939. Many foodstuffs were rationed, and though extra tea and sugar rations were allowed and there were no restrictions on turkeys or confectionary, there were shortages of dried fruit and milk and a coal shortage in London. This year the Boxing Day meetings were at Taunton, where Gerry Wilson rode a treble, and Wetherby, followed by Nottingham on 30th December. Racing at the end of 1940 was like Dr. Johnson's dog walking on its hind legs: "It is not done well, but you are surprised to find it done at all".

CHAPTER 5

IN RETREAT (1941)

If racing people had been feeling mildly relieved at surviving 1940 a series of setbacks at the beginning of the new year reminded them how precarious the long-term situation really was. New Year's Day should have seen the traditional meeting at Manchester, but it did not take place. The only warning was a reference in The Sporting Life of 30th December to its abandonment showing how meetings might have to be cancelled at the shortest notice. Would-be racegoers otherwise had to draw their own conclusions from the absence of the card from the daily papers. In fact, the course had taken direct hits in an air raid on 22nd December. It was back in action for flat racing in May, but there would be no more jumping there until January 1947.

As recently as 23rd December there had been press speculation that Manchester or Cheltenham might be an alternative venue for the Grand National should the application to hold it at Aintree fail. Mrs Topham was determined it should take place there if at all possible, and the 1940 race had been staged successfully. That, however, had been in the fools' paradise when Chamberlain claimed that Hitler had missed the bus. Things would be much more difficult now the world had turned upside down and Liverpool was a target of air raids, so she decided to seek the support of high-ranking officials who would influence the decision. In November 1940 she visited Sir Harry Haig, the Home Office Regional Commissioner in Manchester, and the Chief Constable of Lancashire, Captain Hordern, to persuade them that the race should be arranged provisionally, though she conceded that it would have to be cancelled if the blitz situation did not improve. Sadly for Mrs Topham this did not work. Both men were so deeply unimpressed as to write to the Home Office to say so. Haig pointed out that arranging the race would raise hopes that were likely to be false and that it would be harder to cancel the meeting later than refuse it now: presumably, that had been precisely Mrs Topham's idea.

On 27th November CDC decided that the Grand National should not be held. Weatherbys were notified, and there things seemed to rest. Then, early in 1941, rumours started reaching the Home Office. Col. Vince wrote to J.D.V. Hodge, who was now involved in racing matters at the Home Office, asking if he could discover whether the NHC proposed to hold a substitute Grand National at Cheltenham and, if so, what sort of crowd they expected. Hodge contacted Weatherbys and the clerk of the course at Cheltenham and found that just such a race was being planned for the March meeting. There were only the vaguest ideas about the size of the crowd, but it might be as much as 10,000. Hodge felt that whilst the numbers would be trifling for a normal Grand National, they would be abnormal for Cheltenham and he doubted whether they should allow it.

On 11th January the Gloucestershire Echo, Cheltenham's evening paper, got the story, splashing a back-page lead *Grand National May Be At Cheltenham*. It reported mixed messages from a steward of the meeting, who said nothing was decided, and a "prominent racecourse figure" who said it was practically certain to be run in April. They expected to use the four-mile National Hunt course, though if the race were over the full Grand National distance some of the fences would have to be jumped twice. That seems incredible. A four and a half mile race over the gladiatorial National Hunt course would have involved climbing the whole of the Cheltenham hill by various routes three times: anything still walking at the end would have won.

Three days later the Echo started printing a shoal of readers' letters in the best tradition of Disgusted of Tunbridge Wells. William Johnson reminded readers that the race was being transferred from Liverpool because of the risk of air raids, but the safety of Cheltenham was just as important. He also pointed out that racegoers had binoculars which could be better used by the army. Herbert Cummings said the town was grossly overcrowded and racing at this time served no useful purpose. People should not be encouraged to "rush about the country to race meetings". G.Makins-Smith thought that hotels and restaurants would buy up all available food for racegoers and the poorer residents would go hungry for days. Argus did not think there was much danger of bombing, but objected to the waste of time, money, petrol and food. There was more of the same from Anon, "L", Sanity, Resident, Safety First, "A Burgess", and Sentinel. Mrs B.Crisp wrote a sad letter to say it was an extra worry. She had had infantile paralysis and "could not make a dash for it". Only two swam against the prevailing torrent. Jessie Smith said that people afraid of air raids on race meetings should stay away, rather missing the point that the concern was for Cheltonians and not the punters who put them at risk. Racegoer bluntly criticised them for wanting to save their own skins.

On 17th January the paper reported that Mr Lipson was to ask the Home Secretary to ban the Grand National for the duration of the war. A week later it reported the MP's views at length in a front page lead story about the council's General Purposes and Watch Committee voting unanimously to ask for a ban.

Meanwhile, back at the Home Office, they were wondering what to do. The Chief Constable of Gloucestershire had now told them he would prefer there were no meeting, but he had no grounds for stopping it and there would be no particular difficulties if it went ahead. He thought the crowd might be 15,000. Lord Rosebery came to see Hodge and told him that the National Hunt meeting was already popular and he did not think a substitute Grand National would much increase the crowd. On the other hand, Mr Lipson sent in some letters opposing the race. The Ministry of Transport had no objections provided there were no special trains.

On 23rd January the Civil Defence Executive Sub Committee (CDESC) discussed a memo from the Home Secretary. This marginally favoured allowing the race, but pointed out that holding any race styled Grand National, even though it had little in common but the name, was likely to increase crowds and involve rail traffic on a sensitive part of the system. Had a decision been made then the race might well have been allowed, but CDESC inexplicably decided to seek the views of the Aintree stewards. Then a telegram arrived from Cheltenham Borough Council with details of its resolution, and this seems to have been the feather that tipped the scales.

There was racing at Cheltenham on 29th January. Twelve year old Mr Ted Mumford rode his father's River Fox into sixth place in the Long Distance Handicap Hurdle, but there was still no news of the Grand National. In Parliament Mr Lipson was urging the Minister of Agriculture to ban winter racing "in view of the food position". Next day, CDESC finally decided that "permission should be withheld for the inclusion in the programme of the Cheltenham March meeting of a race to be known as The War National", and Morrison told the Commons this fixture was undesirable.

The racing world was aghast. Looking back from the end of 1941, Bloodstock Breeders Review said Morrison had "dropped a heavyweight bomb in the midst of the NH camp", taking the stewards completely by surprise and appearing to threaten the whole future of their sport. The Sporting Life was apoplectic, denouncing the organised opposition it had discovered in

Cheltenham and unfairly criticising the local press, which had, in fact, reported even-handedly. "If the decisions of the authorities are going to be swayed by the noisy minority of anti-sport faddists" it thundered "the position will be impossible". It lamented that for the first time since 1837 there would be no National - interesting evidence that the Gatwick substitute races of 1916 to 1918 were long accepted as Grand Nationals; only in the 1970s did it become customary to ignore them.

The Echo published two more letters on 1st February, Herbert Cumming and R.F.Stratton both demanding an end to all NH racing for the duration. The Cheltenham racing-haters had tasted blood, and would bite more deeply next year, but something far worse was about to happen.

February 18th was a Tuesday, market day in Newmarket. Though cold and cloudy it was still busy in mid afternoon, with townspeople and local villagers doing their shopping. The White Hart hotel was being redecorated despite the war, and painters were working inside. In the Conservative Club William Jarvis was settling down to a hand of Bridge after cycling from Egerton House, overtaking Snowy Outen walking to town for a haircut. A card school in the less august surroundings of the stable lads' club included Gerry Blum and Fred Winter. Frequent army convoys were passing through on corps exercises.

Suddenly, with no warning at all, a Dornier 17Z plunged out of the clouds from the Thetford direction and flew the length of the High Street, dropping nine high-explosive bombs before banking away southwards. Snowy Outen heard the explosions as he reached the edge of the town and threw himself instinctively to the ground. When he got up it was to see the north side of the High Street in ruins. By chance, a Wellington bomber had just taken off from RAF Newmarket Heath and Sergeant Goodman, its eighteen year old pilot, saw the raider's bombing run. Manoeuvring to intercept, he briefly got into position for his gunners to open fire but, although they scored hits, the Dornier climbed into cloud with the Wellington lumbering in hopeless pursuit. Shortly afterwards, army gunners shot down a Dornier of the same type near Thetford. Although it was never proved to be the same one, Sergeant Goodman was awarded a half-share in the kill. He survived the war and left the RAF as a Group Captain.

There were dreadful scenes in the High Street. The post office, the Marlborough Club and the White Hart had been wrecked. The painters were among 18 dead, and 61 people were injured, nine of them severely. Five houses had been demolished and some shops badly damaged. The street was full of rubble and glass, which was not finally cleared until the Saturday. To make matters worse, communication with the outside world had been lost because the telephone exchange was in the post office, but there seems to have been no panic. Asked in 2006 how he had reacted to the raid, Gerry Blum replied "I got straight on my bike and rode back for evening stables!"

The raid was seen by the military to vindicate warnings they had given the previous autumn before being forced to concede that racing could take place at Newmarket unless it had to be stopped for operational reasons. On 26th February the Home Defence Executive wrote to the Home Office saying they had reconsidered the agreement in the light of recent enemy activity. If enemy pilots bombed army convoys they might do the same to dense civilian traffic. The Commander in Chief considered the proposed meetings highly dangerous for civilians and very undesirable for the military. The qualification about stopping Newmarket meetings for operational reasons must now be invoked.

"This is very awkward," wrote Col. Vince at the foot of the incoming letter, as, indeed, it was, coming just after the 1941 flat fixture list had been agreed after much discussion. "Can we discover how much traffic there is at race meetings? I had thought "operational factors" referred to the threat of invasion, not a single bombing of the place"

This January 1941 Luftwaffe reconnaissance photograph shows Bogside racecourse between Ardeer explosives works, encroaching from the left, and ROF Irvine (lower right). The German analyst has noted barrage balloons on the course with half-brackets marked "a".

Fortified by hearing from the police that Newmarket meetings rarely brought more than 600 cars and 2,000 spectators, the Home Office held its nerve and its line. An internal briefing note confirmed that "operational factors" had been coded language for invasion, and accused the Regional Commissioner and the GOC Eastern Command, who had always opposed Newmarket fixtures, of opportunism. As the government had decided the risks were not such as to warrant prohibiting racing or other outdoor entertainments, the Home Defence Executive should be told "no reason is seen for reviewing [the fixture list] because of an isolated bombing incident near a particular course". This was not callousness but clear-sighted and brave refusal to indulge in gesture politics. The argument nevertheless raged on, with neither side giving ground until, on 24th March, CDESC confirmed that the agreed fixture list should stand.

The difficulties had started in January, when the Ministry of Transport made it clear they were unhappy with the demands racing was making on the railways. In 1940, despite the 3-month suspension, there had been 1,178 special trains taking horses to or from race meetings or the Newmarket sales, 945 of them on the Southern Railway, which could not attach horseboxes to its electric passenger trains. Cheap fares had been abolished but the railways found themselves having to run relief trains to cope with racegoers, who could not be distinguished from other passengers. During long consultations between the interested ministries and the Jockey Club, the Ministry of Transport suggested racing might be confined to Newmarket and Newbury, close to where most horses were trained. The Ministry of Labour argued for more meetings to be on Saturdays and for racing to finish by three o'clock, to avoid delaying workers' transport. The Home Secretary emphasised that there must be some rationalisation and concentration of meetings. The outcome was a draft list of 43 meetings to the end of June, compared with 128 in peacetime, designed to give all parts of the country some racing whilst minimising transport difficulties. The Derby and Oaks were to be at Newbury. In the end, all parties were reasonably satisfied, except for the Regional Commissioner at Cambridge, who objected to Newmarket meetings because they would "definitely have a bad effect on morale both generally and as creating class prejudice". The list was agreed the day before the Newmarket raid.

In the meantime, jump racing carried on, with two or three scheduled meetings a week and less interruption from the weather than in 1940. There were plenty of runners, particularly at

Nottingham and Worcester, despite the majority of races being worth less than £100 to the winner. There was a strange incident at Plumpton on 15th February, when the seven runners in the Cuckfield Handicap Steeplechase found their way blocked by a car crossing the course, forcing them to swerve behind it. All would have been well had the driver not suddenly braked, causing Roman Chief and Sean Magee to hit the car and turn right over. Magee and the occupants of the car were unhurt, but Roman Chief had to be put down.

With no Grand National, the climax of the season was the Cheltenham National Hunt meeting on 19th and 20th March. The programme was the same as in 1940 except for the Juvenile Steeplechase, which failed to fill and was replaced by the National Hunt Moderate Steeplechase. It was a great success. Crowds were reminiscent of pre-war days, though nearly half the spectators were in uniform, and hundreds did not make it to the course "in spite of excellent traffic control by the military, who were putting in a bit of practice", as Bloodstock Breeders Review reported with heavy irony. The Sporting Life thought the meeting had rarely produced higher-class racing.

The Champion Hurdle was the feature of the first day, but attracted only six runners. Solford was odds-on to repeat his previous year's defeat of the 1939 winner, African Sister, but their juniors trounced them. The winner was Seneca, a four-year-old entire, ridden by Ron Smyth and trained by his uncle Vic at Epsom. The horse's only hurdle race experience had been a win over the course the previous December, but he collared the leader, Anarchist, another juvenile novice, at the last and got up by a head in the last few strides.

Roman Hackle, the 1940 winner, was favourite for the Gold Cup, but he had shown in-and-out form and was opposed in the betting by Savon, a winner at the February meeting. The favourite was beaten a long way from home, and at the last fence there was nothing between Poet Prince and Red Rower, both trained by Ivor Anthony. Poet Prince ran on strongly but Red Rower faded and was just run out of second place by Savon. The winner was a chance ride for Roger Burford, who replaced the horse's unfortunate owner and usual rider, Mr David Sherbrooke, who had been hurt the day before.

Two days later the jumping season ended quietly with Ludlow's only meeting, then it was onward to Lincoln for the start of the flat. As in 1940, the meeting was only two days and the course as bleak as ever. There was a crowd of peacetime proportions but evidence of war was everywhere. Many spectators were in uniform, the Clerk of the Course, Captain Malcolm Hancock, in that of the Coldstream Guards, there was a military band, and the sprint handicap known in peacetime as the Brocklesby Trial Plate had become the Home Guard Handicap. The racecard contained helpful hints about what to do in an air raid: the public should, for example, scatter across the racecourse, and would find it safer to lie down during a machine gun attack.

Gordon Richards had been champion jockey for thirteen of the last fourteen seasons, so when he won the first race, the John o' Gaunt Selling Handicap, on Snapdragon it seemed that normal service had resumed immediately. The press had been deploring the poor quality of the entries for the Lincolnshire, the main race of the meeting, and were proved right. The field of nineteen was smaller than usual, Gloaming won easily, and the thirteen lengths between first and fifth were ridiculous for one of the year's supposedly most competitive handicaps. A major factor was the soft going, which affected all early meetings, the first Salisbury meeting of April even being abandoned because of snow.

The approaching season brought another flurry of letters to The Times under the heading *Why Racing?*, started by O.Mordaunt-Burrows of Epworth Rectory, who professed bewilderment that racing could be allowed when it jeopardised the supply of eggs and milk, caused unnecessary travel, diverted labour from civil defence work and consumed paper. He was supported by J.Frankland-West, a poultry farmer, who said that feeding hens with the 5,000 tons of oats eaten by racehorses would produce an "astronomical" number of eggs. The Hon.Gilbert Johnstone, a former member of the NHC, declared that racing was a luxurious waste that caused the public to go without eggs to help bookmakers flourish. A counter attack was mounted by Rowland Meyrick, Clerk of the Course at Wetherby, Mr F.Blain, private secretary to the Aga Khan, and Lord Lambton. "A" felt that racing for older horses and geldings could not be justified, but claimed that dogs and cats ate more than all the horses, and that gambling was as undesirable in peacetime as during the war. The correspondence ended with a measured letter from Lord Harewood, saying that nobody was pressing to indulge their hobby in conflict with the national interest, but the Jockey Club had a duty to ensure the supremacy of the English (sic) thoroughbred and to entertain the public. The weeding-out process would cause the number of horses to fall throughout the season.

The Manchester Guardian, which did not normally cover racing, said in an editorial that it should continue in order to support bloodstock, though many horses would have to be put out to grass. However, it concluded "the racing which survives through the present year will have to be the basic minimum that will keep the racing of the future in existence."

Mr Frankland-West's letter was a manifestation of the horses versus chickens controversy that surfaced regularly in the press and Parliament while rationing of animal feedstuffs was in force. The Daily Express joined the fray with a claim that if the numbers of horses and greyhounds were halved, there would be ten million more eggs and a million more pounds of bacon. Lord Winterton delivered what should have been the knockout punch on 3rd April, telling the House of Lords that if all 6,000 tons of oats allowed to racehorses were fed to hens instead, every member of the population could have an extra egg every four years. It was to no avail: Horses v. Chickens ran and ran.

The Jockey Club was sensitive to this and took action to ensure the weeding-out mentioned by Lord Harewood actually took place, aiming to reduce the number in training to 1,200. This figure may have been chosen because it was same as the one conceded as acceptable by the government in the critical days of 1917. In early April a circular advised owners and trainers to discard moderate horses, particularly geldings, and announced that there would be no selling races from June. The last one was the Bonnington Selling Handicap at Lanark on 31st May. Major MacDonald Buchanan asked the June meeting of the Club whether geldings should be allowed to run when "people are having to get rid of the thirteenth hen". The Duke of Norfolk reminded them he was in a position to know the government's mind on racing, which was that it "catered for two definite and distinct propositions": one was continuance of thoroughbred breeding, and the other public relaxation. Without geldings there would be no big handicaps, and perhaps not enough horses to go round.

For the last time during the war, Newmarket's Craven meeting provided the omens for the classics. Morogoro just beat Sun Castle in the New Craven Stakes, Orthodox won the Free Handicap, with Lambert Simnel third, and Owen Tudor won the Column Stakes decisively. Among the older horses, Anarchist easily won the Babraham Welter Handicap as a reward for his effort at Cheltenham.

The best omen for a long time came at Salisbury on 19th April, when the Myrobella colt (by Bahram) easily won the Hurstbourne Plate in the King's colours. His Majesty had leased this two-year-old from the National Stud, with the wayward Clarence filly, and had them trained by Fred Darling, though the horses he personally owned remained with William Jarvis. The colt was a big, strong and handsome animal. The filly was smaller and initially showed little ability beyond her propensity for injuring members of Darling's staff. It was only after he had applied for a licence to return her to Ireland that she started to please him and plans were changed. The racing public always enjoys royal winners, but in wartime they engendered feelings not just of pleasure but of intense patriotism, and these horses were to provide them in abundance at a time of desperate hanging-on in the face of constantly bad war news. An example came when Merry Wanderer, one of the King's horses from the Jarvis stable, was cheered to the echo after winning the May Handicap at Nottingham.

The Guineas races took place on 30th April and 1st May, by which time the ground had become firm. Lambert Simnel won the Two Thousand under Charlie Elliott from Morogoro, Beckhampton's second string, and Sun Castle. Owen Tudor was only fifth, but Darling and Gordon Richards, knowing how much better than Morogoro he was at home, kept their faith in him. However, Meyrick Good was convinced the horse had shirked it. Lambert Simnel was the Duke of Westminster's second classic winner, the first having been right back in 1906. The One Thousand Guineas went to Lord Glanely's Dancing Time, whose only previous run had been unplaced in a maiden on Oaks day almost a year earlier.

Gordon Richards' first booked ride at Salisbury the following week was in a two-year-old maiden. In the paddock, the Duchess of Norfolk asked if he would look after an apprentice at the start, as the Michel Grove stable were giving him his first ride in public on an unraced and fractious filly. Their reason for unleashing this lethal combination is not clear. The kindly Richards agreed, but as he rode over to speak to the boy at the start the filly lashed out and caught him on the ankle. Realising he was injured, he foolishly jumped off, making an already bad break a great deal worse and putting himself out of action for the rest of the season. This sensational accident diverted attention from the winner of the race, the debutant Ujiji, who looked very promising indeed.

On 4th May Double Summer Time began, with clocks advanced an extra hour until 10th August to allow farm work and daylight travel until late evening. This was repeated, with earlier starting and later finishing dates, for the remaining war years.

Attention was now turning to the Derby and the Oaks. They had been arranged for the first week of June at Newbury but, as in 1940, there was a problem. The military had occupied the course during the winter and, although many had left, they were still using most of the car parks. The chief constable of Berkshire feared the Bath Road would be blocked by parked cars on Derby day and felt the meeting should not be held unless other parking could be arranged. The racecourse company asked the borough council for the use of Stroud Green, a public open space, but the council refused. Unlike their Cheltenham counterparts, they accepted racing on their patch as long as the government allowed it, but they did not want the Derby: it would be too well known in advance and would attract large crowds. The regional commissioner also weighed in, backing up police fears about traffic congestion and emphasising the lack of protection from air raids, of which there had been several around Newbury in daylight.

When the Jockey Club met on 15th April they knew they were in difficulty. Lord Sefton told them the chairman of Newbury council was "very windy about the blitz". Hodge at the Home Office had warned him that if they tried to move the races to Newmarket it might stir up a hornets' nest and possibly "get the whole thing squashed and no racing held at Newmarket at all". Several alternatives were suggested but rejected – Nottingham because the traffic would be unmanageable, Salisbury because of shortage of boxes, and Goodwood because it was in a prohibited area. J.A.de Rothschild even suggested changing the name of the Derby to make it less of an attraction. In the end they decided to let the stewards sort things out as best they could.

Herbert Morrison, who had become aware of the

correspondence flying round his department, wrote plaintively to Vince " Do you know anything about this? I appreciate we refused to allow the Grand National, but I did not know we had sanctioned the holding of the Derby at Newbury". Eventually things calmed down and CDC agreed that the Derby and Oaks could take place at Newmarket's mid-June meeting, where it was originally intended to run some of the Ascot races. The Newbury fixture remained in the programme and kept the two-year-old races transferred from Epsom, the Woodcote Plate and, for fillies, the Acorn Plate.

In the Acorn Plate Fred Darling introduced the King's filly. The Myrobella colt had already paid two successful return visits to Salisbury and now, ridden by Harry Wragg in Gordon Richards' absence, the Clarence filly finished strongly to win well. The next Sporting Life's lead story was *Crack Two-Year-Olds Owned By The King* and ended "May His Majesty win the 1942 Derby and Oaks – at Epsom – with these grand products of the National Stud". The prospect of classic success was real enough. The bit about Epsom was a dream, but dreams were needed: though it was becoming clear that heavy air-raids had ended, recent weeks had seen the Germans end Yugoslav resistance, take Athens, invade Crete, enter western Egypt and sink the *Hood*, quite apart from the introduction of clothes rationing at home. The royal win overshadowed another good performance by Ujiji in the Woodcote Plate. The following week it was announced that the King had named the Myrobella colt Big Game, and that the Clarence filly was to be Sun Chariot.

Derby Day was 18th June, and people once again poured into Newmarket by whatever means they could. There were no special trains, but three trainloads of racegoers arrived by ordinary services, to find only four taxis, which were charging five shillings (about £10 at present-day prices) for the two mile ride to the July Course. There was a continuous procession of people walking across the heath and a stream of cars from the London direction, the road being "black with cars" half an hour before the big race. This was possible because there was still a small personal petrol allowance that could be saved for such occasions. Some of the latecomers rushed the gates, which was considered rather bad form. The Sporting Life thought there were about 25,000 spectators in the enclosures and another 5,000 on The Ditch. Lambert Simnel and Morogoro were made first and second favourites on the strength of their Guineas form, and Sun Castle was also well backed. There were four runners from Beckhampton, with the Wragg brothers on three of them: Harry on Morogoro, Sam on Thoroughfare and Arthur on Annatom. Harry had chosen to ride Owen Tudor, with Billy Nevett booked for Morogoro, but Fred Darling, in his autocratic way, had switched them. This seemed to signal that Owen Tudor was the least fancied of the four, and he started at 25 to1. Despite the rebuff, Harry advised Nevett to ignore Darling's instructions to ride the horse close to the pace, but to drop him out for a late run instead. He then had the perverse satisfaction of seeing Owen Tudor storm past Morogoro as they met the rising ground a furlong out and win comfortably. Meyrick Good reported that of the forty-odd Derby winners he had seen, this one gave him least satisfaction, and there had been few cheers for Darling's seventh Derby win: sour grapes, perhaps?

The following day a far smaller crowd saw Mr J.A.Dewar's Commotion, also trained by Darling, but ridden by Harry Wragg, mow down Turkhana and odds-on favourite Dancing Time to win the Oaks with one of The Head Waiter's characteristic late swoops. Although Commotion had never before run over more than six furlongs, she was well backed on the day.

Before the Derby, the Jockey Club had considered publishing attendance figures so that the Daily Express and Daily Mail did not invent their own, as they had in 1940. These fears were soon justified, one paper claiming that the crowd was at least 50,000, wasting half a million hours of war workers' time. A story of an army convoy being delayed by race traffic added piquancy. The

Sporting Life's "small but vociferous minority opposed to racing" took up the chase in the Commons. First out of the slips was Capt. Montagu Lyons (Leicester East), who asked the number of petrol driven vehicles at Newmarket on 18th June. On being told that the information was being examined, he replied that it was not good enough and a gross public scandal; the Battle of the Atlantic would not wait while it was done. Mr Leach (Bradford Central) asked whether the minister had any idea of the public irritation his inaction was causing. Concerning the convoy, Capt. Margesson, the Minister for War told a questioner that the story was without foundation, but minor problems with the facts were not going to stop the anti-racing lobby. On 26th June, Mr J.J. Tinker (Leigh) asked the Home Secretary if he was aware that there had been 60,000 people and 5,000 cars at the Derby and that they had held up an army convoy for a considerable time. Morrison replied that the actual numbers were less than half those mentioned and, although traffic had been slow, there had been no major blockages. He referred Tinker to the answer already given about the convoy. Replying to other questions he added "We have severely reduced racing facilities, and the point is now reached where we must go on with the very modest programme or abolish racing altogether, which would involve rather serious considerations". Emmanuel Shinwell was immediately on his feet, saying "The government is flying in the face of decent public opinion. Is it desirable to allow these insane and unseemly spectacles to continue?"

Morrison retorted that there was more than one opinion about this. The racing programme beyond September was yet to be set, but it must be considered whether an industry to which some importance was attached should be eliminated.

Shinwell raised the subject again on 2nd July. He emphasised that he was not a killjoy: "I love these things, and so do we all. So do the people of the country. But we cannot afford them now. Why should the workers be called upon to work harder when we can afford this sort of thing? Why should we talk of absenteeism, when this is the real absenteeism?" There was a certain consistency in this, as he had criticised large football crowds as "crazy" at a miners' rally in May. Morrison replied "I have never been to a race meeting and never gambled [and] I must be careful not to let my own prejudices and wishes determine my policy and tempt me to control the enjoyment of other people". However, he warned, some others were trying to use the war as an opportunity to pursue their personal opinion and intolerance.

The Ascot races displaced by the Derby were held on the first day of the First July meeting. Big Game toyed with Watling Street and three others in the Coventry Stakes and Sun Chariot finished fast to head Perfect Peace on the line in the Queen Mary. Both were ridden by Harry Wragg, who also won the Gold Cup on Finis. This was over two and a quarter miles instead of Ascot's two and a half, and even that involved using more of the ground than was normally raced over. In the New St. James's Palace Stakes Orthodox outstayed Lambert Simnel at the end, with Sun Castle a disappointing last of seven. The second day saw the main races of the peacetime First and Second July meetings, with Ujiji just getting up in the July Stakes and Commotion just holding on in the Falmouth. Comatas won the July Cup by a short head after Charlie Elliott mistimed his run on the fast-finishing Poise. Mickey The Greek was favourite, but was always last and never won again.

Racing fell into a kind of torpor for the next few weeks, with some holiday entertainment at the likes of Edinburgh, Ripon, Lanark and Worcester, but lacking the normal landmark meetings of late summer. The main Newmarket Second July races had been brought forward, and although there was a third July meeting featuring some of the Goodwood races, the prize money was so poor that it was a feeble affair (and worse, many of the town's pubs had no beer). There was no attempt at a substitute for York's Ebor

"All profit from race cards goes
to the RED CROSS — 1/-"

THIRSK JULY MEETING,

SATURDAY, JULY 19th, 1941.

2-30 First Race. 5 Fur.
COXWOLD MAIDEN PLATE
of 200 sov.; for two yrs. old. 60 entries.

1 — Mr C. Stuart Brown ... **COROADO GREY**	8	12
Berixe, whi.diagonal st;s & c (*F. Armstrong*)		
2 — Miss J. Clayton .... **ST. LOE**	8	12
Black, white chevrons, blue cap (*Elsey*)		
3 — Mr G. A. Cullington............ **BOMBARDIA**	8	12
Yellow, red x-belts & spots on c (*Flummett*)		
4 — Lord Kilnwilliam .... **COURTLY C.**	8	12
Green, black cap (*Easterby*)		
5 — Mrs E. H. Gasking... **ROYAL MANTLE C.**	8	12
Yellow, green spots, hooped cap (*T. Hall*)		
6 — Lord Harewood .... **THYESSOS**	8	12
Black, yellow slvs, and cap (*Elsey*)		
7 — Mr R. Harland .... **MELIANTHUS**	8	12
Brown, green slvs, red & wh qtd c (*Easterby*)		
8 — Mr J. Hetherton............ **DUAL CONTROL**	8	12
Flame, green collar & cuffs, qtd cap (*Elsey*)		
9 — Mr J. Hetherton ... **SQUADRON LEADER**	8	12
Flame, green collar & cuffs, qtd cap (*Elsey*)		
10 — Mr F. W. Lee.................... **LOANINGMORE**	8	12
Myrtle green, terra-cotta slvs, wh c (*Elsey*)		
11 — Mr A. E. Pilcher.................... **SCRIVEN**	8	12
Primrose, pink slvs, red cap (*Beaton*)		
12 — Capt. C. D. A. Stewart ...... **POPULARITY**	8	12
Chocolate, blue hrd. slvs. yellow cap (*Elsey*)		
13 — Lt-Col.E. Straker **TOWER TYE** (*M. Peacock*)	8	12
Violet, white hoops on body, light blue cap		
14 — Mr L. A. Abelson...... **THRACIAN GIRL C.**	8	12
Blue, grey slvs, hooped cap (*Beeby*)		
15 — Mr S. Webster .... **MARCOM**	8	12
White, blue x-belt, qtd cap (*W. Newton*)		
16 — Lady Fitzwilliam .... **SEA GOD**	8	9
Green, black cross-belts & cap (*Whitaker*)		
17 — ★Mr M. Flemming............ **UNDERSTUDY**	8	9
Cherry, gold hooped sleeves (*Murless*)		
18 — Mrs F. J. Barlow.................... **KILMURRY F.**	8	9
Light blue, crimson stripes (*Walters*)		
19 — Mr W. Barnett **GOOD PAY** (*F. Armstrong*)	8	9
Cherry, blk sash, primrose & wh qtd cap		
20 — Mr G. W. Dixon .... **RENE**	8	9
Gold, blk. slvs. & belt, brd cap (*H. Peacock*)		
21 — Mr J.S.Driver **REJECTED ADDRESSES**	8	9
Scarlet, dark blue sash, qtd cap (*Reddin*)		
22 — Col. T.Dunlop **GLEE MAIDEN F** (*Easterby*)	8	9
Blue, gold slvs, white cap with blue hoop		
23 — Mrs R. C. Fairfax .... **FREE FIGHT**	8	9
Scarlet, blk hrd slvs. & spots on c (*Easterby*)		
24 — Mr J. Farr ... **POLISH STAR** (*H. Peacock*)	8	9
Jade, cream sash and cross-bands on cap		
25 — Mr Marshall Field		
PRINCESSE DU QUART F	8	9
Straw, cherry hooped cap (*R-Rochfort*)		
26 — Mr A. Gibson .... **LA CHANCE F**	8	9
Primrose, brown seams (*H. Leader*)		
27 — Lord Glanely.................... **PRIDE OF CEYLON**	8	9
Black, red, white & blue belt & cap (*Hogg*)		
28 — Mr G. F. X. Hartigan **SONG OF DAWN G**	8	9
Royal blue, gold stripes, crim. c (*R.J.Colling*)		
29 — Mrs D. Henderson .... **SUNNY ANNA F.**	8	9
Turquoise, gold spots & cap (*G. Armstrong*)		
30 — Mr L. Hyman.................... **MUCH ADO F**	8	9
Maroon, gold & turquoise striped (*T. Hall*)		

A typically skimpy wartime racecard. The price had doubled
since the previous Thirsk meeting, hence the emphasis
on the Red Cross donation.

meeting, but a little interest was created by starting nursery handicaps a month earlier than usual, the first being the Highclere Nursery at Newbury on 9th August.

Behind the scenes, summer was spent discussing what flat racing should be permitted, and whether NH racing should be allowed at all. On 2nd April Churchill warned Morrison about a statement he was to make. "Will you kindly let me know beforehand what you think of saying" he wrote. "If anything were done which threatened to terminate horse racing in time of war or ruin the bloodstock industry it would be necessary that the whole matter should be thrashed out in cabinet first".

In early May the Jockey Club sent in its draft programme from July. It provided for 58 days, at two to four days a week until 15th November, unexpectedly including a meeting each at Lincoln and Aintree. CDESC soon agreed, Lincoln excepted, but ordered a review of the fixtures from September in the light of the then prevailing transport situation. Then the atmosphere suddenly changed. Home Office files show that in June fundamental questions about racing were being asked, but the reason is not clear. The row about the Derby probably came too late. One possibility is the attitude of the new Ministry of War Transport, formed in May by amalgamating the Ministries of Transport and Shipping under the especially ennobled Baron Leathers, a specialist in the shipping of coal. A Home Office paper rehearsed the arguments. On the positive side, racing provided recreation and interest for very large numbers of people, and flat racing, at least, was essential to the bloodstock industry. However, it diverted labour from the war effort and tempted workers to absenteeism; crowds held up transport; petrol was diverted to improper use; horses ate food that could be used for cattle or poultry; there was a risk of air attack; money was diverted from National Savings to betting. Interestingly, the paper followed each of the arguments against racing with a counter argument, and warned that restrictions on race meetings would raise similar questions about football and other sports, so it was hardly a model of neutrality. Tom Williams, Joint Parliamentary Secretary at the Ministry of Agriculture, wrote from his sick bed an impassioned letter in favour of racing to his Minister. It ended "The stop racing campaign is engineered by anti-gamblers, religious bigots and others incapable of taking a national view. The feedstuffs campaign has stopped. Now it is petrol. Any old stick will do. The whole thing is magnified out of all proportion and should be strongly resisted by the War Cabinet".

On 30th June CDESC decided there was insufficient reason to stop racing, but the option of meetings on Saturdays only should be explored. It also started a futile and time-wasting search for ways to make it illegal to drive to race meetings. One bright idea was that the police could somehow close the area round a race meeting to motorists who did not have legitimate business there. Maxwell realised immediately that the proposed restrictions could not be enforced but, despite being told this by Vince, Sir Adair Hore of the Petroleum Department insisted that the mere announcement of a Defence Regulation would cut road travel by 75% and that the remainder could be dealt with by turning motorists away at the course entrance. Hodge was sent back to the drawing board but returned with the same answer after consulting the lawyers and the police, and a Home Office paper to CDESC spelled it out that "there is no means at our disposal of enforcing a regulation of the kind contemplated".

A conference with the Jockey Club in July agreed to confine racing at courses other than Newmarket to Saturdays, to end the season on 5th November (thus dropping the Aintree meeting), and to reduce Newbury fixtures for transport reasons. This was a major turn of the screw, but jumping was in worse trouble. In May Hodge sought other ministries' views about next winter's racing, to allow an early decision about rations. The NH stewards wanted three days' racing a week at approved places from early November to late

March. Hodge thought this fitted the policy of avoiding interference with any particular form of recreation and would not now raise public safety objections, but noted that jumping was not as important to the bloodstock industry as flat racing. War Transport said the arguments for continuing were insufficient: permission should be refused because all unnecessary rail travel must be eliminated next winter and there must be the utmost fuel economy in road transport. Then they tried to take over the whole process, holding bilateral talks with the stewards and producing a long paper for CDESC, which described three alternative programmes they had discussed and how they might be made acceptable. This was another clear invasion of Home Office territory, and they were hopping mad, particularly as War Transport had ignored hints to "leave us to handle the matter as usual". A stiff memo reminded them it was the Home Office that advised CDESC on sport and entertainment.

A plan emerged to race in three areas: North at Wetherby and Nottingham, South at Plumpton, and West at Cheltenham and Newbury or Worcester, with 36 to 38 meetings altogether. War Transport vetoed Newbury, and Plumpton was banned by the War Office, but CDESC agreed to allow 30 meetings, on Saturdays only. Asked for a fixture list on that basis, the stewards thumped in an own-goal by including Manchester, Taunton and Southwell, none of which had previously been mentioned and the first two of which were clearly out of the question. After a meeting to thrash things out, War Transport conceded Southwell, provided the fixtures were on Saturdays before or after Nottingham – to allow horses to walk between the courses!

Around the same time, there was a series of Commons questions about rations for steeplechasers from Sir Waldron Smithers, not a character from Dickens or Trollope but the blimpish Tory MP for Chislehurst, who was waging a one-man campaign against jump racing and what he called the "criminality" of training geldings. For the moment, he was unsuccessful and the fixture list was approved on 25th September, allowing twelve meetings at Cheltenham, eight at Wetherby, five at Nottingham, three at Worcester and two at Southwell. It greatly disappointed the racing community.

Flat racing burst back into life in late August, when Big Game scraped home from Watling Street in the Champagne Stakes, transferred to Newbury from Doncaster, and Sun Castle returned to form to beat Devonian, Mazarin and Owen Tudor in the St. Simon Stakes. The stage was set for the St. Leger, this year at Manchester. Sadly, Capt. Robert Busby, the course director and manager, was not there to see it. In poor health since the 1914–18 war, the blitz had mentally shattered him and he died suddenly and tragically, as the Sporting Life put it, in mid-August. There was a huge crowd, and despite traffic problems the meeting was highly successful. The start and finish of the St Leger were sited to be seen easily from the cheap rings, which was well received, and it was a thrilling race. Lambert Simnel faded after half way and Owen Tudor ran badly, but Chateau Larose caught the fading Mazarin over a furlong out, only to be headed on the line by Sun Castle, with Dancing Time running on stoutly into third. The winner was ridden by the Anglo-French George Bridgland, who had fled to Britain in 1940 and joined the RAF.

Most of the important autumn action was at Newmarket. Some of the Doncaster races from the St. Leger meeting were run there the week after the big race itself but, as with the Goodwood races, the prize money was generally poor. The least niggardly was the Portland Handicap, worth £840, in which Comatas showed his July Cup success was no fluke. A month later Fred Darling boldly took on the top juvenile colts, Watling Street and Ujiji, with Sun Chariot in the Middle Park Stakes, and she beat them easily. Her natural target would have been the Cheveley Park, which went to Perfect Peace, who had finished behind Big Game and Watling Street in the Champagne Stakes at Newbury after being second to Sun Chariot in the Queen Mary. The following day Owen Tudor returned to form by comfortably winning the Newmarket St Leger (a long-established race, not to be confused with the Classic), with Chateau Larose second again and Mazarin just holding Dancing Time for third. Newmarket's September sales were very disappointing, but the bloodstock market was holding up reasonably well, a return in mid-summer showing that there were 5,985 mares, stallions, yearlings and foals altogether on stud farms. The October sales saw 350 entries over the three days, and business was buoyant despite bad war news. On 8th October Rue de la Paix won the Cambridgeshire under Tommy Carey, the former PTC champion jockey, who was enjoying a successful season for Walter Nightingall. After being refused a jumps licence in late 1939 he joined the RAF, but was invalided out and successfully applied for a Jockey Club licence for 1941.

The most important event of Cambridgeshire day was a meeting of the Jockey Club, which decided to set up a Racing Reorganisation Committee. Proposing this, Lord Ilchester explained that they needed a plan for action after the war to make racing less expensive and more attractive for owners, encourage breeders, and make racecourses as comfortable and inexpensive as possible for the public. The members were Ilchester himself, the Duke of Norfolk, Lords Zetland, Portal and Harewood and Sir Humphrey de Trafford. The idea was visionary but the members all had important military or government jobs, so it would take a long time. Not content with one enlightened act, the Club then agreed to have an annual meeting to address potential grievances with their tenants, the Newmarket trainers, whom they had sometimes appeared to regard as little better than villeins.

Later in October Filator and Sam Wragg won the Cesarewitch, again over only two miles. Canyonero won a sub-standard Dewhurst, and the Champion Stakes went to the Jack Jarvis trained Hippius, whose lad had looked after the 1899 Ascot Gold Cup winner. Away from Newmarket, Sugar Palm, last in Owen Tudor's maiden on his only run in 1940, gradually came into form and won

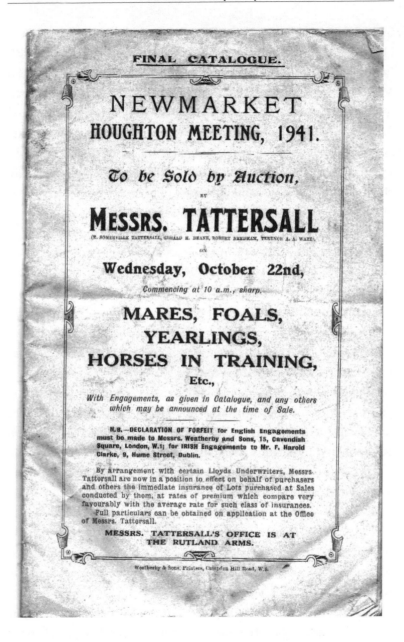

FINAL CATALOGUE.

NEWMARKET
HOUGHTON MEETING, 1941.

To be Sold by Auction,

BY

MESSRS. TATTERSALL
(R. SOMERVILLE TATTERSALL, GERALD H. DEANE, ROBERT NEEDHAM, TERENCE A. A. WATT).

ON

Wednesday, October 22nd,

Commencing at 10 a.m., sharp.

MARES, FOALS,
YEARLINGS,
HORSES IN TRAINING,
Etc.,

*With Engagements, as given in Catalogue, and any others
which may be announced at the time of Sale.*

**N.B.—DECLARATION OF FORFEIT for English Engagements
must be made to Messrs. Weatherby and Sons, 15, Cavendish
Square, London, W.1; for IRISH Engagements to Mr. F. Harold
Clarke, 9, Hume Street, Dublin.**

By arrangement with certain Lloyds Underwriters, Messrs.
Tattersall are now in a position to effect on behalf of purchasers
and others the immediate insurance of Lots purchased at Sales
conducted by them, at rates of premium which compare very
favourably with the average rate for such class of insurances.
Full particulars can be obtained on application at the Office
of Messrs. Tattersall.

**MESSRS. TATTERSALL'S OFFICE IS AT
THE RUTLAND ARMS.**

Weatherby & Sons, Printers, Chapden Hill Road, W.8.

Tattersalls' sales at the autumn 1941 Newmarket meetings saw
brisk business despite bad war news.

sprint handicaps in October at Salisbury, Nottingham and Worcester. He was to be a public favourite throughout the war, and still winning after it. Crown Colony and Cliff Richards won the Manchester November Handicap, held three weeks earlier than usual, for Lord Glanely on 1st November. When flat racing ended five days later the champion jockey was Harry Wragg, now an anti-aircraft gunner conveniently stationed in East Anglia, with 71 winners, ten ahead of Eph Smith. One wonders how many championships this outstanding rider would have won had his career not coincided with that of Gordon Richards.

Jumping was back two days later, with 727 horses in training and few opportunities. 130 ran in six races at the opening meeting at Nottingham, with 29 chasing £118 in the Clifton Maiden Hurdle and 33 in the Colwick Handicap Hurdle. This was not lost on Sir Waldron Smithers, who pointed out to the Minister of Agriculture that it was close to a record for a jumping meeting and that their rations could have been better used to produce milk. The Sporting Life, on the other hand, led with *Bright Send-Off for Chasing* over a typically up-beat story about plucky and enthusiastic jumping people, emphasising that most of the riders were in the forces or munitions work. An exception was Gerry Wilson who, like Gordon Richards and Eph Smith, had failed his medical.

Big fields and good crowds continued for the rest of the year. At Worcester Anarchist, at long odds-on, was only seventh to Red April, but the promising Forestation won two juvenile hurdles at Cheltenham in December. Newmarket December sales were also well attended in spite of dense fog, and brisk business was stimulated by news of a Russian counter-attack: Pearl Harbor was to remain just a dot on the map for a few more days.

Christmas was uneventful at home, with plenty of basic foodstuffs but few luxuries, and factories working full time. Boxing Day being a Friday, there was no racing, but Cheltenham and Wetherby raced next day. The last contest of 1941, the Thorparch

Handicap Steeplechase at Wetherby, was won by course specialist Chesterton, ridden by Jack Bissill. Looking ahead, it had already been announced that the 1942 National Hunt meeting would have to be held on two Saturdays.

To what would racegoers have drunk as they parted for the last time that year? Probably "Victory in 1942", though more in hope than faith. It had been a terrible year, without a speck of light at the end of the tunnel. However, the Empire had begun it fighting alone but now, thanks to Hitler's invasion of the USSR and Japan's attack on Pearl Harbor, two giants were fighting beside us. Or so it seemed. The reality would become that we were fighting beside them, that our war would increasingly become their war. Without realising it, we had just crossed a watershed in world history. Our finest hour had passed and the rest of the century would belong to our new allies.

CHAPTER 6

IN THE BALANCE (1942)

In the first week of January 1942 the Home Secretary again met hostile Commons questions about allowing racing to continue. In the face of heckling he insisted that "There must be recreation within reasonable limitations. I do not think we should too readily adopt the philosophy of progressive misery". Few disagreed with Morrison's basic philosophy, but whether racing fell within those reasonable limitations at all and, if so, how much of it, was another matter. The debate foreshadowed arguments that were to haunt the next few months, starting only two days later when the Jockey Club submitted its proposals for a flat fixture list of 63 days up to 31st July, the majority of them on weekdays, using eleven English courses and two in Scotland. All had featured in earlier wartime lists, but included controversial ones such as Hurst Park, Newbury and Manchester.

The NHC instructed clerks of courses to frame seven-race programmes to squeeze the maximum opportunities from the limited number of meetings, but before they could act the weather closed racing down as completely as in 1940. Unusually for mid-winter, there was good going for the meetings on 10th January at Wetherby and Worcester (where Solford was killed in the Evesham Novices Chase), but by the following weekend everywhere was frozen. Eight consecutive Saturdays were lost, demonstrating at precisely the wrong moment that the absence of a vestigial NH programme would not precipitate the end of civilisation.

The war was going badly everywhere. In North Africa the Germans and Italians had started counter-attacking and took Benghazi on 29th January. The Japanese were advancing swiftly through Malaya, taking Kuala Lumpur and then driving the British off the mainland to make a last stand in Singapore, which had to surrender on 15th February. On 12th February three German warships dashed defiantly up the Channel from the Atlantic and more than forty aircraft were lost in trying to stop them. On the Atlantic itself the battle had spread from the open ocean to American coastal waters when the United States entered the war, and allied shipping losses surged. The tonnage lost in February was greater than any previous month, but that was only the prelude to worse; for many months the country's supplies of oil, wheat and other vital war materials were in acute danger.

Because of the threat to oil supplies the basic petrol ration was reduced from early February, then completely abolished in March. There was also a ban on moving racehorses by rail. It only lasted a month and was hardly noticed because the weather had stopped all racing, but the idea was not dead. The pressing need for fuel economy had put the Ministry of War Transport closer to the heart of government. The obliging chaps who allowed special trains if they did not interfere with other traffic and were not too bothered how people used their petrol ration had gone. In their place were bleakly determined men who saw private motoring in terms of petrol and rubber consumed and knew it was difficult enough to keep goods trains moving in freezing darkness without needless passenger traffic. They were to insist on their message of utmost economy with evangelical zeal for the rest of the war. The department's Parliamentary Secretary, Philip Noel Baker, personified this attitude and was a particularly unfortunate incumbent from racing's point of view. A high-minded intellectual with a Quaker background, he had no time for it and set out to make difficulties at every opportunity.

Early February was, therefore, an unpropitious time for the interested government departments to hold a conference to discuss the proposed fixture list. The elephant in the room was immediately identified by the chairman, Osbert Peake, Under-Secretary of State at the Home Office, who reminded delegates that the principle of whether racing should continue was outside their terms of reference: they must assume it was to continue on the terms of the War Cabinet decision of June 1941 and agree a provisional programme. Representatives of other departments ripped into the proposed size of the programme, dates of meetings and courses to be used. The Ministry of Labour objected to Nottingham because of absenteeism during the last meeting there, but was trumped by War Transport who objected not only to Nottingham but to Hurst Park, Edinburgh, Worcester, Lanark and Manchester because of their remoteness from training centres, and to Thirsk, Ripon and Newbury because of rail congestion. All soon agreed that racing except at Newmarket should be confined to Saturdays and bank holidays to reduce the risk of absenteeism, thereby cutting the programme to 27 days.

The Jockey Club stewards then joined the meeting, and asked if some of the weekday meetings could be held on Saturdays instead. Since they immediately tabled two alternative 37-day programmes, they must have discussed Plan B in detail beforehand. Noel Baker upped the ante by demanding that all racing should be confined to Newmarket and horses trained there – in effect, the solution adopted in the darker periods of the First World War – but the stewards pointed out that Newmarket meetings in this war all had to be on the July Course, which would not stand more than two days a fortnight, and the area where most horses were trained was now around Lambourn. Because the government had requisitioned so much stabling in Newmarket there would not be accommodation for other trainers to move there. Their counter proposal was that horses trained north and south of the Trent should be allowed to race only in those areas respectively, but all should be permitted to run at Newmarket.

Summarising for the Home Office, William Mabane, Parliamentary Secretary, said that the choice was between a severely restricted programme on the proposed basis or a new one that excluded unacceptable courses and days. The stewards should decide whether they could devise an acceptable list, noting in particular that running the Derby on a weekday had caused major criticism.

Morrison was annoyed at this inconclusive end, demanding to know what was actually being recommended and telling staff and junior ministers to discuss a paper for cabinet with him. Before that could happen the Jockey Club put in a proposal for 37 days between 4th April and 29th July, eighteen of them at Newmarket and the rest on Saturdays and bank holidays at Salisbury (6), Windsor (5), Stockton (5) and Pontefract (3). Then, despite the need for a quick decision, there was a pause.

There were others fishing in the troubled waters. The Minister of War Transport received a letter from the Hon. Gilbert Johnstone, who said he had resigned from the NHC in protest at the waste of resources, but flat racing was entirely different and the Classics must be run. "Racing at Newmarket interests the general public much more than racing anywhere else" he asserted, and vested interests that would try to get racing in Scotland and the north should be resisted. Even by the standards of the time, one has to wonder what planet he was on. Sir Adair Hore forwarded to Peake a letter from a lady in Eynsford, who had read an article in the London Evening News and complained in extravagant terms about the use of petrol for travel to race meetings. Although dismissively remarking "We get scores of these", Hore went on to observe that it did illustrate the mind of a good many people, including Sir Waldron Smithers and Mr Lyons in the House of Commons.

Smithers himself was making headway with his anti-jumping campaign despite an approach akin to that of Toytown's Mr Growser on BBC Childrens' Hour. In late January he questioned the Home Secretary about attendances at Cheltenham and cars at Worcester. A month later he wrote to The Times after a report about a disagreement between Salisbury and Wilton Rural District Council and the Ministry of Works. The council had included 42 tons of iron railings at Salisbury racecourse in a return of potential scrap metal in its area, but the Ministry deleted the entry. The railings surrounded the enclosures and without them the public could have got in for nothing. In the exchange that followed the RDC let the cat out of the bag about its true motives by claiming that attending the races was a waste of petrol and tyres, to which the Ministry loftily replied that the continuance of racing was nothing to do with them. Smithers' letter quoted figures about racecourse attendances and how much horses ate as proof that "We are not yet wholly war-minded. Total war demands total effort and total sacrifice". Moreover, he wrote to Cheltenham Borough Council, asking them to help with his campaign to get fodder rations for NH horses diverted to food production and stop the use of petrol for going to race meetings. This struck a chord with the council, which resolved to tell the Home Office that racing should be curtailed during the war and that the frequent Cheltenham meetings were a serious hindrance because the resources of various kinds that were consumed could be better used. The Acting Town Clerk's letter arrived at the Home Office on 3rd March, two months after the latest Cheltenham meeting that had actually been held, but nevertheless contained a catalogue of inconveniences suffered on the "weekly race day", culminating in the complaint that "the whole procedure has given the town an appearance of pre-war gaiety which......the Council consider is quite out of place".

The air raid threat having passed, why should there still have been such strong anti-racing sentiment in a town for which the meetings provided business and, even at that time, some prestige? And would not many of the townspeople have craved a bit of fun to relieve the drabness of wartime? The clue may lie in the revulsion from gaiety: could this have been the legacy of the Reverend Francis Close, who determinedly turned Cheltenham into a citadel of Anglican evangelical rectitude in the second quarter of the nineteenth century? His pet hates were the theatre, gambling and Roman Catholicism, and he proclaimed in 1835 that "Papists and profligacy are essential concomitants of horse racing, for which Cheltenham will soon be paying a terrible price". No wonder he was involved in suppressing the old flat meeting on Cleeve Hill. Long after he left to become Dean of Carlisle, Close's influence lived on in Cheltenham, so perhaps the town was still guided by deeply ingrained puritan instincts, even in 1942.

By now a feeling was building up that something would have to give. There was a Commons debate on 25th February about consumption of oats by horses and petrol for travel to race meetings, and more correspondence in The Times. A few days later it was rumoured that the government was considering new and drastic restrictions on sport, and later that the Home Secretary was to make a statement soon.

The decisive moment came in early March. A meeting of CDESC on the 5th rejected one of the proposed programmes because it included forbidden courses, and then heard from War Transport that they were about to abolish the basic petrol ration, which would make it impossible to sanction the use of petrol for horse boxes (estimated at 15,000 gallons a year). Possible centralisation at Newmarket was again considered, though it was accepted that the idea would only work if the RAF could be persuaded to give back the Rowley Mile and should not be pressed if they demanded alternative accommodation. Then the whole issue was referred to another inter-departmental conference with the Jockey Club stewards, which was held four days later and proved a major turning point for wartime racing. It began with news that the RAF would not release the Rowley Mile, killing the option of complete centralisation and forcing consideration of other ways to economise on transport. The agreed solution was to divide the country into three regions - North, South and Newmarket - and restrict horses to running in the one where they were being trained at the start of the season. This was similar to the earlier Jockey Club proposal, but with the key difference that Newmarket was not to be open to all, except for a handful of races that would allow the best from each region to compete. Up to the end of July these would be the Guineas races, the Derby and Oaks, Ascot Gold Cup, Coventry Stakes and Queen Mary Stakes. Newmarket was allocated eight fortnightly two-day meetings, in midweek except for the Derby meeting, which was to be on a Friday and Saturday. In the north, Pontefract and Stockton were given six Saturdays each, but Noel Baker made difficulties over meetings in the south, where he insisted that transport difficulties precluded Windsor from holding anything more than a single meeting of two days at Whitsun. Consequently, twelve Saturdays had to be allocated to the inaccessible and narrow course at Salisbury, despite being more than the stewards thought it could stand. War Transport agreed that horse boxes could be attached to ordinary trains provided a week's notice was given and they caused no delay or extra demands for locomotives, and trainers could apply to their local Transport Commissioner for petrol to take horses to meetings within a 45-mile radius.

And so the deal was done that shaped racing for the rest of the war. It was ratified by CDESC on 11th March and Hodge wrote to the Jockey Club with the news the same day. Unfortunately, discussion had dragged on so long that the earliest racing that could be arranged was Newmarket's Craven Meeting on 14th April, more than three weeks after the end of the NH season, bringing about the first-ever Easter without racing. It would be 25th April before the northern and southern zones could start. The Sporting Life greeted the new arrangements more positively than its previous form might have suggested, explaining that they had emerged after prolonged consultation with the government and that transport had been the main factor. The restrictions would be "loyally accepted by the hard hit racing and breeding industries". It explained that although the northern and southern zones were described as north and south of the Trent, the actual boundary was an almost straight, imaginary line from Great Yarmouth to Aberystwyth via Peterborough and Birmingham. No reference to this has been found in Home Office or Jockey Club records but the fictional line gave less arbitrary results than the meandering Trent itself, and seems to have been the boundary used in practice: the very few stables between the notional and actual Trents raced in the north.

The weather eventually relented in the second week of March, just in time for the National Hunt meeting to take place over the last two Saturdays of the season. There had been more correspondence in The Times, including a suggestion that it should be abandoned and the prize money given to Warships Week, but it went ahead regardless, and on the first day, 14th March, spring arrived suddenly and unexpectedly. The seven races produced 160 runners, of which 110 managed to complete the course and only 14 pulled up, indicating that trainers had kept horses fitter than might be expected in such desperate weather. There were twenty in the Champion Hurdle, won by Forestation, another four-year-old trained at Epsom by Vic Smyth and ridden by Ron, with Anarchist again run out of it in the closing stages. The winning trainer also owned the horse and gave the prize of £495 to Lady Kemsley's War Relief Fund. Most of the hopefuls for the following week's Gold Cup were given an outing in the steeplechases, with Sawfish and Schubert going for the National Hunt Handicap Chase but most preferring the shorter trip (although smaller prize) of the Grand Annual. Red Rower headed Medoc II at the last and just held on by a neck, with Broken Promise only a length behind, to set up a week's eager speculation about the big race itself.

Spring had made a tactical withdrawal by the last day of the season, which was damp and misty, and Cheltenham not well attended. The opening race, Class 1 of the Lansdown Hurdle, provided a little consolation for Anarchist and Tommy Isaac, who this time successfully beat off all challengers. Twelve started for the Gold Cup, fast run despite heavy ground and effectively decided four fences out, where Solarium and Broken Promise both fell when well clear of the rest. Red Rower, favourite on the strength of his win the previous week, was badly hampered, but Medoc II less so, allowing him to seize an eight length lead on which Red Rower, Asterabad and Schubert could make no impression. Sawfish and the rest were outpaced and Roman Hackle fell, breaking Ron Smyth's collar bone. His discomfort may have been lessened by knowing that he had won the jockeys' championship, albeit with only twelve winners. Wetherby also raced that afternoon and it was there, ending a day of big fields and long-priced winners, that the last race of the season was run. The Harrogate Moderate Chase attracted only four runners, three of which were still in contention between the last two fences, but odds-on favourite Argental dashed clear on the run-in to send the punters home happy. They would have to cherish the memory of jumping for a long time.

The empty weeks that followed were taken up with preparations for flat racing under the new dispensation. Around 400 horses were in training at Newmarket and somewhat fewer in the north, predominantly in Yorkshire, but there were some 750 in the south. There were still 146 licensed trainers, 80 jockeys and 85 apprentices. The Newmarket executive seemed not to understand that the traditional Craven Meeting programme might not meet the demands of zoned racing, and four races did not fill when first advertised. Salisbury, however, had the opposite problem, with colossal entries for the first meeting that compelled the two handicaps to be divided, resulting in a nine race card for which the prize money was barely affordable. The modest amounts on offer

The photographer seems to be alone down the course at the moment Sun Chariot snatches the lead in the 1942 Oaks with the rest already struggling.

brought a complaint from Alfred Allnatt, a newcomer to big ownership who had bought heavily into bloodstock when most others were selling in 1940. Major Gerald Deane, principal at Tattersalls, suggested that the Jockey Club might help out, but this fell on stony ground. Of more general public interest were reports that Gordon Richards was riding work in preparation for his return to the racecourse. This meant that Harry Wragg had lost the rides on the Beckhampton horses, but he was recompensed through the misfortune of Dick Perryman who had suffered career-ending injuries in a car crash, leaving a vacancy for first jockey to Lord Derby. Wragg was the obvious choice and glad to accept: Walter Earl was a more scientific trainer than most, a fine horseman and, as an ex-jockey, easier to ride for than some of the pompous gentry who trained at Newmarket. Furthermore, Stanley House had Watling Street, who seemed as promising a Classic hopeful as Big Game or Sun Chariot.

Radical change was coming in Ireland too. Although the Republic was neutral, The Emergency, as it was known, was making life very difficult. Though poor, the country could largely feed itself, but energy was a different matter. The limitless reserves of turf were good enough for rural, domestic use but unsuitable for industry or railways, and the same was true of the coal from the country's three, small pits. Eire depended on crumbs of coal falling from the United Kingdom's table, and on oil from the same, beleaguered supply lines. 1941 had been a bad year for Irish racing, with the big Fairyhouse and Punchestown meetings lost to a foot-and-mouth epidemic, but 23 courses had struggled on. Even Miltown Malbay in the farthest west had held its annual meeting despite its tortuous, narrow gauge lifeline, the West Clare Railway, being down to a single daily train each way. However, it was clear in the spring of 1942 that something drastic had to be done, and the fixture list was cut almost in half. Racing was to be largely confined to The Curragh and the metropolitan courses at Leopardstown, Baldoyle and Phoenix Park, plus some possible autumn meetings at Naas. Initially, the only concession to the provinces was one two-day fixture each at Galway, Tramore, Killarney and Listowel, though four other courses were later granted meetings. Horse boxes could, if available, be attached to scheduled trains, but motor transport was banned (leading to tales of groups of soberly dressed bookmakers going racing in hearses).

Easter Monday was a bank holiday as usual, though denounced as "a hollow mockery" by The Sporting Life. The only racing was in Ireland, but four London dog tracks were open and there was plenty of football and rugby. Some country folk combined pest control with amusement by organising fox shoots, the curtailed hunting season having finished in February.

At last, on 14th April, the flat season began at what was called the Craven Meeting and greeted like the real thing, despite being confined to Newmarket horses. The afternoon train from London was packed the day before, and even regular visitors found it difficult to find food and accommodation. The problem was that the rationing system was not flexible enough to allow the small town to stock up with provisions for sudden influxes of visitors, worsened by the presence of evacuees and a large, mobile service population. It was a difficulty that Cheltonians had feared, with rather less justification, for their own town, and persisted throughout the war. On the race days there was a shortage of national newspapers and no taxis or buses from the town to the course, although a shuttle service of taxis ran from Six Mile Bottom where illicit users of petrol had prudently parked their cars. A better example was set by the starter, Capt. Allison, who rode his hack to the course. Crowds were up to peacetime levels, with all enclosures except the Members' full, but fields were a little disappointing and several races drew fewer than ten runners. Neither the Free Handicap nor the Craven Stakes was run, leaving the Column Stakes as the most valuable race and this, curiously, was over the last nine furlongs of the Ellesmere Course, finishing downhill into the dip, instead of the usual mile. The most significant race turned out to be the Shelford Stakes, in which Watling Street finished powerfully to win after being hampered. It was generally agreed that he looked capable of staying the Derby distance.

Spring was now in full bloom everywhere despite the cold east wind that had blown ceaselessly since January, but a chill blast of a different kind came with the news that Flight Sgt. Mervyn Jones, hero of the 1940 Grand National, and Capt.D.Marriott, son of the Jockey Club's Newmarket agent, were both listed as missing. Not long afterwards it was reported that Doug Marks was in hospital recovering slowly from "a diseased bone in the back": tuberculosis was one of the great unmentionables in the days before antibiotics.

Attention then turned to the southern three-year-olds, among them the Duchess of Norfolk's six-times winner Honest Penny, Mr Allnatt's Ujiji and, above all, the King's Big Game and Sun Chariot. The filly's temper and behaviour had worsened as her phenomenal ability grew. In the words of Ron Blake "She was a right cow: she bit, she kicked, and when she was upset she laid down – but what an animal!" Even Speedy Holloway, the stable's rough-rider, could not manage Sun Chariot and Gordon Richards had difficulty but, as in the case of Godiva, another temperamental Hyperion filly, there was one person who could. This was a lad called Warren, who looked after her and rode her daily; she was devoted to him and would follow him about like a dog. Even so, it was not always plain sailing; on one occasion she bolted with Warren on the gallops and headed for home so fast that she failed to negotiate the bend into the yard and disappeared at full tilt into a barn. The anxious pursuers were amazed to find horse and rider completely unscathed.

Many racegoers at Salisbury faced a walk of four miles from the station (and four more back again), and the same applied to the unfortunate Tote staff, for whom bus transport had been refused. Nevertheless, there was a good crowd for the first meeting, where the main attraction was the clash between Sun Chariot and Ujiji in the Southern Stakes. The nine races produced a staggering 179 runners despite the modest prize money, 34 of them in the Netheravon Maiden Plate. Sun Chariot looked well in the paddock and was backed down to 3 to 1 on, but she was difficult at the start, where she had developed a disconcerting habit of looking over her shoulder at her rider and trying to go round in circles. Ujiji darted to the front and Richards, obeying instructions, dropped Sun Chariot in behind the leaders. This was a serious mistake, because she refused to take any interest in the race and, tail swishing in protest, cantered in to dead-heat for third behind Ujiji and Mehrali, the latter ridden by Gordon Richards' brother Cliff.

The consensus was that her run was too bad to be true and she remained favourite for the One Thousand Guineas, a judgement proved correct at the next week's Salisbury meeting. Spontaneous singing of the National Anthem greeted the unannounced arrival of the King and Queen to see the royal horses, but Sun Chariot was unimpressed and at first declined to leave the paddock for the Sarum Stakes. Eventually she condescended to be led out by Jack Blake, who then had to run beside her towards the start to make sure she did not change her mind. She was still unhappy when she got there but was off like a shot when the tapes went up and won readily. Afterwards, one of the royal detectives brought Jack a five pound note from the King. It was never spent, but remained a treasured souvenir which was among his widow's possessions when she died. Big Game had his first run of the season in the Salisbury Stakes, easing smoothly into the lead two furlongs out to land long odds-on without difficulty, and Owen Tudor completed a memorable afternoon for Beckhampton by winning the Trial Plate.

The Guineas meeting was only ten days later and on the first day Big Game won the Two Thousand by four lengths in the style an odds-on favourite should. Watling Street was second, ridden by Stan Ellis, a jockey usually seen on no-hopers from various Newmarket stables: Harry Wragg had been put on Umballa, the Stanley House first string, but was soon beaten. Ujiji and Mehrali were fourth and fifth, just behind Gold Nib. The following day Sun Chariot was a bit stubborn at the start of the One Thousand Guineas but was quickly away and never headed. Cheering broke out well before she passed the post four lengths clear of Perfect Peace, and Fred Darling actually smiled as she was led in. The only disappointment was that the King and Queen were unable to be there. Walter Earl again chose his first string wrongly, with Harry Wragg on Equipoise finishing well behind third-placed Light of Day under Ellis. Among the zoned races the Bedford Maiden Plate was won by a filly called Ribbon, trained by Jack Jarvis and destined for a career of heart breaking near misses. Her owner was Lord Rosebery, who was now spending much of his time in Scotland, where he had been Regional Commissioner since early 1941.

Whitsun weekend saw sport of all kinds, including football, cricket at Lords, the Rugby League cup final, top-class athletics, and racing at Pontefract and, for the first time in two years, Windsor. Despite cold weather and government exhortations not to travel, there were big crowds, but only those at the race meetings attracted press criticism. For some reason, 10,000 at Windsor was reprehensible but 35,000 at Roker Park passed without comment. The Metropolitan Police were said to be investigating the legality of taxi journeys by which some spectators had reached Windsor.

The Jockey Club met twice in April and noted that there were now 1,800 horses in training, which Lord Sefton said was too many. They made important changes aimed at encouraging the younger horses but reducing overall numbers by excluding all but the best older ones. Up to three two-year-old races per day were to be allowed from 1st June, but five-year-olds and upwards would be excluded from handicaps, though every card was to have a weight-for-age race for older horses. Nursery handicaps would again start on 1st August. The issue of The Sporting Life that carried this news also reported that the recently doubled entertainments tax was to be passed on in higher admission charges at Newmarket. There were big discounts for the forces but the charge for the grandstand and paddock was to be 26 shillings, and the silver ring eight and elevenpence. These equate to roughly £37 and £13 in present terms. The charge for Tattersalls at Windsor had been an eye-watering 28 shillings.

War news in May was still bad, with shipping losses worsening, new German offensives in Russia and North Africa and the Philippines surrendering, though the Americans had prevented a new Japanese advance at the battle of the Coral Sea. It is not surprising that this was the month when the government turned against NH racing. The NHC submitted a surprisingly tentative suggestion in April that there might be 24 Saturday meetings from November 1942 to March 1943, using only Cheltenham and Wetherby and involving no more than 400 horses. Fatally, as it transpired, they emphasised that this was not a request to continue racing but an offer to help organise a limited programme economically. When the Home Office made its usual consultations, the Ministry of Agriculture had no objections and, provided there was no interference with transport, neither did War Transport. The Ministry of Labour was happy in principle but feared Wetherby races might somehow disturb workers at nearby R.O.F. Thorp Arch. It was the Home Office itself that blocked the idea. A memo by C.S.Petherham, who had succeeded Rucker in early 1941, summarised the history of wartime jumping and the present position, concluding "As even the National Hunt Committee seem to be a little luke-warm......on the whole the best course would be for steeplechasing to be suspended altogether". On 21st May CDESC made the self-contradictory decision to tell the NHC that there was no hope of facilities being given, but it was possible that a skeleton programme might be allowed when the time came and a delegation would be received if they wished.

Sir Waldron Smithers' day of triumph was 4th June, when he was allowed to bowl a full-toss question to the Home Secretary about the government's policy on NH racing, to which Morrison replied that, subject to a final decision, it would not be permitted next winter. When the stewards' delegation met the various departmental representatives on 9th June all parties agreed that maintenance of public morale was the only argument for continuing jumping and each department explained its pet objections. There was then a convoluted discussion in which the stewards argued for meetings at Newbury, Windsor and Worcester as well as Cheltenham and Wetherby, and Noel Baker appeared to say that he did not mind people travelling to meetings at Windsor and Cheltenham but he strongly objected to horses doing so. In the end, Peake told the stewards there was very little hope, but CDESC might change its mind if they proposed a bare minimum programme and could demonstrate a month-by-month fall in the number of horses in training since last season.

As the Derby meeting approached, racing found itself basking in the unaccustomed spotlight of favourable public attention, thanks to the royal Guineas winners, now hot favourites for the Derby and Oaks. Picture Post, a photo news weekly with a million circulation, featured Big Game on the front cover and an inside article of five pages, a huge amount by wartime standards. When the King and Queen went to Beckhampton to see their horses working Fred Darling let his staff's families know that they could stand at the crossroads to see them arrive, provided they told nobody else and there was no clapping or cheering, but all they saw was a glimpse of the royal car sweeping past and a wave from the Queen. Sun Chariot was on her very worst behaviour, defying every attempt by Gordon Richards to get her to go – until Templeton gave her a tap with his whip, at which she bolted into a ploughed field, went down on her knees and squealed with rage. In the end she did consent to take part in the planned gallop, but it had been a tense morning and very different from the relaxed atmosphere when the royal family went on an earlier occasion to see the King's personally owned horses at Egerton House. After watching the whole string canter up two by two there had been a leisurely tour of the stables and finally, while the King had lunch at Harewood House, an impromptu game of rounders between the apprentices and some of the royal party! There seems to have been less fuss than for Lord Derby's visits to Stanley House, which were preceded by general tidying up and the use of air spray, with staff in white coats for the actual visit.

Walter Earl was having enough trouble with Watling Street without visits from his owner, the horse having a reputation as "an utter bastard" who intimidated his lad and kicked at trees on the way to the gallops. Earl was becoming worried about his big bet on him for the Derby and, at Harry Wragg's suggestion, decided to ride Watling Street at exercise himself, which kept him sweet enough to train.

To enable the Derby to be run on a Saturday, the Oaks preceded it for the first time ever, on Friday, 12th June. There was a good crowd, though abolition of the basic petrol ration was now being felt and the car parks were only half full. After the second race some cars were seen coming up the course, but there was little curiosity until they stopped just short of the enclosures and the King and Queen got out and walked slowly along beside the rails to rapturous cheering, the King in Air Marshal's uniform and the Queen in a pale mauve dress, long coat and straw hat. They had come to watch Sun Chariot. She was 4 to 1 on for the Oaks but got into another filthy temper as soon as she left the paddock. Out of sight from the stands she spoiled three attempts at a start and then, when the gate did go up, careered off to the left on the unrailed course and lost many lengths. She was still tailed off when the field came into sight, and ran wide as they made their one turn at the top of the Bunbury Mile. Until this point Richards was in despair, but then she started to make up ground. Half a mile out she had caught the tail-enders, in another furlong she was with the leaders and in the dip she was clear, coasting up the hill to win effortlessly by a length. As in the Guineas, the cheering broke out as soon as she took the lead and there were scenes of delight when the King led her in.

Derby day was overcast with some morning rain to make it uncomfortable for the crowd. The King and Queen were there again, with His Majesty this time in army khaki. Big Game looked magnificent and started at 6 to 4 on, but became stirred up after the long canter to the start and pulled hard early in the race. It probably made no difference: after moving up to dispute the lead with Hyperides a quarter of a mile out his run suddenly came to an end and he faded to finish sixth. As Richards had suspected, he did not stay a mile and a half in top-class company. For a moment Hyperides looked the winner, but he was headed in the last fifty yards by Watling Street, who charged up the hill with one of Harry Wragg's perfectly timed runs, Ujiji finishing third. Lord Derby was not there to see his winner. Not only was he elderly and unwell ("This will buck him up!" remarked Lady Derby as she led Watling Street in), but he was following the example of the Earl of Durham in the Great War by supporting racing whilst denying himself the pleasure of actually going. War or no war, Stanley House put up the flag with which they always celebrated big winners.

Analysing the results in an article looking forward to the St.Leger, The Sporting Life's Augur confined his attentions to Watling Street, Hyperides and Big Game. He disagreed with those who thought Sun Chariot could have won the Derby. "The filly has no pretensions to beat Hyperides [who is] greatly superior in every respect" he declared.

Negotiations over fixtures for the second half of the season should have been straightforward, but the waters were muddied by transport issues and the Jockey Club's attempt to include some banned courses. They also sent a letter explaining the difficulties of running Epsom horses at Salisbury. To race there on a Saturday the horses had to leave by motor horsebox at 6.00 a.m. on Friday for Esher station, whence rail horseboxes attached to a scheduled train got them to Salisbury in the early afternoon. They then walked five miles to overnight stabling where there was hardly any accommodation for their lads, and another five miles to the course on race day. After running and cooling off they walked four miles back to Salisbury station for a train that got them back to Esher in the small hours of Sunday morning. The proposed solution was to allow Epsom horses to run at Newmarket instead, involving a longer road journey to join the train, but arrival close to stabling and to lodgings for lads. It was claimed this would also even up the number of horses eligible to run in the Newmarket and southern areas, apparently overlooking the fact that Epsom horses could run at Windsor (perhaps because this was before any racing had actually taken place there). At this point War Transport flung a spanner into the works by making it known that they proposed to stop transport of horses to meetings from 15th September, though they had no objection to Epsom horses running at Newmarket until then. At first it seemed that the ban applied to both road and rail, which would have stopped racing everywhere except Newmarket, but it soon became clear that it applied only to rail, the ostensible reason being the anticipated increase in travel because of new concessions to servicemen. Given the 45 mile limit on road transport, this was a major new constraint and would limit Epsom horses to Windsor, most Wiltshire horses to Salisbury and exclude some isolated stables from racing altogether.

The Jockey Club proposed 38 days racing, fourteen of them at Newmarket, five at Salisbury, six at Newbury (failing which, eleven at Salisbury), two at Windsor, three at Stockton, two at Pontefract, and six at Thirsk (failing which, six at Stockton and five at Pontefract). They wanted seven open races at Newmarket and would run the St.Leger on a Saturday if asked. The upshot was that on 18th June CDESC approved a programme without racing at Newbury or Thirsk, agreed the seven open races (later increased to eight), with the St.Leger on a Saturday, and allowed Epsom runners at Newmarket instead of Salisbury until 15th September. They also asked War Transport to review the strict 45 mile limit on road transport and authorised the transfer of Salisbury meetings to Windsor if desirable in the light of the outcome. The Jockey Club was also warned that racing at Newmarket might have to be suspended in August because of "government requirements" – secret aircraft trials at RAF Newmarket Heath. War Transport tried to wriggle out of the commitment to review the mileage limit that everyone else thought they had given but, pressed by Hodge, soon agreed to allow up to fifteen miles extra for stables that would otherwise be isolated from any course. Very few were affected, but it may not have been a complete coincidence that the only large one was the Duke of Norfolk's stable at Arundel. Four of the days provisionally allocated to Salisbury after 15th September were given to Windsor, and a fifth was later transferred at short notice, officially because of the state of the course but really because of large military and civil exercises in the Salisbury area.

The next milestone was the meeting featuring the three open races normally run at Ascot. The Aga Khan's Nasrullah, trained by Frank Butters, won the Coventry from Dorothy Paget's Straight Deal, who started relatively unfancied despite having won well at Salisbury, but none of the fillies in the Queen Mary, won by Samovar, were destined for greatness. Ribbon, who might have run in it, instead scored a hard-fought win in one of the zoned races. The main race of the meeting was the Gold Cup, which was considered important enough for a commentary on the BBC Forces Programme and decisively won by Owen Tudor. He was making amends for a disastrous failure at Salisbury after his earlier win there and was quickly packed off to stud before he could lapse again. The going was now firm everywhere, contributing to the first walkover of zoned racing when the smart juvenile gelding Fleur de Lys frightened off all others in the Yeovil Stakes at Salisbury.

Except for the rout of the Japanese by the Americans at Midway, the war was still going badly on all fronts, but the saddest news for the racing community was the death of Lord Glanely in an air raid at the end of June. It was a small consolation that all 134 of his horses in training and at stud were bought by Mr. Allnatt at the time of the July sales, where there were some remarkable prices despite the bad news.

In July thoughts were turning towards the autumn. The open races normally run then were being brought forward to beat the rail transport ban but it was announced that the Autumn Double races would not take place, as they could not be run in their normal form. The Home Office was looking ahead, too, deciding that even talking to the NHC about a programme would seem like a partial commitment. Instead, they consulted other departments about finally banning jumping. The Ministry of Labour fully agreed, War Transport thought it would simplify matters, and Agriculture agreed provided a ban did not prejudice the decision about 1943 flat racing. Petherham prepared a briefing for CDESC recommending that NH

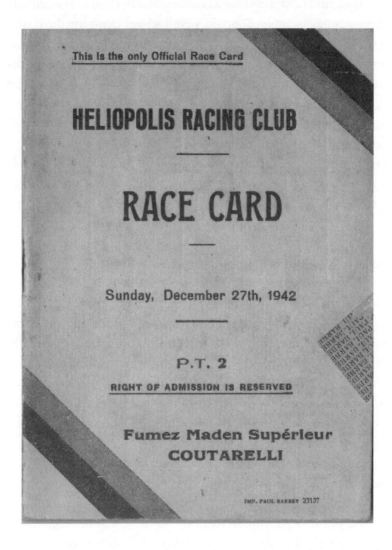

There were no British meetings at Christmas 1942 but there was one in Cairo, where expatriate Britons had long been involved in racing. Tommy Weston was among those who rode there during his military service.

racing should be stopped for a combination of reasons: the shipping and feedstuffs situation, difficulties with winter transport, the relative unimportance of jumping to the bloodstock industry, the low entertainment value of a minimal programme, and objections that had been raised to Cheltenham and Wetherby. CDESC readily agreed and the Home Office prepared a press notice and a letter to Sir Humphrey de Trafford, the senior steward, telling him that NH racing could not be allowed in 1942/3 because "the present need for extreme economy, together with the additional strain on transport services during the winter months have made this decision necessary". In a hand written reply to Peake, de Trafford hoped that better war news next year would enable discussions to start again, concluding "The National Hunt stewards quite realise you have done your best to help us, and we are most grateful".

The news broke on 10th September and was not well received in racing circles. Bloodstock Breeders Review thought that when they had given wholehearted co-operation "it seemed hard on the jumping folk that their modest requirements were refused", this being the first time the government had not maintained its sympathetic attitude towards racing. The Sporting Life's first report was quite low-key, but its lead story the next week reported letters of protest from "nearly all classes of the civil community" and the fighting services. The article then turned into a classic example of the paper's editorial spluttering outrage, denouncing the minimal impact the ban would have on the war effort but noting that it would "please the vociferous minority of kill-joys – if anything can be said to bring pleasure to that doleful section of the community, who probably do more to clog the war effort than a thousand race meetings". Expostulatory letters to the editor appeared for some weeks afterwards.

Windsor returned to action over August bank holiday weekend, with a large crowd on the Saturday but a smaller one on the Monday because of transport problems. There were few cars but many cycles, with boats and a two-horse coach plying their trade between town and course, where military and civilian police busily checked leave passes and identity cards. Newmarket's late August meeting featured two open races on each day, starting with the Rous and Champion Stakes. The former, a five-furlong two-year-old race, was an oddity among the open races in not having a prestigious peacetime counterpart: the Rous Plates at the Ebor and St.Leger meetings were only part of the supporting programmes and the York race was a seller. Only four ran and Lady Sybil, the mainstay of Capt.Tommy Hogg's stable, struggled to land long odds-on from Samovar, but a classy five ran in the Champion Stakes. Big Game was favourite on the assumption that the shorter trip would help him redeem his Derby failure, but he was turning into a bit of a thinker and had finished behind Ujiji in an inter-stable gallop hosted by Joe Lawson, Ujiji's trainer, at Manton. On the day, Big Game was invincible and came through to win smoothly from Afterthought and Ujiji, with Hyperides fourth.

Next day the Nunthorpe Stakes attracted mainly older sprinters. One of the few northern horses to run in open races, The Pale, was clear until the last furlong only to be caught by Epsom-trained Linklater, ridden by Eph Smith, with old Mickey the Greek and Honest Penny finishing in the ruck. Half an hour later there was drama before the Middle Park Stakes, for which Nasrullah was odds-on and Ribbon was challenging the colts, when third favourite Straight Deal suddenly dumped Tommy Carey at the start and galloped away from the course. He went several hundred yards before being caught by Snowy Outen, who happened to be taking a short cut from Egerton House to the course and rode him gently back towards the start. He had taken too much out of himself to figure in the race and finished sixth behind Ribbon, who battled on bravely to hold off Nasrullah.

The last open races were run at the St.Leger meeting on 11th and 12th September. Watling Street and Sun Chariot, neither of whom had run since the Derby meeting, were first and second favourites for the big race, with Hyperides the only other seriously fancied. Sun Chariot's temperament had mellowed somewhat during the summer and Darling decided to try her against mature horses over the St.Leger distance. Using the Manton gallops again and ridden by Warren, she ran against her usual lead horse Massowa, Bakhtawar and, just to make sure, Bo-Tree, a tough stayer cum hurdler borrowed from George Todd. The other three took turns to set a strong pace but a furlong from the end Sun Chariot cruised up to Bakhtawar, who was leading, and left them for dead. When Bakhtawar was beaten only two heads in the Jockey Club Cup they knew Sun Chariot was a near certainty for the St.Leger, but such was the security of information in those days that Watling Street still started clear favourite. It was a one horse race. Sun Chariot, who now allowed herself to be held up, tracked the field for nearly a mile and then steadily made ground to lead into the dip and canter effortlessly home ahead of the hard-driven Watling Street and Hyperides, giving the King his fourth Classic winner of the year. Gordon Richards maintained she was the best filly he ever rode, and in the first half of the twentieth century only Pretty Polly and Sceptre could be compared with her.

Lady Sybil and Samovar had repeated their Rous Stakes placings over the extra furlong of the Cheveley Park on the previous day, and in the Dewhurst Straight Deal just failed to hold the Aga Khan's Umiddad, ridden by Doug Smith. The winner had scored first time out when unfancied in a Newmarket maiden in July and now looked as serious a Classic prospect as his owner's Nasrullah.

Then, suddenly, the leading players left the stage. Big Game, Sun Chariot and Watling Street all went to stud within a week and the leading Classic prospects came out of training to await 1943. It was left to those they had overshadowed to seek consolation prizes in their own zones now that the travel restrictions were in full operation. Among those who succeeded were Massowa, Fortunate

Lady, Harroway, Jamaica Inn and the repeatedly disappointing Seasick, who scrambled home in the Southfield Maiden Stakes, the very last race of the year, on 4th November. Of the rest, Areley Kings won four in a row in the north for Fred Armstrong, and Reg Day's Pink Flower won three at Newmarket. Vic Smyth's Historic won maidens at the last two Windsor meetings, where Forestation and Sugar Palm picked up a race apiece. The last Pontefract meeting featured a "Substitute November Handicap" which was definitely not the real thing, being confined to northern zone three- and four-year-olds. Excluding older horses from handicaps had had some perverse results, the better handicappers, particularly Germanicus and The Pale, being able to farm weight for age races, where they conceded less weight than they otherwise would.

Bloodstock Breeders Review felt the season had been highly satisfactory and in many ways this was true. In the north the number of horses and the opportunities for them were well balanced, the two courses were easily accessible and, though both left handed, the Stockton billiard table and the Pontefract Alps provided contrasting challenges. Newmarket fields were occasionally on the thin side, but generally the numbers of horses and suitable races were well matched. The insoluble difficulty was the monotony of the same horses meeting eachother repeatedly on the same course, usually with similar results. Horses trained at Newmarket are sometimes mentally affected by their surroundings and now there was no opportunity to ease the stress. The worst difficulty was in the south, where division of races and bigger fields were the inevitable consequence of the larger number of horses. Lord Sefton called a meeting of trainers at the last Windsor meeting and urged them to get rid of the worst, but that was not really the answer to the structural problem. Though Windsor is an easy track and Salisbury stiffer, they are both idiosyncratic in shape, and Salisbury was remote and unable to offer attractive prize money. Furthermore, it had only got away with eighteen days' racing, including a spell of twelve

Saturdays out of fourteen, because of favourable weather and heroic efforts by the groundstaff. A third and more orthodox course was needed to share the load: there was one, obvious candidate but no obvious way of getting hold of it. Tote betting had also taken a knock in 1942, with on-course turnover falling to £1.41 million, compared with £1.79 million in 1941, although credit betting had held steady in real terms at £0.43 million.

At last there was better war news. Shipping losses had peaked, the Eighth Army had defeated Rommel at El Alamein and Americans were landing behind him, and the Russians were counter-attacking at Stalingrad. Everyone was cautious after earlier disappointments, but on 10th November Churchill pronounced it "The end of the beginning". The turning point looks so obvious now that it is easy to overlook his genius in spotting it at the time. In celebration, church bells were allowed to be rung for the first time since 1940.

One result was a good attendance at Newmarket December sales and high prices for anything worth having but, with no actual meetings, racing was really in hibernation and waiting for 1943. Other entertainments were far from dormant, with greyhound racing enjoying unprecedented popularity and providing a lifeline for bookmakers. According to Cyril Whiterow it was "money for old rope; prices were very tight and you only needed one skinner and you were O.K." There was also plenty of football (though with nothing serious at stake) and rugby, and theatres and restaurants in London were packed to capacity. Bell ringing was allowed again for morning services at a Christmas that was the most austere of the war to date, but the year ended with hopes that were, for the first time, rational and not just intuitive.

CHAPTER 7

IN THE DOLDRUMS (1943)

The course needed to ease pressure in the south was Ascot, among the best in the country, able to accommodate huge crowds, close to a station with trains from three directions, and within the 45-mile radius of most stables in the zone. Manton, Beckhampton and Stockbridge were just outside the limit but had got away with running horses at Windsor the previous autumn. Despite more than three years' disuse the course was still being maintained, though the stands were looking shabby. However, there were difficulties. It was royal property, administered through the King's Representative at Ascot, and the unique annual meeting normally set the highest standards in racing and social terms: run-of-the-mill Saturday meetings might seem like musical comedy at Glyndebourne. Also, the army was occupying some of the buildings needed for race meetings and was likely to resist attempts to move the soldiers or work round them.

In December 1942 Sefton had asked Peake whether there would be any objection to using Ascot for most of the meetings formerly allocated to Salisbury, where the Jockey Club would only want "odd days" for local trainers. He thought the only likely opposition would be from the War Office, who had staff in the grandstand. He added that the King "would like to get away from the idea of a Royal Ascot after the war" and it would be easier to do this if racing took place there before the end of the war. It is not clear what the King meant, as no other record of his views has been found. Taken literally, he wanted to do away with the Royal meeting, but there is no evidence that His Majesty had developed such radical views, and the traditional meeting resumed without debate in 1946. It seems more likely that he wanted Ascot to be no longer solely royal, but accessible as an ordinary racecourse too. Or perhaps Sefton was playing the "King" card to win Peake over and inflated the importance of a casual remark. In any event, there was no discouragement when other departments (even War Transport) were first consulted and on Christmas Eve Peake wrote to tell Sefton that it was up to him to deal with the War Office if he wanted to proceed further. Sefton replied that the Jockey Club proposed to ask for fixtures for the two Saturdays in every four that the course inspector thought Ascot would stand, and one each at Salisbury and Windsor.

When Sefton and the King's Representative, now Sir Ulick Alexander, approached the Secretary of State for War, Sir James Grigg, they were firmly knocked back, and he remained immovable when Peake wrote to explain the system for authorising racing and assure him that it would be up to the Home Secretary to deal with any political fallout. Grigg replied that the army could simply leave the course but the Ascot Authority did not want that – they wanted rent from military occupation and racing as well, which the army would not agree. He concluded "I will clear out altogether and you can take the onus of starting Ascot again, or I will continue in occupation, in which case there will not be any racing. If you feel unhappy about this the Home Secretary may like to bring the matter up in cabinet". CDESC agreed it would give the wrong impression if soldiers were moved out just to allow racing but thought there must be some way of racing without disturbing them. Despite this, the deadlock remained and Sir John Anderson was brought in to bang heads together. At an informal meeting on 1st

February attended by Grigg and Morrison themselves, Grigg explained that he objected to temporary evacuation of buildings because it was "undesirable that members of the armed forces should receive the impression that, in the view of HM Government, horse racing was of such importance as to justify the disturbance". Anderson suggested making permanent adjustments between the accommodation occupied for military and racing purposes, an obvious solution that had somehow eluded the parties to the dispute and, after some later negotiation of details, a deal was done.

By now discussion of the fixture list to July had started, with the Jockey Club proposing 45 days - fourteen at Newmarket, seven at Ascot, Stockton and Pontefract, and five at Salisbury and Windsor. An important change was that they wanted to add the Coronation Cup to the open races and run all of them except the Guineas at Ascot. They also wanted rail travel to open races and allowances of petrol for essential officials and for taking horses to regional meetings. Petherham's first reaction was that although the general shape of the programme was acceptably similar to 1942, there were major security problems over holding Classics or bank holiday meetings at Ascot: there would be huge crowds and it was outside the London defence area, with no balloons and, he thought, no guns. Other departments were more doubtful. Agriculture wanted the programme cut by a third, to match reductions in animal feed rations, and War Transport wanted a 25% cut in the programme, half the southern meetings to be at Salisbury, and no racing on bank holiday Saturdays. Sefton and Mr Weatherby met Petherham and agreed a reduction to 39 days and to running the Oaks and Derby on a Friday and Saturday at Newmarket, but they stuck out for Ascot holding the other four open races. When this was reported to an inter-departmental conference Noel Baker argued at first for the full 25% cut, but eventually went along with a decision to ask for a reduction to 36 or 37 days and won his point about holding no meetings on bank holiday Saturdays. All departments agreed that open races must be confined to Newmarket. The stewards joined the meeting and offered an unspecified "bold cut" in the programme for the second half of the season, when the number of horses would have fallen, in exchange for keeping 39 days before then. This was accepted: Newmarket would have twelve days, the two northern courses six each and the three in the south five each. A few days later War Transport agreed to allow rail transport to open races and to raise the road travel radius to 50 miles, putting all northern stables within reach of both courses and all southern ones within range of Ascot and Windsor.

At the CDESC meeting on 3rd March which formally authorised the arrangements it seems that, in Noel Baker's absence, the War Transport representative made a rash commitment to more flexibility over the 50-mile limit. News of this reached the Jockey Club, perhaps via the Ministry of Agriculture and the Duke of Norfolk. Over the next few weeks there were requests by Epsom and Sussex stables for petrol to go to Salisbury, followed by complaints when no flexibility was forthcoming, and insistence by Noel Baker that the 50 mile limit was strict and unchangeable. It culminated in sharp recriminations between Peake and Noel Baker after War Transport still refused to budge at the next CDESC meeting.

Good war news continued in early 1943, with Tripoli falling to the Allies on 23rd January and the German surrender at Stalingrad on the 31st, and Russian advances throughout February. January was almost frost-free and spring began exceptionally early, blossom starting to come out by mid-February – the best jumping weather of the war, but no jumping to go with it. On the darker side, William Jarvis died after an operation in late January. The staff at Egerton House had not realised the seriousness of his illness, but it had been announced four months earlier that the King's personally owned horses were to be trained by Captain Cecil Boyd-Rochfort. The Sporting Life of 8th February included a tribute from Doug Marks, still in hospital in Mansfield, describing Jarvis as not just his guvnor but his adviser and friend and the finest gentleman he had ever known.

Two weeks earlier the paper had led with a tirade by the volatile Major Deane of Tattersalls, excoriating the government for calling up stable staff, particularly very small apprentices, and giving details of the progressive effects on a particular stable. He claimed the lads were too small to be any use to the forces, and that women were not up to looking after entire horses. Some of this was undoubtedly special pleading by a racing and bloodstock obsessive who was still looking at the war through the wrong end of the telescope, but he had a point. A surprising number of jockeys were invalided out of the forces and although Jackie Sirrett is the only one known to have been discharged explicitly because of his size, it was probably an unspoken reason in other cases. Shortages of stable staff, particularly work riders, had been a problem since early in the war. Gerry Blum and Snowy Outen recalled stables staffed entirely by old men and boys, the latter being replaced by other boys as they reached call-up age. The elderly lad who looked after Hippius has already been mentioned but he was not alone. In 1941 Fred Wood, who rode racing in the 1890s, was riding work for Fred Butters (Frank's younger brother) and H.G.Southey, winner of the 1913 Cambridgeshire on Cantilever, was working for Ted Leader. In October 1942 a 77-year-old lad called Bill Evans was doing his two and riding work for a Newmarket stable: he had to be lifted into the saddle because of his rheumatism but once up he was fine. Girls were appearing in Newmarket yards by 1941 and Jack Jarvis had at least four in 1943, but they, too, became increasingly liable to conscription. The Jockey Club thought the issue worth pursuing and asked for a meeting with Ernest Bevin, the Minister of Labour and National Service, who heard them sympathetically. Although nothing could be done retrospectively he agreed that only lads medically graded 1 or 2 would be called up in future, and he had no objection to stables recruiting Irish staff (though this would not have interested Fred Darling, who would give Borstal boys a chance but refused to employ Irish lads).

As the new season approached The Sporting Life reported that there were fewer horses in training, an estimate extrapolated from data for 19 leading stables which may not have been correct. At the February conference the Jockey Club gave figures of 482 horses at Newmarket, 491 in the north and 781 in the south – slightly fewer than the total of 1,800 quoted in April 1942, but that had probably included some that were really jumpers. On the other hand, there had definitely been falls in the number of trainers (125), jockeys (73) and licensed apprentices (67). Opportunities for older horses were to be increased by dropping the ban on their running in handicaps.

Fine weather lasted through March and until the first meeting, held at Windsor on 10th April. There was a big crowd and plenty of runners, though not so many as to force division of any races and they were a mainly moderate lot. It was the same when the northern season began at Stockton the next week, but the quality was a bit better at Salisbury, where Dorothy Paget's Orison colt won the Manton Maiden Stakes impressively. The Craven Meeting took place the following Tuesday and Wednesday, but was a shadow of its normal self. A Free Handicap had been framed for information, with Lady Sybil, Nasrullah, Umiddad and Ribbon at the top, but there was no question of running the actual race, nor was there a Craven Stakes. With the Column Stakes down to an insignificant £212 the most valuable race was a handicap worth a scarcely more significant £310, but the Newmarket regulars still clung to their ideal of the meeting as the start of the season proper and 3,000 were there. The editor of Bloodstock Breeders Review observed that they seemed bright and mostly well dressed, the course pretty in the sun and beeches, limes and chestnuts all out. He returned to London by road, scarcely meeting another car and noting that the signposts removed in 1940 had been put back like the railway station name boards

Walter Earl (right) speaks to Harry Wragg on Herringbone as Gerry Blum leads her in after winning the 1943 One Thousand Guineas. Jack Jarvis, Ribbon's trainer, is on the left.

restored some months earlier. The previous day the Prime Minister had told the Commons that church bells could again be rung normally, another sign that the fear of invasion had finally passed.

Easter Monday fell on its latest possible date, 26th April, when Pontefract held its Substitute Lincolnshire for northern stables, though the main focus was on Windsor. There was a bus strike and police stopped and checked every car going into the town, but spectators reached the course by all kinds of transport, including a governess cart at a charge of four shillings. It was worth it when they got there. Straight Deal, easy winner of the feature race, the Upper Sixpenny Stakes, and Sugar Palm, who just beat Mehrali in the Copper Horse Handicap, were among five winners for Tommy Carey, but the day belonged to Gordon Richards. His win on Scotch Mist in a division of the Cannon Yard Stakes was the 2,750th of his career and hailed as the one that took him past Fred Archer's total, and he was cheered all the way from winning post to unsaddling enclosure. However, Archer's total under Jockey Club rules was 2,748, and Richards had beaten this, apparently unnoticed, at Newmarket five days earlier.

One reason for the oversight may have been that attention was on the Report of the Racing Reorganisation Committee, alias the Ilchester Report, published on 15th April. This was racing's equivalent of the Beveridge Report, which the government had accepted in principle a few weeks earlier. It is, unfortunately, not possible to do it justice here, but Appendix 4 gives a summary of the more important and interesting recommendations.

The committee had been appointed in 1941 "To consider the whole future of racing in general, and in particular with reference to the encouragement of owners and the greater comfort and convenience of the public". As with Beveridge, the threat to the country's whole way of life seems to have stimulated radical consideration of how to make life better when the opportunity came (it may also have been a subconscious way of reinforcing the belief that the opportunity would someday actually come, despite ominous signs to the contrary). It is clear from their description of "The Problem in Outline" that the authors saw the racecourses as the villains and owners and the public as their victims to an unacceptable extent, which was probably not far from the mark. They pointed out that the attractiveness of racing in England (sic) for the general public, as distinct from the regular racegoer, had fallen far behind countries where the sport was more recent in origin. Racecourses were disinclined to cater for potential spectators beyond those directly concerned with racing, despite the fact that the new money for improvements depended on attracting larger attendances. The alterations needed to bring courses up to standard might seem drastic for a traditionally minded and conservative country, but this was the time when they could most easily be made.

A few of the recommendations were of their time only and of little interest now, and some were explained in more detail than seems necessary, but many simply happened sooner or later and are now taken for granted. Only a few perpetuated flat earth attitudes, such as the rejection of on-course commentaries (they would "only lead to confusion") and overnight declarations, which would encourage stay at home backers who contributed nothing to racing or its finances (true enough at the time). The most radical and controversial suggestions came in the final section of the report, which cut across the capitalist assumptions of most racing people by asserting that the need for racecourse companies to pay dividends to shareholders was inherently bad for racing: some courses were surplus to requirements and should be told to close, and the Jockey Club should take a controlling interest in eight or nine of the rest and run them on a non-dividend basis. This was powerful and revolutionary stuff from five peers and a baronet.

Despite wall to wall coverage in The Sporting Life, the immediate reaction was rather muted, perhaps because many people thought it was something for the indeterminate future and shared the view of Lord Rosebery, who told the Jockey Club that, like the Beveridge Report, it was "a very excellent plan when we have the money for it". How many of the recommendations would eventually be adopted was also unclear, as it was known that opinions within the Jockey Club were divided on some important points. Letters appeared in the paper for several weeks, but they were less than visionary and tended to focus on detailed points that displeased the writers concerned.

The Aga Khan had taken the second retainer on Gordon Richards' services and he was available to ride Nasrullah in the Two Thousand Guineas because Fred Darling's three-year-old colts were sub-standard and he had no runner. Nasrullah was one of those horses driven mad by Newmarket but there was no way of getting him away from the place to work or race, so Frank Butters was having great difficulty training him. He took to holding up the string with displays of temperament and Butters had to use all kinds of subterfuge to get him to work at all. Nasrullah had a preparatory race in the Chatteris Stakes on 5th May, when he was reluctant to leave the paddock and had to be led to the start by a mounted policeman. He won easily enough, with Lady Sybil well beaten, but he only ran at all because officialdom had bent over backwards to accommodate him, provoking another explosion by Major Deane. The punting public, however, was prepared to overlook this waywardness and installed him as favourite for the Classic.

By contrast, Ribbon fought tenaciously to win the Upwell Stakes by a short head from Open Warfare after meeting interference, with Herringbone a close third after also being hampered. Ribbon had hardly grown during the winter but the public loved her for her courage and she was the other Guineas favourite. What they had, perhaps, overlooked was that the Upwell Stakes was over the Beaufort Course, the first seven furlongs of the Bunbury Mile, a very different proposition from the full Mile with its steep, uphill finish.

The awe-inspiring sight and sound of bombers roaring across the Rowley Mile course to clear The Ditch by perilously few feet on their take off run had become familiar, but it was only a matter of time before one failed to make it. There had been a bad crash the previous December and there was another on 12th May, just before the scheduled date of the Guineas meeting, when a Stirling of 75 Squadron clipped the top of The Ditch and crashed on the edge of the July Course near the five furlong start. There was a bald announcement that the meeting had been postponed for a week, leaving those not in the know to wonder why.

The rearranged meeting produced the customary huge crowd despite several hundred would-be spectators getting no further than the London termini, where there was no room on the trains. Most of those who reached the course walked at least some of the way -

up to fifteen miles in a few cases. Barely a length separated the first five in the Two Thousand Guineas, in which Sam Wragg got Kingsway's head in front of Pink Flower right on the line and Cliff Richards finished fast on Way In to beat his brother on Nasrullah for third. Nasrullah should have won but hesitated, ran on briefly, then stopped again. Straight Deal was outpaced in the last furlong and finished sixth. The One Thousand was just as close. Samovar made the running at first but faded a quarter of a mile out, where Ribbon led and looked the winner only to be caught close home by Herringbone, who held on by a neck as Ribbon came back at her. A couple of lengths behind, the fading Cincture and Open Warfare just beat J.V.Rank's Why Hurry, who was having her first run of the season.

The Guineas had been preceded by the first Ascot meeting on 15th May. There was an immense crowd: almost 11,000 paid to go into the enclosures, but there was no way of knowing how many more thousands watched for nothing on the Heath. Every Reading line train out of Waterloo after 8.30 left passengers behind and for a time bookings had to be suspended altogether. Passengers were also converging on Ascot from the Reading direction and the Aldershot line, besides thousands walking or cycling there, but there were only 130 cars. Among the minority who neither walked, cycled nor caught the train were the King, in Field Marshal's uniform, and the Queen.

Sugar Palm and the Orison colt, both hot favourites, and Major Deane's St.Valery were among the winners on the eight race card, Tommy Carey rode a treble, Arthur Wragg a double, and Cliff and Gordon Richards had a winner apiece. Then, at about 5.45, it was time to go home and the trouble really started. The problem was that wartime railway timetables were geared to the hours people typically worked – all day Mondays to Fridays and up to midday on Saturdays – so the crowds that had squeezed into half-hourly trains to get to Ascot found only hourly ones to take them back. Foreseeing difficulties, the Southern Railway had sent its Deputy Traffic Manager to take control and, by dint of loading trains to 50% above their nominal capacity, the last of the weary queues of racegoers were on their way by 9.25.

Newspaper reports next day described crowds fighting to get home and women fainting in the crush, although the Deputy Traffic Manager's report to War Transport said that if there were any such incidents they had not occurred on railway premises, and that crowd control had been adequate. Nevertheless, the bad publicity reached the top echelons of government, with Anderson asking Morrison to investigate criticisms he had received. Morrison decided it was all War Transport's fault and wrote to Noel Baker about the difficulties and hardship endured by those who went to the races, but the reply amounted to "We told you so!": War Transport had opposed racing at Ascot; they had warned this would happen, but nobody would listen; they had been pressurised into conceding a generous Ascot programme, and now they had been proved right; the railway company had done well in difficult circumstances. By the time a copy reached Anderson there had been a smaller-scale repetition at the second Ascot meeting, though mitigated somewhat by lengthening the trains. He decided to get a report from the Chief Constable of Berkshire, Commander The Hon. Sir Humphrey Legge, in case he could suggest anything to help at the impending Whit Monday meeting. Legge reported that the crowds had behaved extremely well despite waiting hours in queues, concluding in a sympathetic tone not always associated with the police that those who managed to get to the races "must return home very tired after a gruelling wait in queues and an extremely unpleasant, overcrowded rail journey". Noel Baker's reaction was that there was nothing War Transport could do: it was an issue of principle and they would not compromise.

By Whit Monday the draft programme for the second half of the season was being discussed and War Transport were pressing hard for

Ascot to be dropped from the list, together with all August Bank Holiday racing, so they must have been irritated by the almost lyrical tone of Legge's report on the Whitsun meeting. About 13,000 were in the enclosures with an estimated 25,000 more on the Heath where "many families with small children took advantage of this agreeable spot and many picnic parties were to be seen". The crowd had behaved extremely well, train and bus travellers had been content to wait in queues until accommodation was available, the station had been cleared by 8.30, the county police had had no difficulties and the railway police deserved congratulation. He concluded "I recommend that the meetings at Ascot be continued, for there is no better course nor more agreeable surroundings for a day's holiday in the fresh air".

Problems over getting to racecourses were not just for spectators: the arbitrary rules about using petrol for horses, jockeys and racecourse officials and their inconsistent interpretation were discussed with exasperation at the Jockey Club's May meeting. Lord Zetland said that when he drove to Stockton to steward he was waved through by the Durham police, only to be challenged at the course by an inspector of the Petrol Control Department. This official told him that his reason for using his car was "no use at all", although it would have been different had he been an owner. When Zetland told him that he was an owner besides a steward he changed his tune and said it was alright to use the petrol. Sefton explained that, technically, nobody was allowed petrol to go racing and though concessions had been agreed with Regional Petroleum Officers their attitudes varied. Some jockeys could get petrol to ride work but not to go racing. Some trainers had no trouble, but his own [Atty Persse] would not be allowed petrol if he put on the application form that it was for going racing – he had to say he was taking his staff to Windsor or Salisbury. On the other hand, another person was going to all the meetings in a chauffeur driven car simply through being a director of Kempton Park, where there had been no racing for four years! Relations with the Ministry of War Transport were unsatisfactory and the stewards had had "a terrible tussle" with them. In 1942 local officials had been allowed to wink at six or seven miles over the limit but Lord Leathers now insisted that the 50-miles was absolute and was unmoved by arguments that stables and racecourses were in fixed positions and the Jockey Club could do nothing to bring them closer. The Ministry had eventually allowed a maximum of fifteen Epsom and Sussex horses to go to Salisbury meetings, co-ordinated by Walter Nightingall, and although this was "niggling and stupid" it was proving adequate. Nevertheless, Sefton and Rosebery advised against a further approach to the ministry for fear that it might cause petrol allocations to be stopped altogether. What nobody admitted was that there were ways and means of getting petrol if you knew the right person, like Cyril Whiterow, a small bookmaker, who recalled having his car taken to a garage and filled up by a friendly government official who was entitled to petrol.

Postponement of the Guineas meeting cut the interval before the Derby and Oaks to little more than three weeks and resulted in fewer of the Classic contenders than usual having a race in the meantime. Of those which did, Umiddad beat the Derby outsider Herald in the Fakenham Stakes, though not well enough to inspire confidence in him for the big race, but there was some serious punting on Tropical Sun after she easily beat several other Oaks fillies and St. Valery over a mile and a quarter at Windsor. After three fair runs in 1942 she had reappeared in May to win a maiden easily on the testing Salisbury course and looked another progressive Hyperion filly from Beckhampton: it was not yet clear that 1943 was a poor year for Chateau Darling. On Oaks day, which was dull and damp and with a surprisingly small crowd, she was favourite in preference to Ribbon, who had not raced beyond a mile before. Accounts vary as to what happened when the tapes went up: either Ribbon whipped round or she was baulked when another filly did so, but she lost ten lengths and almost all chance. Tidworth was leading half way up the straight, but in the dip Charlie Elliott got Why Hurry in front of Tropical Sun and she ran on stoutly to hold off Ribbon who dashed up the hill, gaining with every stride, to fail by only a neck. It seemed a poor reward for such courage – and there was more bad luck to come.

This year the meeting included a mixture of Epsom and Royal Ascot races for the first time. The other open races on Oaks day were the Coronation Cup, won by Hyperides from Shahpoor and Ujiji, and the Queen Mary Stakes, for which Picture Play was favourite after an effortless win at Ascot on her first appearance. Her day would come, but this time she was beaten by the more experienced Fair Fame and the Charwoman filly (later named Mrs Mops).

Though a wartime Derby was better than no Derby, there was a feeling that this one was without any real savour and the crowd not as large as in former years. The majority were in uniform and military police were checking identities, but one thing that never seemed to change was the dirty and smelly refreshment bars. Way In, High Chancellor and Merchant Navy were the first three in the Derby betting on the strength of their staying on in the Two Thousand Guineas, but they were all as chopped for finishing speed as they had been that day. George Bridgland made most of the running on Persian Gulf, but was headed a furlong out by Nasrullah, running a thoroughly genuine race this time, only to be passed by Umiddad who, in turn, was unable to resist Tommy Carey's decisive swoop on Straight Deal. This gave Dorothy Paget her only Classic winner and the day turned into her best ever in flat racing half an hour later when the Orison colt, now named Orestes, won the Coventry Stakes. The Derby winner had not been much backed by the public, but they were pleased for Miss Paget and cheered as she led him in. The verdict of the press was that Straight Deal was "a fine specimen of a perfectly trained horse" and had won on merit, whilst Why Hurry had been lucky.

The last of the open races normally run at Royal Ascot, The Gold Cup, was not run until the next Newmarket meeting, in early July. As in the two preceding seasons, it was run over two and a quarter miles, using some ground not normally raced over in peacetime but still a quarter of a mile short of its Ascot distance. There were eight runners and Hyperides was a strong favourite, but Ujiji and High Table had the race to themselves until High Table weakened a quarter of a mile out and Ujiji went on to win unchallenged.

The fixtures for the second half of the season had been agreed by now, but only after much delay and acrimony. As early as 19th May the Jockey Club had put in proposals for 32 days' racing (later increased to 33) between 2nd August and 23rd October, with the same eight open races as in 1942, and by the first week of June the Air Ministry, Home Office and Ministries of Agriculture and Labour had all confirmed they had no objections. That only left War Transport, but on 11th June Hodge had a letter from his opposite number there to say that they were not happy, quoting the Railway Executive as feeling that there should be no Ascot meetings because the train service was inadequate and none on August Bank Holiday "at any price". His Minister also still wanted a 25% reduction in fixtures for the year compared with 1942, but the 32 now proposed would make 71 for the full season, considerably more than he had expected. The result was that instead of the programme being nodded through, another of the all too familiar conferences of Parliamentary Secretaries had to be called to try to agree recommendations. At the meeting Noel Baker pressed strongly for the 25% cut, exclusion of Ascot and the veto on bank holiday racing, but he was on his own. Tom Williams of Agriculture supported adding the 33rd day so that the season could finish on the same date in the north and south and Malcolm McCorquodale of Labour and National Service thought that restraints should be kept to a minimum because racing provided valuable recreation for tired workers. He thought it would be difficult to close Ascot in mid-season but suggested they might warn that it must not be used next year. When Peake suggested a programme of 28 days Noel Baker provisionally accepted it as a compromise but demanded the transfer of the bank holiday meeting to Windsor and firmly refused to agree anything finally until he had again consulted the Railway Executive.

It was now late June and arrangements for August meetings needed to start urgently. On the 28th Lord Sefton wrote a "Personal and Urgent" letter to Morrison about the delay, expressing surprise that the draft programme had not been accepted, since it was less than in 1942. So far, he said, "the general public has accepted the situation with great good humour and behaved throughout in the most orderly manner in putting up with disappointments and delays". Using Ascot had been beneficial; it was the best course they had and access to the Heath was free. Next day Petherham briefed Morrison and Peake that War Transport were to report verbally to CDC. There are two interesting manuscript notes on file from that date: one in Peake's writing says "I had a casual word with Lord Leathers last week about this; he thinks Mr Noel Baker is a little unduly obstructive where racing is concerned", and one by a frustrated Morrison adds "War Transport will get a tick off from me for being obstructive and slow".

There was a meeting of the full CDC on 1st July at which, according to Petherham's note to Hodge, "there was a good deal of straight talking, especially in respect of the delay by the MWT". Noel Baker was defeated. Although the 28-day programme was confirmed, the committee felt there should be no interference with legitimate recreation without substantial reason, that there were insufficient grounds for stopping Ascot meetings, and that the bank holiday fixture should not merely take place but do so at Ascot. Next day Morrison replied to Sefton's letter, apologising for the delay and contriving to stick up for War Transport whilst leaving no doubt that it had all been their fault. Sefton replied in his own handwriting to thank Morrison personally for his help and understanding, but slipped in the point that everyone must now recognise that the further cut in fixtures meant that the irreducible minimum had been reached.

There was one more, small ripple over the fixture list when Lord Wigram and Mr Rous of the Sports Committee of the Red Cross came to ask Peake at the end of July if the government would sanction a charity race meeting for them. They had been egged on by the Jockey Club who, besides feeling uncomfortable about their own modest donations, saw it as a way of getting an extra meeting, and the idea had also been leaked to the press. When Peake told them that race meetings were unprofitable at present they replied that they thought owners would donate their prize money and bookmakers their profits. Peake was privately amused at their naiveté and wondered what they thought the position of winning backers would be, but his formal response was that they should approach the Jockey Club, because any such meeting would have to come out of those already allocated. His note to Petherham concluded that he did not expect to hear any more about the proposal. He was right.

The war situation continued to improve during the summer, with U-Boats leaving the Atlantic and the Germans routed near Kursk. A piece of bad news from racing's standpoint was the irreparable damage to the Torquay racecourse buildings in an air raid. On 10th July the Allies invaded Sicily with the assistance of Gunner C.Smirke of 66th Light Anti-Aircraft Regiment. Some time later a rumour started circulating in Newmarket that he had won a gallantry award, and soon reached the staff of Frank Butters, a trainer famously distrustful of jockeys.

"Have you heard Charlie Smirke's won a medal, sir?" one of them enquired.

"No. What for?" replied Butters.

"They say he stopped a tank, sir"

"Not surprised. He stopped everything I ever put him on".

Among jockeys who really were decorated were the NH riders Bob Everett, who won a DSO in the RAF, and Bruce Hobbs, the youngest person to ride a Grand National winner, who not only won an MC in 1943 but was twice wounded. Others involved in combat at various times included Sam Wragg, Joe Caldwell, Jack Fawcus and Vic Mitchell, the last two being taken prisoner. Tommy Weston and Richard Duller both had ships sunk beneath them: Duller was captured but Weston survived three days on a raft and went on to ride at wartime meetings in Egypt. As might be expected, a good number found themselves in the Royal Army Veterinary Corps. Some served overseas, where Tommy Hawcroft suffered serious illness, and John Sables was killed in an accident in 1944, but many were at Doncaster racecourse, regimental headquarters and site of No. 1 Royal Veterinary Hospital, commanded at first by Col.Slocock, a former Jockey Club vet. They included Billy Nevett and Doug Smith, who were able to continue their racing careers and enjoyed a more congenial war than many servicemen. Harry Wragg was also able to combine racing with military duties. He had managed to badger his way into the army in July 1941 despite a medical grading of C3 because of an old leg injury and served first as an anti-aircraft gunner at Mildenhall and later in the Guns Operations Room at Gorleston, both ideal postings for riding work and racing at Newmarket. Jockeys who were in the forces had to make time for riding by exchanging duties with other men, and though colleagues were prepared to do this and commanding officers to allow it, particularly if the arrangement produced useful tips, it resulted in some unsociable hours and was not a soft option. Others combined riding with farming or munitions work, but a few leading riders were medically unfit for service, such as Gordon Richards and Arthur Wragg as former TB patients and Eph Smith, who was deaf.

As the war progressed training grounds came under pressure from the demands of agriculture and the need to accommodate the hordes of Americans who were arriving. War Agriculture Committees naturally saw gallops and stud farms as suitable for cultivation, irreplaceable though they might be in racing terms, and some catastrophic losses were only narrowly averted. In April 1943 the Newmarket stud owners reached a compromise agreement with the Suffolk War Agriculture Committee, and in July Epsom trainers beat off a threat to their gallops by agreeing to help the Surrey committee cultivate some semi-derelict land. This coincided with a boom in agricultural land prices as investment companies tried to accumulate long term holdings of good quality land.

The American forces already had major supply depots at Aintree and Newbury racecourses, the latter disappearing under miles of railway sidings, and an air force unit at Hurst Park. Haydock Park and Leicester followed later and long-occupied Wincanton was also transferred to the US army. Americans also briefly camped on the downs at Beckhampton, but Fred Darling managed to save the gallops by arranging for them to move across the road onto farmland, in exchange for which Darling trained a horse for the farmer. He was good at persuading local farmers, particularly those who were his tenants, to help him get round tiresome wartime restrictions: one would provide an odd bag or two of oats to supplement the rations legitimately obtained from the corn merchants in Calne; another grew an unauthorised patch of clover for him in the middle of what was supposed to be only a cornfield; yet another saved him the choicest hay from the middle of mature ricks.

On 2nd August, an uncomfortably hot day, the King and Queen joined the bank holiday crowd at Ascot to watch three races. They went into the paddock to see their filly Sunblind saddled for the Eton Stakes, in which she was just beaten by Samovar, and presented Fred Darling with a painting of Sun Chariot by Munnings. Ujiji made his final appearance in the Old Windsor Stakes over the Old Mile before going to stud. It should have been too short a trip but

Construction lorries approach the judge's box up what had been
the straight mile as Newbury racecourse is transformed
into a military supplies depot.

Cliff Richards got him up to win cleverly from Gordon on Fun Fair,
the hot favourite. A couple of weeks later the results and betting
returns at Windsor were announced by loudspeaker, a ground-
breaking innovation reported as having been well received (though
there were doubtless a few who wondered where this kind of
pandering to vulgarity was going to end). There were no open races
in August, but some of the St.Leger candidates had preparatory races
in their home zones, with Nasrullah winning a three horse event at
Newmarket, Tropical Sun beating Merchant Navy at Salisbury and
Why Hurry finishing third to Straight Deal at Ascot.

With September came the Nunthorpe Stakes, in which
Linklater gave Epsom trainer Bill Smyth the most important success
of his career so far. Sugar Palm had twice beaten the winner earlier
in the season and started favourite, but could not go the pace until
it was too late. Earlier the same day three of the four runners in the

Whepstead Stakes were St.Leger hopefuls. It was an unsatisfactory dawdle and sprint in which Umiddad led throughout and won by two lengths, with Herringbone, Pink Flower and Ribbon finishing within half a length of eachother. Nobody was much the wiser afterwards.

The Rous Stakes on the first day of the St.Leger meeting was won by Dorothy Paget's sprint-bred Lady Maderty filly (later Lady Wyn), with the odds-on Happy Landing only third. The race turned out to have little longer term significance, but the Cheveley Park stakes next day was a key showdown between most of the season's top juvenile fillies, and it appeared to confirm the form of the Queen Mary and to fit Garden Path into the picture. As expected, Fair Fame came out on top, with Garden Path third after again misbehaving before the race, Mrs Mops fifth and Picture Play seventh. The St.Leger itself was a rough and controversial race. Tropical Sun was in front approaching the dip but behind her Umiddad and Ribbon were getting the worst of a barging match as the beaten Why Hurry came off a true line, and it was Straight Deal who took a slight lead at the foot of the hill, only to be passed close home by Ribbon who had fought back doggedly. She looked sure to win, but Harry Wragg drove Herringbone up to her right on the post. Most of the crowd thought Ribbon had held on but the judge, Major Petch, gave the race to Herringbone by a short head. Straight Deal was a close third, with Persian Gulf, Tropical Sun and Nasrullah finishing in a heap just behind him. To the end of his life Jack Jarvis was adamant that Ribbon had been robbed, but close finishes on the July Course in pre-camera days were notoriously difficult to judge. The still photographs of the race are inconclusive, as is the Gaumont British newsreel film (on the sound track of which the eerie sound of bombers warming up their engines can be heard in the background).

Only the day before, Lord Willoughby de Broke had raised the possibility of "photographs of the finishes of races" at the Jockey

Club meeting, the main business of which had been planning for inspection of courses needed after the war. Sefton reported that they had tried to get the Inspector of Courses, Major Gorton, out of the army, but had failed despite his being over military age, holding only a desk job at Southern Command HQ and being keen to leave. Sefton could not understand this: he had, after all, told the army that "it was a matter of great importance to the future of horse racing…" It was also noticeable that buyers at the St.Leger sales, where the number of lots was about 60% of the peacetime volume, seemed to be expecting normal racing in 1944 or 1945, as they were seeking ready made racehorses.

The back end of the season was shorter than in 1942 but the racing was not so desultory, as there were four open races and regional substitutes for the autumn double. Nasrullah redeemed himself by winning the Champion Stakes like a really good horse, beating Kingsway, Umiddad and Pink Flower, and went off to one of the most successful stud careers of the century. In the Middle Park Orestes only just held on from Happy Landing, with Garden Path third. It provided a useful comparison with the earlier open juvenile races but the value of the form was felt by some astute commentators to be doubtful. During the last month of the season each zone staged a Cambridgeshire and Cesarewitch, but over distances which, with the exception of the Northern Cesarewitch, varied by at least a furlong from the peacetime races. The winners' prizes of around £750 at Stockton and £850 at Newmarket and Ascot were worth having and apart from the Newmarket Cesarewitch, in which Germanicus beat only six others, there were plenty of runners and strong betting markets. The Ascot races were run on the same day and attracted a Tote Double pool of a record £16,217 out of a total £90,000 for the meeting. Pontefract's Substitute November Handicap on the last day of the northern season also attracted a large field and strong betting. Nine races at Windsor the same day produced 170 runners altogether but only three in the Championship Cup, in which Sugar Palm was trying to win his seventh race of the season in eight starts. Despite the tiny field, he somehow managed to get boxed in when Mehrali challenged Linklater close home and seemed to get up, only for Linklater to be adjudged the winner.

The season came to its earliest-ever end on 20th October at Newmarket on an autumn day of rare beauty, with blue wash skies and a translucent atmosphere. The previous day Ribbon had been unplaced in the Jockey Club Cup behind Shahpoor after one, final misfortune: whilst exercising on the Heath she had fallen and bolted after being frightened by a jeep and probably should not have raced. On the last day the Alington Maiden Plate was won comfortably by the favourite Ocean Swell, a Blue Peter colt trained by Jack Jarvis, with the unfancied Tehran finishing fifth. Jarvis immediately prophesied that Ocean Swell would win the Derby, and both would become names to conjure with. That was not the fate of Effervescence, who won the Dewhurst stakes but was destined to end a long and fairly undistinguished career at the likes of Lewes and Brighton. Finally, Tommy Lowrey won the Bluntisham Maiden Plate on Sir Victor Sassoon's Big Sam and it was all over until Easter Monday next year.

In terms of numbers of races, days' racing and total runners the season had been the nadir of the war, but the median value of races, which had closely matched pre-war levels in real terms since April 1941, shot up in the second half of the season. This was largely because of the higher prizes that Ascot was able to provide. Tote betting also recovered from a slump in 1942, with on-course turnover back to its 1941 level and credit betting up 50%.

What would a day at the races have been like in 1943?

In short, expensive and exhausting. The first challenge was simply getting there and back. Beyond walking or cycling distance, using public transport was almost unavoidable by 1943. Earlier in the war, according to Peter Willett, people in remoter areas had a small extra petrol allowance which they might have been able to save up and some others, such as vets, had plenty. Those with petrol gave lifts to others and everyone showed great ingenuity in getting to the races by hook or by crook. Later, the squeeze gradually tightened and a ban on driving for pleasure from August 1942 closely followed abolition of the basic petrol ration. Anyone arriving by car could expect to be questioned, like Lord Zetland, by a petroleum inspector and those using taxis might find the police checking whether they had exceeded the permitted distance. Reports of convictions for using petrol illegally or excessive taxi rides regularly appeared in the press, although there were some ingenious defences: a bookmaker who took a taxi from Doncaster to Newmarket successfully claimed that Tattersalls' ring there was his place of business, whilst another pleaded that his age and infirmity made using taxis essential. For most the only option was scheduled buses and trains, with no cheap fares and many passengers standing, often followed by a long walk to the course. Afterwards, when everyone left at the same time, there was the prospect of a long wait in a queue even to get on a bus or train at all.

On arrival at the course there was a good chance that military police would check the leave passes of the many in uniform and that civilians would have to show their identity cards. Admission charges without the discounts for those in uniform were much higher than now in real terms, partly because of the heavy entertainments tax they included. Racecards normally cost a shilling (the 1943 equivalent of about £1.40), of which the racecourse gave half to Red Cross funds, but only provided the minimum essential information in the smallest possible space. They did not include form summaries, and neither did daily papers to any extent: broadsheets typically gave racing about an eighth of a page.

For refreshment there were sandwiches (usually cheese or corned beef) and cups of tea or glasses of beer – everyone interviewed about their memories mentioned that there was never a shortage of beer at race meetings – and at Ascot the Red Cross would provide a glass of water in exchange for a donation. In most other ways, however, a wartime meeting was much like a peacetime one. And that was an important reason for making the effort to go: for a few, precious hours it might as well have been 1933 or 1923. It is unlikely that many beyond the core of Newmarket faithful went to every possible meeting. Looking back in 2005, Bill Parrish recalled the day he and some friends went from Wisbech to see the 1941 July Cup as a rare and special treat, and that is how many would have seen a day at the races.

In October Major Deane fired a double-barrelled blast at the Jockey Club, first with a letter to the News Chronicle criticising the cutting of opportunities for certain types of horse and the Club's attitude to calling up apprentices, and then with a thousand word article in The Sporting Life saying they had done insufficient to put owners' and breeders' cases to the government. The members were not at all pleased. They noted at their November meeting that Deane was a director of Tattersalls who were "in effect, employees of the Club", and seemed annoyed that the servants were getting uppish. They were also angry with Marcel Boussac, who had headed the owners' list in France. They felt he was racing under the auspices and protection of the Nazi occupiers and noted that two of his horses trained by Steve Donoghue had been seized by the Trading With The Enemy Department, though Mr Holland-Martin explained that the legal status of French citizens as enemy aliens was complicated. The stewards agreed to investigate further, but all seems to have been forgotten by the time Boussac was dominating Ascot and the Classics shortly after the war.

The same meeting decided that the coming year's Classics should again be abandoned and reopened, and heard about negotiations for Jockey Club Racecourses Ltd. to take over "a certain racecourse". Tantalisingly, there is no clue in the minutes as to which one. The company was formally floated in December with capital of £10,000 to take over several courses following the

Ilchester Report proposals, which prompted Sir Loftus Bates to write to The Times warning against the report's recommendation about compulsory closures. One involuntary closure, which turned out not to be permanent, occurred when Worcester Racecourse Company was liquidated after the Racecourse Betting Control Board refused to bail it out of rent arrears to the city council. The most durable decision of the Jockey Club meeting, however, was to replace the apprentices' riding allowance of 5lbs with the now long-familiar sliding scale of 7lbs, 5lbs and 3lbs.

The year ended in a burst of optimism, with accommodation at the December sales barely adequate for the number of lots and some of the later ones being bought at prices beyond their apparent worth by over-anxious bidders. The NH stewards announced that sufficient courses would be available as soon as racing was permitted again, and The Sporting Life ran a series of articles reviewing, region by region, how soon courses could be available "if the war ended next month". Nobody seriously thought it would end that soon, but it reflected the feeling of expectation, some of it unrealistic, that was spreading through the country.

CHAPTER 8

IN EXPECTATION (1944)

Mid winter produced several weeks' frustratingly ideal jumping weather again, until a miserably cold spell began in mid-February. News of the Allied landings at Anzio and the end of the siege of Leningrad kept public morale high, whilst on the home front the radical Education Bill and early plans for a national health service were published, all seeming to point towards a Better Tomorrow. It was clear, too, that Second Front Now was no longer just a slogan daubed on walls by USSR sympathisers but about to become a reality, with an invasion of the continent not far away. Countless thousands of Americans had arrived in recent months, changing daily life in much of southern Britain and adding phrases like "Got any gum, chum?" and "Overpaid, over-sexed and over here" to the national lexicon. There was no way of hiding the widespread training, manoeuvres, accumulation of materiel and sheer numbers of servicemen. The year's first issue of The Sporting Life led on *Threat to Racing in the South* over a story about the feared impact of plans for manoeuvres by mechanised units near gallops. In reality, few trainers lost their gallops, even in Wiltshire and Hampshire, which had virtually become an armed camp, but some others were less fortunate: the inhabitants of Imber and Tyneham had been evicted from their villages in December 1943 with words of appreciation for their involuntary sacrifice and a promise of a post-war return which has yet to be honoured.

With no possibility of surprise as to the invasion itself it was vital to conceal from the Germans where and when it would happen, so the Jockey Club's announcement in early January that it might defer any of the year's Classics by up to 28 days at the stewards' discretion, though understandable, was unhelpful. On 3rd February Sir Findlater Stewart of the Home Defence Executive forwarded a letter to the Home Office from Lt. Col. J.V.B.Jervis-Read of Supreme Headquarters Allied Expeditionary Force. Headed "Most Secret", it said they were "most anxious that big public events such as the Derby should take place as usual to avoid giving the enemy any clue as to the target date for Overlord". Jervis-Read was to be warned about any proposal to cancel or postpone a national event, and four days later there was an unfamiliar face at the table when the Parliamentary Secretaries met for their biannual row about the fixture list. This was Lt.Col.Wild of SHAEF, who told the meeting that cancellation of meetings could give the enemy valuable information. Either racing should be abandoned now or, preferably, a normal wartime programme published with the usual provisos about abandonments at short notice. The list to the end of July submitted by the Jockey Club was practically the same as for 1943, proposing an extra day per region (making 42 days instead of 39) because the period covered was a week longer, but with another request to run all open races except the Guineas and Coronation Cup at Ascot. A note by Hodge on 30th January said there was no reason to object, provided the list for the second part of the season was correspondingly shorter, but the Air Ministry felt it inadvisable to attract large crowds to Ascot in the next few months and that all open races should remain at Newmarket. Hodge also remarked that the 1943 Whit Monday Ascot meeting had brought 38,000 but "circumstances might arise by the end of April [which was crossed out and "May?" substituted in an unknown hand] which required the abandonment of the meeting, but we have no grounds for suggesting a change at present".

After hearing Wild, Noel Baker let it be known that he favoured abandonment of all racing for the season, for which the railway companies were pushing (with good reason, he thought). His ministry would not press the point for the moment, but fixtures must be reduced to a minimum and there could be no more rail travel to open races. It might be possible to allow road transport instead, but he had not yet consulted his advisors and would let the Home Office know in due course. The meeting eventually agreed to allow 36 days by cutting two from each zone but this was overridden by Peake and Lord Leathers next day. According to Peake, Leathers thought that if there were any racing at all (and he had been persuaded that there should be), it must be exactly as in 1943 – 39 days for a period one week shorter than currently proposed. He added that "Mr Philip Baker in pressing for a reduction on last year's programme was doing so without authority and should not have taken this line". There would be no difficulty about a modest allocation of petrol for taking horses to open races. On 9th February Peake and Petherham met Sefton and Mr. Weatherby and agreed a list of 39 meetings to the penultimate Saturday of July, twelve each for Newmarket and the north and fifteen in the south. All open races were to be at Newmarket, with travel by road only, for which the Jockey Club would agree petrol rations with War Transport, though the possibility of cancellations at short notice was emphasised. Petherham asked Hodge to prepare a suitable note for CDC, gleefully pointing out that "it is clear that Noel Baker has been thrown over by his minister", and Peake wrote to Leathers agreeing that 39 days over the same number of weekends as in 1943 would be easier to sell than 42 over a longer period. He believed the arrangements were "perfectly fair and will protect the government from the charge that they have singled out horse racing for special curtailment as compared with other sports such as football and dog racing. They will also stand up against the criticism, however ill-informed, that special favour....is being given to the Jockey Club". It only remained for the arrangements to be put to CDC, which received them with some irritation and instructed that racing programmes should in future only be put on its agenda if there were disagreements to resolve.

Around this time the government was nearly drawn into a spat between the Jockey Club and Irish racing interests. Paul Emrys-Evans, Parliamentary Secretary at the Dominions Office, asked Peake's advice about a letter from John Maffey, the United Kingdom Representative to Eire (effectively ambassador in Dublin). Maffey, who had a good relationship with prime minister De Valera and understood Irish sensitivities, was concerned about the consequences of the Jockey Club's rebuffing a request to lift its ban on Irish horses and those returning from Ireland to Great Britain. This had been made to Lord Hamilton of Dalzell by the Earl of Granard, an Irish peer who had sat in both the House of Lords and the Senate of the Irish Free State. Hamilton had responded with an abusive letter about Irish neutrality and persuaded the Jockey Club that the ban should not be rescinded, despite opposition from Sefton and others. Maffey wondered whether the UK government had to acquiesce in this. He felt the Club's policy had major importance for Anglo-Irish relations, adding "I can imagine no sphere of interest in which bitterness could be more easily stirred, nor in which we could hope to establish a happier relationship more fruitfully". Fortunately, the nettle did not have to be grasped, because War Transport's policy could be quoted as making the whole idea unrealistic – horses would never get beyond their port of entry because of the embargo on moving them by rail, and no petrol would be allowed either.

A fortnight later the idea became absolutely unworkable with the suspension of travel between the UK and Eire to protect D-Day security following De Valera's refusal of an Allied demand to expel Axis envoys. Shortly afterwards the imminence of the invasion seemed to be further signalled when Churchill warned the country that "the hour of our greatest effort is approaching". However, there was frustration in Italy, where German resistance at Monte Cassino was preventing the allies from breaking the Gustav Line, and in Burma there was desperate fighting at Imphal and Kohima.

In March the PTC emerged briefly from suspended animation when the stewards met representatives of the Midland and District Pony Racing Association, which had been running meetings in various parts of the country, though not, apparently, under PTC rules. They intended to hold 23 during 1944 for wartime charities and also had grandiose plans for a Northolt-style course near Nottingham when peace returned. Because the PTC was a recognised turf authority, pony meetings counted as flapping if not sanctioned by it and held under its rules, making anyone who organised or participated in them liable to be made "disqualified persons" under all recognised rules of racing. The members of the MDPRA must have been men of sufficient status for this to matter to them, because they agreed to cancel their 1944 meetings and to hold those on the new course under PTC auspices. Ironically, there would have been no chance of holding a wartime programme under the PTC's rules because it was subject to the same governmental regulation as the Jockey Club and NHC and no fixtures would have been authorised.

Others did not give a fig about recognised turf authorities and carried on organising flapping meetings regardless, and the authorities did not try to stop them. The Jockey Club seemed unperturbed, in contrast to its attitude in the First World War, when flapping had a higher profile and filled the gap when rules racing was confined to Newmarket or completely suspended. For its part the government had enough to do without trying to control a diffusely organised activity that made no demands for petrol or feedstuffs and had little impact on public transport. Flapping probably enjoyed a boom in the Second World War, but it is difficult

SUNNY HILL RACES————1945

FIRST RACE 2 P.M.

President—Mr. W. H. Spendlove	*Chairman*—Mr. J. S. Hoult.
Handicapper & Starter—Mr. W. Hardy.	*Assistant Starter*—Mr. H. King.
Clerk of Course—Mr. F. Spendlove.	*Clerk of Scales*—Mr. C. Cliffe.
Hon. Veterinary Surgeon—Mr. J. Else.	*Gate Entrances*—Mr. S. T. Parker.
Judges—Messrs. W. H. Spendlove & T. Kitching.	

Stewards—Messrs. S. Hoult, H. A. Groome, A. Brealey, H. B. Dunn, H. S. Kidd,
H. Morley, F. Richardson, R. Green,
St. John Ambulance—Mr. A. D. Waddington.
A Medical Officer will be in attendance on the Course.

NOTICE TO OWNERS.

Any objection to be lodged immediately after the Races to the Secretary accompanied by a deposit of £1, which will be returned if objection is sustained, otherwise it will be forfeited.

In the case of a dead heat, stakes will be divided.

Owners and Jockeys must attend at the Secretary's Tent 15 minutes before each Race.

The Committee have, at their discretion, power to cancel or alter any Race. Entries only accepted on these conditions.

NOTICE TO THE PUBLIC.

During the running of the Races, the Public are requested to assemble outside the Fenced Enclosure of the Course, and not on the Track.

Every reasonable precaution will be taken during the running of the Races, and the Management do not hold themselves liable for any accident that may occur.

The Management have the power to exclude, at their discretion, any person from all at any place under their control.

Weighed-in : BLUE FLAG.   Objection : WHITE FLAG.
Objection Sustained : GREEN FLAG.   Objection Over-ruled : BLUE FLAG.

NOTICE TO JOCKEYS.

The Signal for Starting will be by the Fall of a WHITE FLAG.

In the event of a False Start a RED FLAG will be waved about fifty yards from the Starting Post.

Jockeys must weigh-in as they have weighed-out.

The decision of the Judges and Stewards is final.

NUMBER CLOTHS to be returned to the Secretary after each Race.

This flapping meeting near Derby had flat and trotting races. It seems to have been well organised, with a full set of officials, entries made in advance, handicapping by weight and proper medical and veterinary cover.

to be certain because it was unregulated and without central organisation, consequently leaving few traces. However, there is some anecdotal evidence. For example, in east Dorset, never a flapping stronghold, wartime meetings sprang up at Wallisdown and West Morden, and references in The Sporting Life in August 1945 imply that it was thriving generally that summer.

Though providing welcome entertainment, flapping from the participants' point of view was not for the faint-hearted. Doug

Jemmeson, who was exempt from military service as a blacksmith's apprentice, looking back in 2007 at his days as a flapping jockey in the north east painted a picture of a rough and ready sport where almost anything went if you could get away with it. Races were mostly between one and two miles at weights around eleven stone, with handicapping by distance rather than weight. There were some "hurdle" races, though the actual obstacles varied widely, as did the courses - some were excellent, such as Belmont, near Bishop Auckland, but they were usually very tight, a mile at Easington being four times round. Riding bends was a skill essential to success so, being a farrier, Doug would put a big nail in the outside of horses' shoes to give a better grip. Horses were entered on the day and often ran two or three times, not always under the same names or with the same results (one owner had a mare that ran as Black Beauty, Coal Dust or Beautiful Dreamer, and almost identical greys called Don't Know and Can't Tell), and the last event each day was a consolation race for those which had not won earlier. Win prize money rarely exceeded five pounds and most bets were in shillings rather than pounds, but some people would go to any lengths to land a touch, including intimidation of other horses' riders, rough-riding during races (often leading to fights afterwards) and doping. Dope was usually administered as powder in a handful of grass and had quick but temporary effects, so a delay at the start could be enough for it to wear off. And yet there was some honour and respect. Jockeys rode for the kudos and excitement and were not paid except, perhaps, a few shillings from an owner's winning bet. The best were respected for their skill, among them Ted Scott and Eddie Fletcher, both of whom sired Grand National winning jockeys. Doug's career blossomed after he earned Ted Scott's respect following a race when he got up his inside and nearly beat him. As they pulled up Scott said "Young man, don't you *ever* come up my inside again, *or I will cut you in two!*" Unlike most teenagers, he promptly apologised and Scott took him under his wing, later putting him on many good horses. Unfortunately, Doug's refusal to lose any race on purpose ended his race-riding career after the war when he was brought down by someone determined he was not going to win. He was unconscious for a week, and his parents called a halt.

The 1944 flat racing season began on Easter Monday, 10th April, with about 1,850 horses in training, of which just over half were two-year-olds and two thirds of the rest three-year-olds. There were 460 at Newmarket, 540 in the north (almost all in Yorkshire) and about 850 in the south. The numbers of jockeys and licensed apprentices had jumped to 110 and 88, but the 130 trainers were only slightly more numerous than before. The early April weather was depressingly cloudy, with the return of Double Summer Time only giving the opportunity to see more grey sky, but there were crowds reported to be "on a fantastic scale" for the opening meetings at Windsor and Stockton. The Upper Sixpenny Stakes at Windsor produced what proved to be only the first of a series of upsets to three-year-old form when Orestes, favourite at 4 to1 on, failed to get past The Solicitor, a Beckhampton cast-off now trained by Victor Smyth, but the most significant race of the day (and the most significant in the north for years) was the first at Stockton, the Carlton Stakes. Of the nineteen two-year-olds the only one seriously backed was Sir Eric Ohlson's Dante, a strong, handsome colt by Nearco, trained at Middleham by Matthew Peacock, and the result was never in doubt: Dante led a furlong out and won easily.

This year each zone staged its own Free Handicap, the Newmarket version being run at the Craven meeting. Lord Rosebery's Roadhouse won, but none of the twelve runners had performed with distinction in 1943 and they were not destined to improve. The Column Stakes had been lengthened to a mile and a quarter and was won comfortably by Ocean Swell, the favourite and one of the few top three-year-olds to maintain his reputation, but the odds-on Happy Landing failed to hold off Borealis in the

Shelford Stakes. A one-day sale accompanied the meeting but, against what had now become the trend, attracted little business.

Free Handicap day at Newmarket was also the date of Downpatrick races, of no importance in itself (though unusual in being an all jumping Irish meeting), but it was the first racing in Northern Ireland since May 1940 and the first jumping in the UK for over two years. The profits went to the Northern Ireland Agricultural Red Cross Fund. It was, however, under INHS rules and outside the domain of the London government departments, so was perhaps not even the single swallow that did not make a summer. In fact, the Irish racing authorities were again having to review their programme because of the desperate transport situation in much of the Republic. There was an acute petrol shortage and although the Great Northern Railway of Ireland, which operated both sides of the border, could get locomotive coal because of its UK activities, the Irish government had made the Great Southern suspend services on many branches and run just a single train only two days a week on other lines. Despite these difficulties, the year eventually saw 90 days' Irish racing against 79 in 1943.

On 21st April the 15th Scottish Reconnaissance Regiment left Pontefract racecourse, and were probably glad to go: the first meeting of the season was next day and the previous autumn they had had to clear all their kit and bedding out of their quarters in the stands and tote for each meeting, and put them back afterwards. Free passes for the races and a convenient number board from which to hang scrambling nets for training were poor compensation. The main race there was another running of the Substitute Lincolnshire Handicap, whilst at Windsor Beckhampton's Distingue became the latest top three-year-old to fail when Midge Richardson on Norah Wilmot's St.Athans held off his challenge in the Southern Free Handicap. The following Saturday the Northern equivalent at Stockton produced a disappointing field of nine distinctly moderate animals. On the same day the Clerk of the Scales at Salisbury found himself weighing out G.Richards for Division 2 of the Apprentices Handicap. This particular G.Richards was thirteen and carrying a weight cloth containing nearly two stone of lead. On enquiry it transpired that G stood for Gordon and he had no other names, which was no help at all. Rejecting the boy's suggestion that he might be called Gordon Richards the Second, he decided he must incorporate his master's name and be called Gordon Waugh Richards. G.W.Richards scarcely rippled the surface of flat racing but was destined, long afterwards, to become one of the most successful northern jumping trainers of the century.

Signs that the invasion was imminent continued to mount. Visitors had been excluded from a ten mile coastal strip from The Wash to Lands End from the beginning of April and at the end of the month all travel abroad was banned. It was evident that some day soon racing might have to be cancelled overnight or even on the morning of a meeting for military transport reasons and Mr Weatherby wrote to ask the Home Office exactly what the procedure would be. The departments conferred and agreed that War Transport would tell the Home Office, who would tell the local Chief Constable, who would tell the Clerk of the Course!

Supposedly classy three-year-olds continued to get beaten. Tudor Maid reappeared at Salisbury from her Beckhampton winter quarters as favourite for the Southern Stakes, only to fade suddenly and finish nowhere behind Growing Confidence from George Beeby's stable. At Newmarket Roadhouse and Ocean Swell finished behind Borealis and Fair Fame was beaten by Monsoon, but Tehran looked promising in winning the Culford Maiden Stakes, and in the Chatteris Stakes Garden Path easily disposed of Honeyway and Effervescence on her reappearance. When he came to preview the Guineas races The Sporting Life's Man on the Spot confessed he could not remember a spring when so many of the reputed best three-year-olds had been beaten. This all pointed to the probability that they were a below average generation and that the Classics might take less winning than usual, a fact not lost on Walter Earl. After consulting The Hon. George Lambton, one of his predecessors at Stanley House, who had started training in 1892, Earl decided to take on the colts in the Two Thousand Guineas with Garden Path. No filly had won it since Sceptre in 1902 but he knew she was above average, whereas the colts were not, and he had an ante post bet at a good price because the bookmakers were assuming she would go for her natural target, the One Thousand.

The Guineas meeting was well attended but the numbers in uniform were lower, another indication of imminent military action. On the first day Picture Play won the One Thousand Guineas easily. She was trained at Foxhill by J.E. Watts for Jim Joel and ran without a preparatory race, despite which she left the likes of Fair Fame, Mrs Mops and Monsoon trailing in her wake. Earl knew from the running of his stable's Queen Nitocris that Garden Path could have won it, but he must have been just as excited when Lord Derby's two-year-old Sun Stream, a Hyperion filly, won a division of the Bedford Maiden Stakes in a canter on her first appearance. Garden Path's chance was now obvious and she started favourite in a field of 26 for the Two Thousand, which was run in a rainstorm. Tehran, a complete outsider, made the running to the dip, where Garden Path swept past and held on by a head from Growing Confidence with Tehran third, only heads in front of His Excellency, Vigorous and Happy Landing. It was a popular win but Lord and Lady Derby were now both too infirm to come to Newmarket to see it and were represented by Lady Stanley, their daughter in law.

The Fillies Maiden Stakes at Pontefract the next Saturday did not, at first sight, seem out of the ordinary, but joint favourite with the eventual winner, Trixie From Tad, in the second division was an unraced Hermia filly, trained at Middleham by the wily Fred Armstrong. This was the first British runner for the Maharajah Sir Pratapsinha Gaekwar of Baroda, who had contacted Armstrong without ever having met him and asked him to start buying horses

Harry Wragg looks across at the fast-finishing Growing Confidence
(Ken Mullins) as Garden Path wins the 1944 Two Thousand
Guineas. The crowd has abandoned the lower steps
of the stand because of the rain.

with a view to eventually establishing a stud. The filly, later named
Her Highness, and a colt called Baroda Squadron were the advance
party of what rapidly became a large and successful operation, only
to disappear just as quickly when the Maharajah was deposed by the
Indian government in 1951 and lost much of his wealth.

On the hottest Whit Monday since 1933 six of the nine
favourites won at Ascot, among them Neola, a very smart two-year-
old trained by Fred Darling for J.A.Dewar, whilst Dante murdered

the opposition at Stockton for the third time: the betting was 1 to 4 Dante, 4 to 1 Langton Abbot, 50 to 1 the other ten. The Sporting Life's Augur had to concede that, though the hype about Dante could only be a product of the fevered imagination of clueless northern yokels, he did seem to be a useful colt.

Suddenly, the war scenario started to change rapidly. Monte Cassino fell at last on 18th May, forcing the Germans into full retreat when the allies broke through the Gustav Line, and on 4th June the Americans entered Rome. On the 6th came the momentous news of the Normandy landings, but a week later something happened that the government had long anticipated, feared and tried to prevent. In the early dawn a Royal Observer Corps post in Kent spotted a small, strange aircraft with a glowing exhaust. Hardly had they sent the code word ("Diver") they had been given for this eventuality than its engine cut out over Swanscombe and it fell to the ground with a huge explosion: the doodlebugs had arrived.

D-Day was also Coronation Cup day and there was speculation in the morning that the meeting might be cancelled, but it went ahead with a small, almost entirely civilian crowd that was quiet and serious: the country had been disappointed too many times for anyone to be confident or jubilant. The race was won by Persian Gulf from High Chancellor, with Umiddad and Kingsway well beaten. The winner was trained at Newmarket for Lady Zia Wernher by Capt. Cecil Boyd-Rochfort and ridden by Bobby Jones.

In former years The Times could have been relied on for some purse-lipped disapproval as the Derby meeting approached, but not this time. A leader on 13th June headed *Normandy and Newmarket* said that the flow of news across The Channel would be reversed for a few moments on Saturday – troops would be waiting for the Derby result. "The pattern of daily life in this country has somehow survived nearly five years of war" it continued "and, although there is nothing intrinsically meritorious in holding a race meeting, it does afford a curiously heartening proof of stability". Whilst being careful about imputing thoughts to servicemen or prisoners of war, The Times was sure they would want the race to be run, concluding "It is our Derby, and those who are most remote from it may, perhaps, when they hear the result, feel for a precious, fleeting moment the most closely drawn into the magic circle of home".

There was only a moderate crowd for the Oaks, run on firm going, with hardly any in uniform and fewer women than usual, and nobody bothered to dress up. Picture Play was favourite, as would be expected, from Tudor Maid, who had redeemed herself with an easy win at Windsor, but there was a tremendous punt on the maiden Hycilla, a Boyd-Rochfort horse. The Newmarket touts had spotted that she was coming on in leaps and bounds after her promising first run a month before and she started at only 8 to 1, having been offered at 100 to 1 in early May. In the race itself Picture Play led into the dip but broke down and finished sixth. Queen Nitocris led briefly but could not quicken and was passed by Hycilla, vainly pursued by Monsoon and Kannabis.

Queen Nitocris alone had represented Walter Earl in the Oaks because Garden Path was taking on the colts again in the Derby, though Growing Confidence was a narrow favourite to beat her this time. Derby day was unpleasantly windy but there was a better crowd and more servicemen, including Americans ("some of them coloured" noted Bloodstock Breeders Review). Garden Path had every chance less than a quarter of a mile out but injured a suspensory and finished in the ruck like Picture Play. Billy Nevett had already gone for home on Ocean Swell and held on in a finish of heads and necks from Tehran, Happy Landing and Abbots Fell. Jack Jarvis was ill at home a couple of miles away and missed seeing what turned out to be his penultimate Classic winner, and Lord Rosebery was also absent because of his duties as Regional Commissioner for Scotland. In the open two-year-old races Sun Stream beat nine rivals who had already won eleven races between

them in the Queen Mary, including Fille du Regiment and Sweet
Cygnet, and in the Coventry Stakes Dante became the first northern
horse to win an open race under the zoning system. Even The
Sporting Life had to admit it was a sparkling performance.

The Jockey Club met during the Derby meeting and authorised
the trustees to underwrite whatever amount the stewards decided in
loan stock for the three or four racecourses which Jockey Club
Racecourses Ltd was considering buying. They were also told that
a committee was being set up to look into the possibility of photo
finishes, the members of which were later named as the Duke of
Norfolk, Sir Percy Lorraine and Major J.B.Walker, and the Club
agreed to be represented at a conference called by the Racecourse
Association to discuss the televising of racing. This sudden interest
in technology had begun at the Club's April meeting, at which a Mr
Moore of Broadcast Amplifiers Ltd was appointed as technical
advisor on "broadcasting", which seems to have meant public
address systems on racecourses.

The Racecourse Betting Control Board had met on the same
day in April, to be told that the Derby Recreation Company had
notified them there would be no further racing there because the
borough (as it then was) council had refused a new lease when the
99-year term expired in 1945. This was victory for Derby's
counterparts of the Cheltenham miserablists, particularly an
alderman who regularly asserted that the races brought "scallywags"
to the town. Although things were looking bad at Torquay and
Loughborough, Derby was only the second confirmed wartime
casualty among racecourses. The first was Llanymynech, where the
liquidator was at work and would present his final report in
September. The situation at Worcester was uncertain but hopeful, the
city council having told the RBCB that they might re-let the course
after the failure of the tenant company, or run it themselves.

D-Day came in the midst of the discussion of the fixture list for
the second half of the season. The Jockey Club had proposed only

one more day than in 1943, giving a total of 68 for the season, with the same open races, and had given up asking for open races at Ascot, but War Transport still wanted a Parliamentary Secretaries' meeting. When it was arranged they wrote to Petherham saying that the meeting must take the matter seriously; they wanted to bring it before CDC and the cabinet. One factor was that Noel Baker was under pressure from his party. The Labour conference had been cancelled for transport reasons and the Party Secretary, Jim Middleton, wrote to Noel Baker saying that this was being unfavourably compared with allowing race meetings. "Is there any real answer that an intelligent person could appreciate?" he rhetorically enquired. When the inevitable meeting took place it deviated somewhat from the well-trodden path, as everyone accepted that the draft programme was reasonable in itself. Instead, there was heart-searching about criticisms like Middleton's, and 1940-style anxiety about giving the impression that the war was not being taken seriously. It was thought impractical to stop racing whilst allowing other kinds of recreation, a decision which, in any case, could only be taken by the War Cabinet. Noel Baker announced that his department was not going to oppose the continuance of racing, to the surprise and irritation of Peake, whose file note said that "in these circumstances the meeting seemed a little pointless". He felt the question now was whether they should let sleeping dogs lie or ask the cabinet for a positive decision to continue racing. The risk of going to cabinet would be uninformed discussion unless there was an explanatory paper, and he felt Churchill would not want to spend much time on the issue at this juncture.

In the end, Morrison went to cabinet with a long paper by Hodge entitled "Attendances at Sports". This pointed out that flat racing had come down from 330 days before the war to 67 in 1943, and jumping from 270 to nil. In contrast, greyhound racing had been cut from 104 to 52 days per track, and football was unrestricted except for being organised regionally and confined to Saturdays and holidays. Racing had, therefore, suffered greater reductions than comparable sports, though not from a desire to discriminate, but for transport reasons; however, the stopping of movement of horses by rail and of race specials for spectators meant that the problem was now purely one of handling crowds on stations and trains, not of providing more trains or rolling stock. Football crowds of 40,000 were allowed in some areas, with 90,000 at Wembley and 135,000 in Glasgow. Average racing crowds were 13,641 at Ascot (though Hodge was forgetting the thousands on the Heath), 21,597 at Stockton and 5,783 at Newmarket, which included 1,098 servicemen. Morrison added a note of his own saying that "according to press reports, horse racing has recently been resumed in Moscow. My personal view is that the case for further restrictions is not strong [though] the matter is one in which in present circumstances there might be a minor Parliamentary storm". The War Cabinet minutes for 12th June show that the Ministry of Agriculture supported Morrison and that Leathers said that stopping racing would not release any more trains. The Secretary of State for War carped that he could not reconcile the proposal not to curtail racing further with the decision to ration concessionary travel by dependents of service personnel, but the cabinet "expressed general concurrence" in the Home Secretary's views. On 21st June the programme was agreed without reference to CDC and appeared in the Racing Calendar next day. The last threat to racing continuing had been overcome.

Three days after the first flying bomb, the Chief Constable of Windsor, Ralph Wellings, wrote to the Home Office expressing concern about the potentially catastrophic results of an air raid on a race meeting there. The course was on an island in the Thames with the only escape route over two, narrow bridges and they were now getting crowds of up to 25,000 – nearly five times what had been expected when racing resumed in 1942. He thought a larger course should be used and no Saturday or bank holiday meetings held at Windsor, apparently not understanding that those were the only days when racing was allowed. The reply from Miss Livingstone, who did the spade work for Petherham and Hodge, said it had been decided to continue with racing and that crowds in areas affected by flying bombs were expected to reduce, as was happening at greyhound meetings and other entertainments. Wellings was still worried and telephoned to ask if the Home Office had any objection to a message being given over the course loudspeakers if the army warned that a flying bomb was approaching. He proposed to instruct the crowd to lie flat. Mr Lee, who took the call, told him in a rather off-hand way to do whatever he thought fit.

The next Windsor meeting was on 1st July and the crowd was down to about 12,000 because there had been a rainy morning for the first time since racing resumed there, although it brightened up a bit by the first race. As the runners were preparing to leave the paddock for the sixth of the eight races the warning sounded. Exactly what happened is not clear, because accounts conflict in such basic details as the direction in which the missile was travelling, and some have definitely been embroidered. The most dramatic of them claim that its engine cut out above the course but, according to Ron Blake, who was there with the Beckhampton horses, it was still spluttering when it passed, though he remembered the sense of helplessness everyone felt when advised to take non-existent cover. The bomb fell several hundred yards away on the disused council refuse incinerator, damaging over three hundred buildings and injuring about sixty people but causing no deaths. Racing continued as though nothing had happened and the incident went unmentioned in both press and form book. One of the unanswered questions is how the ARP record of 3.27 p.m. for the explosion of the bomb and the form book's 3.34 for the "off" time of the delayed race, starting five furlongs away from the paddock, could both be right. Mr Wellings wrote again to the Home Office to emphasise that his fears had been justified and that the races must surely now be stopped, because Windsor people were sure the bomb had been aimed at the course. This was pretty unlikely. One can imagine German commanders aiming a V1 at the King's well known castle, but not scanning the sports pages for a race meeting to bombard, and this was the only example during the entire war of anything like an attack on a meeting. At the Home Office they were coolly rational. Lee, who happened to know someone who had been there, considered it unlikely that the bombs could be targeted so accurately and Hodge thought they approached so fast that it made no practical difference that the crowd could not disperse as easily at Windsor as elsewhere. He thought the risk "not in excess of that which it has been decided to take", and Lee wrote to tell Wellings so.

Despite this, the doodlebugs were soon affecting racing, because a new evacuation of children from London started later that week. This imposed great stresses on the railways and the meetings at Salisbury and Ascot on the next two Saturdays were cancelled as a result. Windsor, ironically, went ahead on July 22nd, though only 7,000 came, but War Transport would not agree a Jockey Club and Home Office request for the following week's Salisbury meeting to be transferred there, and that, too, was abandoned.

On 24th July the Daily Herald featured a story headed *So Racegoers Come Before Evacuees*, claiming that around the racing and sales week it had taken ten days for the Newmarket billeting officer to find accommodation for 32 mothers and 84 children. Councillor Bertie Newton of the local evacuation committee said "Some of the people in this town have behaved very badly. Racegoers have been given priority and that is not right. It is not the cottagers who refuse to help, but the people living in some of the big houses". A refugee mother said that being inspected by the gentry made them feel like puppies in a shop window, and a stableman told the paper he had not seen a racing man looking for a bed. This touched a nerve at the Home Office and Morrison asked the Regional Commissioner, Sir

Will Spens, for a report. Spens replied that his investigating officer had found general difficulty, no worse in Newmarket than elsewhere, in billeting women with children, but none in billeting unaccompanied children. The problems peculiar to Newmarket were that those who regularly let rooms to racegoers did not want them taken by evacuees and that owners of bigger houses resented interference with their ability to entertain. He suggested warning the Jockey Club that racing would be restricted if there were any more trouble, but Petherham pointed out that the Jockey Club had no control over the offenders and that the real answer was for the billeting officer to use his powers of compulsion without fear or favour, so Spens was told that no action would be taken as it would prove futile.

On the racecourse, apart from Umiddad narrowly winning a rather feeble renewal of the Gold Cup and a fourth consecutive win for Neola, Fred Darling's latest smart juvenile filly, little of note happened during the disrupted programme for July, but at Ascot on August Bank Holiday another brilliant two-year-old burst onto the stage. This was Lord Astor's Court Martial, a Fair Trial colt trained by Joe Lawson, prompting The Sporting Life to conclude that the juveniles were the best since 1941 and the overall quality of horses the best of the five wartime seasons to date – a surprising claim in view of the obvious mediocrity of most three-year-olds. A couple of weekends later Orestes at last managed to struggle home for his only three-year-old win, and on 30th August Sugar Palm's long career reached its peak when he got up in the last few strides to take the Nunthorpe Stakes. Summer racing ended on the first Saturday of September with Abbot's Fell winning a meaningless, three-runner St Leger Trial Stakes at Windsor and fourteen undistinguished northern handicappers ploughing through a mile and a half of holding ground in what Pontefract was pleased to call the Substitute Ebor Handicap.

By this time the Allies had taken Paris and the V1's were being countered by various means, including attacking them with fast fighters, such as Tempest Vs and Spitfire XIVs, deploying hundreds of anti-aircraft guns on the coast and providing 2,000 extra barrage balloons, and by the Allied advance overrunning their launch sites. On 7th September the evacuation of London was suspended and refugees started to stream back. Duncan Sandys of the Ministry of Supply announced that "the Battle of London is over", but next day there were big explosions in Chiswick and Epping as the first V2s landed. These were rockets with 2,000 lb warheads which arrived from the stratosphere at 3,500 miles per hour without warning and against which there was no defence except destroying the launch sites. They were to make London life frighteningly insecure for over six months. Other bad news during September included the failure of the Arnhem operation and the death in a flying accident of Frank Furlong, who had ridden Reynoldstown to his first Grand National win in 1935 and survived crashing in the sea in 1941. Literally on the brighter side, modified street lighting was allowed again in non-coastal areas.

The day before the St.Leger meeting, Hodge wrote to tell Mr Weatherby that the Jockey Club's application for supplementary meetings to replace the three abandoned because of the evacuation had been granted, but CDC had refused an extra day per zone on top of that. These requests had been made a month earlier but Noel Baker's customary prevarication had delayed a decision. When the Club met the following day a letter from Lord Portal told them that the Treasury had refused consent for the issue of loan stock to finance buying the share capital of three racecourses they proposed to take over in the near future. The reason for this disappointment was the government's policy of preserving capital investment funds for post-war reconstruction and they hoped the setback would be only temporary. In fact, it was not temporary at all: the government's policy was an unavoidable necessity for the years of austerity ahead. The scheme was dead and the one big initiative from the Ilchester Report that had been vigorously pursued had become one of the Might Have Beens of racing history.

In the Rous Stakes Fille du Regiment won her fourth race in five attempts and was sent off to stud without racing again. The other outstanding two-year-old filly from Beckhampton, Neola, tried to win her fifth in the Cheveley Park, and Gordon Richards always believed she had held on at the finish, but Sweet Cygnet was judged the winner by a head, with Sun Stream a short head third.

St Leger day's weather was lovely and there was a large but mainly civilian crowd, who afterwards queued as patiently as ever for buses and taxis, hitched lifts on lorries or simply walked to the station. Hycilla was the narrow favourite but pulled too hard and was finished a long way out. Teheran, Borealis and Ocean Swell had it to themselves over the last three furlongs and finished in that order, with Teheran's stamina helping him beat off successive challenges from the other two. As a result the Indian Army Comfort Fund was £4,000 better off, the Aga Khan having given 75% of his winnings to it throughout the war.

Less than a fortnight later Hycilla was back for the Champion Stakes and, fitted with the special noseband she had worn in the Oaks, settled easily and beat her sixteen opponents comfortably. Dante faced only three opponents in the Middle Park and won unextended.

In October the season bustled towards its close. On the 7th the regional Cambridgeshire and Cesarewitch races at Ascot and Stockton all produced large fields, Fun Fair's second Ascot Cambridgeshire win causing The Sporting Life to hail him as the best wartime handicapper. At the following week's Newmarket meeting there was rather disappointing turnout for their Cambridgeshire, and no Cesarewitch at all. The Dewhurst was won by Sir Alfred Butt's Paper Weight, with whom Frank Butters had cleverly run up a sequence of wins in lesser races, but it was the best he ever achieved. Ocean Swell, on the other hand, proved himself to be the traditional sort of Classic and Cup horse by winning the Jockey Club Cup, becoming the first outright Derby winner to do so, showing speed enough to win over a mile and a quarter in the spring and the stamina for two and a quarter in the autumn. The northern season ended at Pontefract on the Saturday of the same week, where Gaekwar's Pride was the Maharajah of Baroda's second winner of the season, Baroda Squadron having scored at the previous meeting. The Substitute November (sic) Handicap led to one of Raceform's more unusual footnotes - "Start hidden by haystacks. Time shown is actual time taken from the hand of the man holding the bell, who had sight of the start". On the same day Sugar Palm was acclaimed champion sprinter after a spectacular winning charge at Windsor, his seventh on the course. The southern season ran on for another three Saturdays of large fields but mundane racing, each course staging a replacement meeting for one lost in July, and ending at Windsor on 4th November. Although there had been only one more day's racing than in 1943 there had, because of divisions, been 85 more races – equivalent to a hidden twelve days extra.

In late October The Sporting Life, which had been appearing only on Mondays, resumed publication on Wednesdays too, but what would there be to write about? One possibility was National Hunt Racing. In July the NHC had put out a statement hoping there would be a prompt announcement when racing became possible again, which stimulated a long article noting the exemplary patience shown by jumping owners and trainers. The paper assumed that NH racing would not start again until the war with Germany was over, but hoped it would resume in 1944-45 - it was not clear whether because of victory or despite the absence of it. The article contained a distinctly suspect list of jump jockeys who were said to be farming or doing munitions work. It included Hubert Applin and John Hislop, who were both amateurs, and the latter of whom was neither farming nor making bombs but waiting to be dropped behind enemy lines in a hazardous SAS mission. The first concrete development came on 12th October in a personal letter from Lord

York racecourse with prisoner-of-war huts behind the cheap
enclosure and livestock grazing nearby, but the stands and
the course itself are untouched

Rosebery letting Morrison know that the NHC was to apply for a
few fixtures from the end of the year as a result of his encouraging
remarks in an earlier telephone conversation. Rosebery rehearsed
the traditional NH assurances to government about how small,
undemanding and harmless the sport was, but asked for a decision
in principle before going into more detail. Next day, Peake received
his own letter, this time from the Duke of Norfolk, saying much the
same in rather more importunate terms. Peake sent a note telling
Petherham that although NH racing was fine entertainment and
might boost morale, it had no bloodstock value and the transport,
feedstuffs and psychological implications were such that they should
resist the proposal until organised resistance in Europe was over.
Petherham reminded the other interested departments of the reasons

for suspending jumping in 1942 and asked for their views immediately. 550 horses were ready to be trained, including up to 150 now running on the flat and it would take two months to get them fit if and when feed coupons had been issued. Though there were no security reasons for forbidding jumping, he wondered whether a resumption might seem to indicate that the war was almost over. When they replied it was not War Transport but the Ministry of Agriculture who were hostile, because there would be criticism from farmers whose livestock feed was severely rationed. They thought the present level of flat racing was enough to maintain a nucleus of bloodstock and an expansion of racing might worsen the shortage of labour in stables. The inevitable result was the summoning of yet another of the Parliamentary Secretaries' meetings for 30th October, by which time the NHC had sent in a draft programme. This suggested racing on Boxing Day and every Saturday from 6th January to 31st March, with one meeting in the north and the south each day, using Cheltenham, Plumpton, Nottingham, Wetherby and Catterick. There would be open races at Cheltenham for the Champion Hurdle and Gold Cup and at Nottingham for the Grand National, and the travel limit should be raised to a hundred miles. Hodge and Petherham wondered whether to consult Cheltenham Borough Council, but decided against it because less racing was proposed there than in 1942 when, they thought, Sir Waldron Smithers had been behind the council's objection in any case.

When the Parliamentary Secretaries met Norfolk, Lord Willoughby de Broke and Mr Weatherby, almost every aspect of the plan was queried and alternatives suggested (including absurd ones like substituting Pontefract or Thirsk, where there had never been jumping, for Catterick). Windsor now looked a better bet than Plumpton, and there were doubts about Nottingham being derequisitioned in time. Almost the only definite conclusion was that the fifty mile limit had to apply, throwing the running of open races into doubt. Three days later the War Cabinet got involved and sorted things out in quick time: racing could resume on Boxing Day but the fifty mile limit must apply, making a revised programme essential and open races inadmissible for the present, though open to reconsideration later. The Ministry of Agriculture greeted this with heavy hearts. R.A.Franklin, Hodge's opposite number there, wrote sourly that "We shall now have to do our best to defend the War Cabinet's decision in the event of any criticism from the poultry industry about the further use of feeding stuffs for non-essential animals". A file note by Peake recorded that 546 horses were available (137 in Epsom and Sussex, 175 in Wiltshire, Berkshire and Gloucestershire, 150 in Yorkshire and 84 elsewhere). This was Peake's last involvement with racing: within days he had been moved to the Treasury and replaced at the Home Office by the Earl of Munster.

The NHC came straight back with a programme using only Windsor and Cheltenham in the south and Wetherby and Catterick in the north, plus a request for extra petrol for Epsom and Sussex horses to go to Cheltenham like the concession that allowed them to reach Salisbury. By 16th November the programme had been agreed and CDC notified. Within days horses started to appear from where they had been tucked away on little farms all over the country (though only those which were in Great Britain on 1st June 1941 and had remained there since were allowed to race) and the names of almost forgotten trainers and jockeys started to reappear in the press.

December was a month of miserable weather, with rain, snow and frost and no sunshine at all. It was cold but fine for Tattersalls' five day sale, where there was a big crowd that made accommodation in Newmarket as hard as ever to find. Many were from Ireland but few from further overseas. Prices were exceptionally high and 679 of the 760 lots were sold, producing a record aggregate of 571,722 guineas, the yearlings averaging 938 guineas apiece. The annual Thoroughbred Breeders Association meeting was exceptionally well attended and sympathetically received Rosebery's annual presidential tirade urging more racing. The Jockey Club also met in December and decided, for the first time during the war, that they could allow the entries for next year's Classics to stand, instead of abandoning the original races and reopening them with the "New" prefix.

By mid-December the finishing touches for the jumping season were in place. The NHC was to award a temporary travel allowance for horses of sixpence a mile for up to a hundred miles, and one selling race would be allowed per meeting. There were reported to be 111 trainers, 98 jockeys and twelve amateurs with permits (though at that time amateurs only needed a permit if they had ridden at least ten winners, so the number of amateurs actually riding would be more than twelve). Then it all went flat: the coldest Christmas since 1890 saw frozen ground that forced the opening meetings at Windsor and Wetherby to be cancelled. Incomparably worse than that, the Germans launched their surprise counter offensive in the Ardennes on 16th December and the Allies ended the year furiously fighting the Battle of the Bulge.

CHAPTER 9

IN VICTORY (1945)

The weather relented for the Cheltenham meeting on 6th January but the crowd was smaller than hoped because some had decided not to chance it, and Wetherby was again frosted off. The 93 runners for seven races were a mixture of veterans returning from a sabbatical of almost three years and former flat racers which had never jumped an obstacle in public. As if to prove that NH racing had not changed, the programme started with a selling hurdle. It was won by Birthlaw, who had made his hurdling debut in 1938, ridden by Frenchie Nicholson and trained locally by Charlie Piggott. Forestation and Seneca were back for the Berkeley Hurdle, the former finishing all out to beat Brains Trust, a horse bred by Dorothy Paget but sold off cheaply after one unsuccessful run on the flat in 1943. Farther West, another old Champion Hurdle contestant, won the novices chase and the venerable Schubert and Cliff Beechener made all the running to win the New Year Chase. Prize money was a shade better in cash than at the corresponding 1942 meeting but in real terms it had fallen, which was to be the trend for the whole season.

One thing that was like the old days but should not have been was the Great Western Railway running the usual, non-stop special from Paddington. Mr Lipson was attacking Noel Baker in the

Commons within days. Was it proposed to run such trains for every meeting, he asked, and, having refused repeated requests by Cheltenham's council and chamber of commerce, would the minister now arrange for a daily fast train to meet the business community's needs? Noel Baker replied that there had been a serious breach of the instructions forbidding railway companies to run race specials and the minister was taking the necessary action, but, he regretted, heavy essential traffic on the line meant no additional fast trains could be provided. A week later Lipson was back like a terrier with a rat: who ordered the train; what disciplinary action had been taken; how many coaches had there been; how many passengers; how much coal was used; how much did it cost; would the taxpayer have to meet this? Noel Baker squirmed again: it was the GWR's fault and the Chairman had apologised to the Minister and would deal with those responsible. The eleven coach train had used six tons of coal but there would be no cost to the taxpayer.

The weather closed in again and the heaviest snow for three years fell in the south, followed later by bitter frost which brought temperatures in Kent down to 8F (minus 13C) and froze the edge of the sea at Dover. It was little better in the north and the rest of January's racing was lost. For a time it looked like a repeat of 1942, though Tattersalls' overflow sale went ahead, with prices similar to those in December. Across the Channel fighting continued during the same, appalling weather in the Ardennes, the Allied counter attack finally cutting off the "bulge" in the middle of the month, and on the eastern front the Russians captured Warsaw.

The Sporting Life printed articles of general interest during the interruption, including two by Leonard Jayne which contrast sharply in retrospect. One was about likely post-war PTC venues, with optimistic speculation about local interests reopening the still-intact Portsmouth course and unspecified new tracks opening in the north, midlands, South Wales, the south west and Berkshire or

Sussex, plus one at Southend. It was a pipe dream; almost none of it came to pass. The second was a perceptive article based on experience at Northolt, advocating commentaries at racecourses and contradicting the Jockey Club view that "any form of audible broadcast during the progress of a race can only lead to confusion". Among others, George Picken of Woodcote wrote to disagree; most racegoers could read a race and the answer was not to confuse them with commentaries but make sure they could all see. On 31st January the paper carried a short report that the BBC would soon announce plans to televise the Cup Final and the Derby, but this can have been of only limited interest even to the few who would have been able to receive television but for its having remained suspended since 1939.

The weather improved by early February and in the third week briefly became quite spring-like. Racing resumed at Cheltenham on the 3rd and by the next Saturday an avalanche of horses was ready. 191 ran in eleven races at Windsor (a record for a NH meeting that still stands) and the northern season opened at last with 91 in six at Catterick, so more than half the horses in training ran that day! Brains Trust won at Windsor and more old friends returned, including Red Rower who also won at Windsor and Venturesome Knight, favourite at Catterick despite his fifteen years, but brought down at the water. The Easby Novices Chase there descended into farce, with Priority Call making all the running to win in a glacially slow time by only three lengths from Kilton, who had been remounted after falling at the first fence. None of the other thirteen got round. There had been talk of extending the season to make up for lost meetings, but urgency was added to running horses wherever possible when the Duke of Norfolk announced that it must end as planned on Easter Saturday to make way for what he called "racing proper". This prompted E.S.T.Johnson to write from Chester to The Sporting Life to complain, as he had five years earlier, that jumping owners were being unfairly treated. The following

Saturday saw 146 runners at Cheltenham and 113 at Wetherby, but it was the 175 at Windsor on the 24th that precipitated a crisis. Jumping there took place over the same ground as "racing proper", which was due to start on 14th April. The course was now in shreds and there were still two more NH meetings to come. The inspector recommended that these should not take place, or the early flat meetings would be in jeopardy. The NHC had already put out feelers to the Home Office about transferring them to Fontwell Park. Petherham told Hodge that he had no idea where Fontwell was, but he had no objection if War Transport agreed. The same went for proposals to run the Champion Hurdle and Cheltenham Gold Cup as open races (Grand National plans having been abandoned). After some confusion the Fontwell proposal was dropped, the next Windsor meeting cancelled and the other transferred to Cheltenham, which would race on the last three Saturdays of March with an open Gold Cup on the 17th and Champion Hurdle on the 31st.

There was a very large crowd on Gold Cup day. It cost thirty shillings to get into the reserved enclosure and ten shillings for the public enclosure, roughly £37 and £12 at present day values, with forces in uniform at half price. Though the big race was open, it might as well not have been because there were no northern runners. The record field of sixteen was a mixture of the geriatric and the inexperienced: five of the runners were aged thirteen or more and another five had not won a chase between them. The favourite was Red Rower, bred, owned and trained by Lord Stalbridge and ridden by Davy Jones. Jumping indifferently for most of the race he struggled to keep in touch, but passed Schubert and Paladin at the last and drew three lengths clear to take the derisory prize of £340. Schubert was second, Paladin third and the ancient Poet Prince fourth. Suffering a rush of mud to the brain, The Sporting Life excitedly proclaimed that the winner had beaten Golden Miller's 1935 record time, only to have to admit in its next edition that the distance of this year's race was three furlongs shorter. A fortnight later the Champion Hurdle also attracted sixteen, including two from the north. Seven of them were four-year-olds and there were several older novices; only Red April and Forestation represented the old guard. The favourite was Triona, a winner of two juvenile hurdles, but the race was a dawdle and dash in which he exhausted himself by failing to settle, and it also put paid to the chances of Forestation, who needed more of a stamina test. Brains Trust led coming to the last and just held on from the fast finishing Vidi, with Red April a close third. Gerry Wilson, who was now training nearby, had managed to conjure an improvement of nearly a stone from him against Forestation compared with their running at the January meeting. Wetherby again closed the season a few minutes after Cheltenham's last race, with Unofficial and Billy Parvin taking the £100 for the Bramhope Novices Chase. The verdict on the short season was that it had been successful, with big fields and big crowds at every meeting.

March was the last month of the air war against Britain. The last serious raid on London by conventional bombers occurred on the 3rd, the last V2 fell on the 27th and the final doodlebug the following day (at Swanscombe, where the first had come down). The Allies were squeezing Germany from east and west, the Americans liberated Manila on the 4th and in Burma, Mandalay fell on the 20th. A new chapter in racing opened with the formation of the Racegoers Association at a meeting in London, but another closed when Steve Donoghue died, leaving thousands feeling they had lost a personal friend. He had been champion jockey for ten consecutive years from 1914 and won fourteen Classics, including six Derbies, but, like other jockeys who have dominated their era, he was a flawed genius. A fine horseman, fearless round Epsom, charming and generous, he was also vagueness personified, naïve, unpunctual, only dimly aware of the meaning of loyalty and pretty hopeless with money, but the public adored him.

The flat season started on 2nd April, the earliest since 1941. The Jockey Club had pushed the boat out a little further when applying for fixtures, their first draft running only to the end of June but asking for 40 days instead of the 29 allowed for the same period in 1944. They also wanted to include four days at Thirsk in the northern programme, to race on Whit Saturday, run three extra open races and hold the Queen Mary and Coventry Stakes at Ascot. They had not done their homework properly: they soon found that Thirsk was still in military hands and hurriedly had to ask to hold the meetings at Catterick and Redcar instead. Hodge took a relaxed view in his briefing to Petherham, noting that the increased number of meetings would be a reversal of previous policy but that "restrictions on racing have been stringent, and a discreet increase is unlikely to embarrass us in dealing with other sports". He also thought the security objection to open races at Ascot was less and that they need not question the proposal if War Transport had no problem. Nevertheless, there had to be a Parliamentary Secretaries' meeting for one, last time. Even Noel Baker did not query the size of the programme, and agreed that the Redcar meetings could be held elsewhere when he vetoed racing there because of local rail transport difficulties. He would not allow Ascot on Whit Saturday, but was happy enough with Stockton. His misgivings about Ascot open races were brushed aside on the grounds that they were two-year-old races and, therefore, "of no great public interest". Munster briefed Morrison the same day and soon almost everything was agreed: the Redcar meetings would go to Catterick and the only outstanding issue was Whit Saturday at Ascot, about which the Jockey Club was to negotiate direct with War Transport. They got nowhere.

There were now 166 licensed trainers with 2,569 horses between them, of which about 50% were in the southern zone, 30% in the north and (because the figures now included jumpers) only 20% at Newmarket. 1,091 were two-year-olds and 681 three-year-olds but, again because of the NH factor, there were also 278 aged seven or more. Easter Monday fields were huge and so were crowds, swept along on what The Sporting Life called "waves of optimism" about the end of the war. There were 25 runners in Pontefract's feature, a final repetition of the "Substitute Lincolnshire", but that was topped in the most valuable race of the day, the Bagshot Handicap at Ascot, in which 29 barged their way round the Swinley Course. On the whole, though, the sport was mundane and the first significant results did not come until the next Saturday's meetings, when Dorothy Paget's Sun Storm was hard pressed by Court Martial in the Trial Stakes at Salisbury and Dante made his first appearance over a mile in the Roseberry (sic) Stakes at Stockton. He was 10 to 1 on, with Gaekwar's Pride and Donah at 20's against and the other seven at 50 to 1. The result was a foregone conclusion (though a few critics thought Dante could not have won by more than the actual margin of four lengths), and greeted with wild enthusiasm. "It might be thought that the pride of the North had just won the Derby!" sneered The Sporting Life. "A large portion of the huge crowd rushed to the paddock and for several minutes cheered the colt and his jockey, W.Nevett".

The Craven meeting regained a little of its pre-zoning lustre when the Free Handicap, one of the new opens, reverted to being an actual race instead of a paper exercise for information only. The winner was Grandmaster, trained at Epsom by Walter Nightingall, not for Dorothy Paget but Mr M.Freedman, though ten days later Miss Paget's Mrs Feather, trained by Ossie Bell, beat him at Salisbury. The King's Rising Light became a serious Guineas candidate after he won the Column Stakes, reversing placings with Sun Honey from their meeting the previous autumn, and Ocean Swell easily beat Borealis in a match for the April Stakes over a mile and a half.

The day afterwards, overshadowed by news of President Roosevelt's death, the Jockey Club met to lift the ban on Irish horses and hear about progress on several fronts. The BBC had initially continued to resist broadcasting racing results, but Raymond Glendenning was now saying that they were to start doing so almost immediately – but only on Saturdays: that, of course, meant that Newmarket results would be broadcast on Derby day only. The photo finishes committee reported and it was agreed to give the new technology a season's trial at one course, preferably Newmarket, but the main business concerned getting the Rowley Mile back into use. It had been de-requisitioned in February and the RAF had left the course itself in excellent condition except for 200 yards either side of The Bushes (which had disappeared, though it would later become clear that all was not lost). This section had had to be re-turfed and could not be ready for the Derby meeting, but that was academic because of repairs needed to the silver ring stand and the bars. There would be a very big claim against the government and licenses to start the work were being sought. Though not recorded in the minutes, the stewards were trying to inveigle the Home Office into intervening with the Ministry of Works on their behalf. Sir Humphrey de Trafford wrote personally to Munster on 18th April but was firmly told that the department was not going to get involved on behalf of the Club or any of the many other bodies that might try it on. Elsewhere, York and Hurst Park were de-requisitioned during April and although Hurst needed considerable work to become raceable, York could be ready very soon.

A minor milestone on the road back to normality was passed at the low-key First Spring meeting at Newmarket with the running of the first selling flat race for nearly four years. Mr R.F.Watson went to 1,100 guineas for Lord Derby's Widdicombe Fair, which turned out to be a better bargain for his Lordship than Mr.Watson.

On the evening of Tuesday, 1st May German radio announced that Hitler had died and, with the Russians fighting their way through Berlin and the other Allies pressing in the west, speculation about an imminent surrender rose daily. However, a palpable sense of frustration was creeping in by the weekend when the expected

Farther West (P.Lay) leads at the water jump in the 1945 Cheltenham Gold Cup as the eventual winner, Red Rower (Davy Jones), jumps clumsily just behind, followed by The Hack (Jack Moloney).

announcement still did not come, and the capture of Rangoon in the meantime was little consolation. When it came, the release of the news was a shambles. The surrender document was signed at 2.41 on the morning of 7th May with scores of journalists in attendance, but they were sworn to secrecy and their copy retained by the censor pending agreement between the Allies about how to handle the announcement. The Russians were insisting on delaying until a formal ceremony some 36 hours later, but everyone had reckoned without German radio, which broadcast the news in the early afternoon and was picked up by the BBC monitoring service. At this point a leading American correspondent decided that the deal with the censor was a dead letter and managed to phone a report via his agency's London office. Finally, at 7.40 p.m., the BBC interrupted a recital with a comically legalistic Ministry of Information announcement that it was "understood that" the Prime Minister would make the announcement next afternoon and tomorrow would, therefore, be "treated as" Victory in Europe Day and "regarded as" a holiday, as would the day after. Reactions varied from relief, joy, singing, drinking, embracing total strangers and dancing in the streets to a curious sense of flatness and disappointment and an uneasy realisation that the Far East war was nothing like over. By eerie coincidence the first night of peace in Europe was marked in some places, including north London, by prolonged and violent thunder like that of the night before war broke out.

One place with dancing in the streets that evening was Newmarket, where VE Day was also One Thousand Guineas day. The crowd was bigger than usual for this day and the enclosures were well filled an hour before racing, including the Members', where attendance had been sparse throughout the war. Fewer were in uniform, but there were more women than usual, some very smartly dressed and hats more in evidence, though most stuck to wearing coats and skirts. The men wore the lounge suits, brown shoes and soft hats that had become standard during the war years. The bars were well stocked and well patronised but no drunks were to be seen.

Sun Stream, proudly led up by Gerry Blum, who stood out as unusually tall for a stable hand, was favourite for the Classic in preference to Exotic, despite having been beaten by her over seven furlongs at the previous meeting, and Mrs Feather. She led well inside the last furlong and won by such a comfortable looking three lengths that Meyrick Good's report said he could not remember a jockey riding as confidently as had Harry Wragg. Little did he know: like other Hyperion fillies ("they were all bitches", according to Gerry Blum), Sun Stream was becoming difficult to train. It could take half an hour to get her to the gallops, and when she arrived she just wanted to tear off at top speed. The only way she could be made to get the trip was to keep her close behind other horses until the last moment and then pull out for one, short run. It looked brilliant when it worked but was a nightmare to execute, and she would have been done for if anything got past her again.

On the same card was the Spring Stakes, the second of the extra open races. It was for two-year-olds and, presumably because of the limits on prize money for juvenile races before the Derby meeting, was worth only £317. Its only point seems to have been to provide early comparison of two-year-old form between the zones. The winner was Fine Lad, trained locally by Henri Jelliss for Baron de Rothschild.

Dante was even money for the Two Thousand Guineas despite being known to have what was thought to be a minor eye infection, with only Court Martial, Sun Storm and High Peak seriously backed against him in a field of twenty. Dante was always among the leaders and ran on strongly, but could not quite peg back Court Martial, whom Cliff Richards had driven to the front in the dip. They were followed home by the outsiders Royal Charger and (significantly, as it was to prove) Chamossaire. It was a grave disappointment for Yorkshire, but Meyrick Good loved it – the oiks had been put in their place. He would make no excuse for Dante and thought he had thrown his head up in the finish. Good might have done the same whilst running flat out with a malfunctioning eye.

On 10ᵗʰ May, the first working day after the VE holidays, a letter from Mr Weatherby arrived at the Home Office, telling Munster that the Jockey Club was to submit a draft programme for July on a regional basis, but wanted to discuss the whole situation from August onwards. However, the end of war with Germany had changed the world even as the letter made its way through the postal system: a note in Petherham's writing says "DR 42 (B) under which we controlled all forms of sports and games has now gone. There is therefore no need for the Jockey Club to submit their proposed fixtures to us". It only remained for Munster to pass on this joyful news, though adding that transport problems were still severe and future programmes should first be cleared with War Transport. As a first step, the Club got War Transport to agree an extra day for both Newmarket July meetings and to racing on some Fridays as well as Saturdays in the other zones, and there were to be several more open races in July at both Newmarket and Ascot. Another sign of impending normality was a warning by the NHC (in particular, for some reason, to organisers of horse shows and hunter trials!) that the rule making anyone involved in unlicensed racing a disqualified person would be enforced again.

By the end of May public attitudes had changed completely. Sir Robert Bruce Lockhart, a diplomat at the Foreign Office observed "Seventeen days since VE Day and never have I seen a nation change so quickly from a war mentality to a peace mentality. The war has disappeared from the news......sport and the election now fill the front pages". The election had been called because Churchill's coalition government resigned on 23rd May after the Labour Party decided to withdraw rather than continue until Japan was defeated. Lord Leathers remained Minister of War Transport in the caretaker government that took over, but Noel Baker was replaced as Parliamentary Secretary by Peter Thorneycroft. Voting was to take place on 5th July but the logistics of counting the votes of millions of service people overseas would delay the results for three weeks. Most people felt the war was over. Despite fierce and bloody fighting in the Far East and fears that conquest of the Japanese mainland would take until well into 1946, or even 1947, it was almost as if the winning team had heard as they came off the field that the Second XI still had a few wickets to take in their away game. As in early 1940, the country was in a kind of denial, though the reasons were complex. Part of it may have been colonialist attitudes: fighting black, brown or yellow people the other side of the planet was something British forces had done fairly routinely for a couple of centuries, and was not in the same league as wars on the European doorstep. Also, so much emotional capital had been invested in the war with Germany that there was not much left for the Japanese conflict which was, in any case, an overwhelmingly American affair. Ultimately, though, sheer exhaustion may have been the decisive factor – perhaps Britain could not face more war after even briefly relaxing. Whatever the reasons, it was deeply hurtful to those with family members still in danger far away.

The third and most valuable of the new open races was the Newmarket Stakes for thee-year-olds, run over a mile and a quarter in late May and clearly intended as a Derby and Oaks trial. Paper Weight was favourite despite not having run since winning the 1944 Dewhurst, but one of Arthur Wragg's leathers broke at the crucial moment and he finished nowhere. The winner was Lord Rosebery's Midas, who had also not run since the Dewhurst but easily beat Grandmaster, Blue Water and Rising Light and now became one of the leading contenders for the Derby. The only filly to take part, Sweet Cygnet, made no impression and finished last.

Sun Stream was backed down to 6 to 4 favourite for the Oaks, but in reality it was longer odds against her even getting the trip. Harry Wragg tracked filly after filly and had her behind the wall of four leaders as they left the dip. Working across to the outside he pounced in the last fifty yards and got her head momentarily in front as they passed the post: a few strides later she was an exhausted fourth, but it was just enough. She was the 17th Earl of Derby's twentieth and last Classic winner and her efforts made him leading owner for the season, and Walter Earl leading trainer, but she never ran again.

There was an immense crowd on Derby day, some getting in free after the turnstiles were overwhelmed. It included American, Canadian and Indian servicemen and remained good-natured throughout despite the crush and (in contrast with the Guineas meeting) an ever increasing number of recumbent drunks. The King and Queen were there to see Rising Light. Dante was favourite in the Derby field of 27, but Court Martial was comparatively unfancied because, being by Fair Trial, he was thought unlikely to get the trip and High Peak, Midas and Sun Storm were all preferred to him. High Peak just led a quarter of a mile out, with Court Martial and Chamossaire well placed, but Dante was too good for them all and drew away up the hill to win like a top class horse by two lengths. He was the first northern winner since 1869 and the jubilation at the course was nothing to that at Middleham, where the Bell was tolled and a Dante Ball was held soon afterwards. Meyrick Good had the grace to concede that "In my long experience [which went back to the 1890s] I have never seen a Derby colt sent to the post more perfectly trained". Matt Peacock, who was responsible for the perfect training confined himself to remarking "Aye, he goes a bit".

The last race on Derby day was the Horningsea Handicap, the winner of which, Golden Cloud, was the very last sent out by the Hon. George Lambton. He had been training at Newmarket almost continuously since 1892 and had produced thirteen Classic winners, all but one of them as private trainer to the Earls of Derby. He had already written his memoirs, *Men and Horses I Have Known,* a classic of racing literature, by the time the 17th Earl replaced him in 1933 as being too old at 73, but he then set up a public yard at Kremlin House. The flow of winners continued season after season, but in the summer of 1945 time was up at last: soon after Golden Cloud's win he handed over to his son, Teddy, and died two days later.

There were other departures that summer. Charles Wood, who had ridden nine Classic winners and once been champion jockey in the Victorian era, despite being warned off for seven seasons, died aged ninety. Unlike many of his contemporaries, he was no fool with money and left £60,000 after 45 years of retirement. Just before the Derby meeting the legendary Charles Marriott retired because of ill-health from his position of Jockey Club agent and clerk of the course at Newmarket. He had served the Club for fifty years and assiduously protected their interests in a style somewhere between autocracy and tyranny. Though his attempt to keep the RAF off the Rowley Mile got no further than waving his walking stick in protest, he later saved the precious Limekilns gallops from destruction when it was feared enemy planes might land on them. The Jockey Club members paid glowing tributes to him at their July meeting. They even had a whip round - *with contributions limited to one pound each*!

There were arrivals and returns, too. At Stockton on 19th May the Australian Edgar Britt had his first rides in Britain after being brought from India by the Maharajah of Baroda, and it was again possible to see three Wraggs or (less often) three Richards brothers in the same race with the return of Sam Wragg and Colin Richards from military service. Doug Marks, restored to health at last, had also been granted a jockey's licence, but got few rides and was to find his future first in jumping and then as a trainer with a name for managing difficult horses.

Bruce Hobbs went to Buckingham Palace in early July to receive his Military Cross for heroic observation work close to enemy positions in North Africa in 1943, and John Goldsmith, a NH trainer before the war, was given the DSO. He carried out three missions in occupied France and "by bluff and daring" had escaped from Gestapo arrest.

Mid-summer racing after the Derby saw the Coventry and Queen Mary Stakes return to their natural habitat at Ascot, the winners being Khaled and Rivaz, both owned by the Aga Khan and trained by Frank Butters. The following week Borealis got his own back on Ocean Swell by beating him in the Coronation Cup, still run at Newmarket, with Hycilla third. Fields were still large and division of races frequent in June, but greater opportunities were starting to open up. Newmarket's First July meeting was the first three day fixture since May 1940 but, because of firm going, produced only 127 runners compared with 161 in two days in 1944. There were two open races daily, including the July Cup, July Stakes and Stud Produce Stakes, but not many runners from other zones and the successful interlopers were not the usual big guns: Sweet Cygnet, trained at deeply unfashionable Kinnersley by Tom Rimell, beat the Aga Khan's filly Naishapur in the Falmouth Stakes and the Stetchworth Handicap went to Johnny Dines' modest Epsom stable through Star Lover. Unlike Sweet Cygnet, who was the outsider of three, Star Lover was a warm favourite on the strength of winning over Ascot's gruelling two and a half miles – the same course as the Gold Cup at the July meeting there, when Ocean Swell came out on top. He easily beat Tehran, the odds-on favourite, with Hycilla and Borealis only fifth and sixth. It was his sixth win in sixteen attempts and he was also placed six times, making him the pre-eminent wartime stayer. The other open race on Gold Cup day was the Royal Hunt Cup, but the field of fourteen was disappointing by peacetime standards.

On 15th July the unloved Double Summer Time, which had formerly lasted until mid-August or even September, was brought to a premature and permanent end.

Fridays were added to northern and southern meetings at Catterick and Salisbury on 20th July, and the extra day at the Newmarket Second July meeting featured the first Princess of Wales's Stakes since 1939. The imminent end of zoned racing had been announced with publication of the August programme and the last regional meetings were on 27th and 28th July. Windsor raced both days, but Pontefract on the Saturday only, because of uncertainty about how many spectators would come on a Friday. The last zoned race of all was Division 2 of Pontefract's Fillies Stakes, and was won by Queen Eleanor, ridden by Percy Evans and trained at Malton by Cecil Ray.

The unrestricted fixture list, admittedly covering only August, looked remarkably like the zoned one, with meetings both north and south on Saturdays, August Bank Holiday and some Fridays, plus two mid-week ones during the month at Newmarket. A significant change, however, was the addition of Brighton to the southern courses and Redcar to those in the north.

In the world beyond racing the new era was starting to look unpredictable and uncomfortable. The election gave the Labour Party and its radical policies a clear mandate for the vast and daunting task of post-war reconstruction, and at the Potsdam conference the victorious Allies were already falling out at the start of what was to become the Cold War. The Americans had finally taken Okinawa in June and were bombing the Japanese mainland, but when President Truman's ultimatum to surrender unconditionally or face utter destruction was rejected the appalling prospect of an invasion in the face of a fanatically determined enemy seemed inevitable. Then there was a dramatic change, even more appalling in its way.

Few of those who went bank holiday racing at Ascot or Stockton on 6th August would have reached home in time to join what had become the national ritual of switching on the six o'clock radio news, but the millions who did heard that the Japanese city of Hiroshima had been destroyed by a new kind of bomb. Exactly how was not immediately clear – some listeners misunderstood the explanation and thought the bomb had somehow harnessed the power of the sun – but many quickly realised that something new and unimaginably terrible had entered the world, even though it might shorten the war. Three days later Nagasaki was similarly destroyed and on 14th August Emperor Hirohito ordered his people to stop fighting in the face of this "cruel weapon", to avoid "the collapse and obliteration of Japan and the total extinction of human civilisation". By the time the news broke in Britain, with an announcement that next day would be VJ Day and the 16th a holiday also, it was midnight and many people set off for work next morning unaware that they need not do so. There were celebrations, of course, with flags and singing and dancing, and pubs allowed to open until midnight but it was altogether lower-key than VE Day, an inevitable result of the feeling that the "real" war was already over.

While politicians and the military set about tidying up the formalities of surrender and, cautiously at first, occupying Japan, racing was going through a humdrum spell and The Sporting Life was filling up its pages with stories of discontent. On 11th August a letter from Tom Sharpley (Junior) of Enfield complained that bookmakers discharged from the forces and wishing to bet at dog tracks had to join a waiting list. The issue of the 18th proclaimed that *Lancashire Demands Racing* over a story grumbling that Manchester had been left out of the fixture list and that pony racing (presumably flapping) was an inadequate substitute. On the 22nd the main story was about a chronic shortage of stablemen at Newmarket that was thought, for some unexplained reason, unlikely to improve much through demobilisation: trainers returning from war service were restricted not by any difficulty in finding horses or owners, but grooms. The headline on 25th August was *The Dead Hand On Racing*. The story told readers not to blame the Jockey Club for the failure of racing to expand as fast as other sports, but the government. The Home Office and Ministry of Agriculture were no longer involved and the "niggardly concessions" were down to the Ministry of Transport, which was now the controlling body and only wanted to keep racing to a minimum. The public wanted racing, something said to be not lost on the flapping promoters who were hampered by no authority.

On the racecourse August saw Rising Light win his St.Leger preparation race at Ascot, followed by Baroda Squadron at the reopened Redcar and Chamossaire, Naishapur and Blue Smoke at the two Newmarket meetings. Unfortunately, there was to be no such race for Dante, the odds-on favourite. His eye problem was not

The paddock at York before the first race on 1945 St.Leger day.

The number-board men relax after putting up the St.Leger
runners. Their perch looks more secure than that of the
newsreel crews on the stand roof.

just a temporary infection but a progressive disease and on 25th August Matt Peacock had to take the heartbreaking decision to scratch him from the Classic. Dante was retired to stud and soon became completely blind.

Brighton returned at the end of the month with the kind of down-market seaside fun in which it had always specialised, one of the winners being Date Palm, Sugar Palm's considerably less able half-brother, also trained by Frank Hartigan for Major A.Bonsor.

And then it was the first Saturday of September again, with preparations complete for the formal Japanese surrender early next morning. The last wartime meetings were at Ascot and Stockton. As usual, racing at the southern meeting started and finished earlier than in the north, so the very last wartime race was the five o'clock at Stockton, the Farndale Maiden Stakes (Division 2) over five furlongs. The odds-on favourite was Wisecrack, trained at Malton by J.C.Hollowell and ridden by Charlie Spares, a journeyman jockey better known over hurdles in the south before the war and now riding on the flat in the north, but destined to become one of the more improbable riders of a Derby winner. When the tapes went up at 5.01 Ken Gethin popped the Theodoric colt out smartly and kept him ahead until the last furlong, but Wisecrack sailed past to win by three lengths from Superlative. The also rans streamed over the line and last of all was Bats Wing, ridden by Joe Taylor, thus completing a strange piece of symmetry (or, perhaps, asymmetry): Taylor had been on the last winner at Manchester on the fateful Saturday in 1939 and so had ridden the last horse to finish first in peacetime and the last one to finish last in wartime.

Soon after 9.00 a.m. local time on Sunday, 2nd September Japanese government representatives signed the unconditional surrender document on the US battleship *Missouri* in Tokyo harbour. The war was formally over.

★ ★ ★

York reopened on Tuesday, 4th September. It was the first three-day fixture anywhere except Newmarket since the 1940 Aintree meeting, the first mid-week racing away from Newmarket since June 1941, and the first real taste of peacetime normality. Many of the familiar Ebor meeting races were run, including the Gimcrack Stakes, the Nunthorpe (won by Golden Cloud), the Great Yorkshire and the Ebor Handicap itself. The Rous Stakes had lost its starring role and returned to the chorus as a seller again, but top of the bill was the St.Leger, back in Yorkshire if not quite back home. Naishapur was favourite but never looked like winning and the race went to Chamossaire from Rising Light.

A week later there was a final meeting on the July Course before it went into hibernation, to return in 1946 in its normal guise as the setting for a brief, summer idyll instead of a better-than-nothing wartime bolt hole. The next Newmarket meeting was on the Rowley Mile, where the opportunity to make some improvements for spectators had been taken whilst putting the buildings in order. Cuttings had been taken from the old Bushes and Major Gorton, now clerk of the course, was arranging for them to be planted with due ceremony. Lanark rejoined the fixture list in late September and Worcester, under the auspices of the City Council, in October, though there was an unfortunate incident at the first meeting when 25 people were injured in the collapse of the Tote building onto which spectators had climbed because of overcrowding. On 20th October jumping re-started at Taunton, the first overlap with the end of the flat season since 1940. Flat racing finished on 1st November, more than three weeks short of the peacetime norm, but by then Fontwell Park and Wincanton had joined the NH programme, to be followed quickly by Southwell, Worcester, Wetherby, Cheltenham, Catterick and Windsor. Together they provided a steady four cards a week on Fridays and Saturdays until reinforced by more courses in the New Year. The Boxing Day programme of three meetings was close to the usual pre-war four, with Windsor deputising for Kempton Park as it had in 1939 but Wetherby again having to be abandoned, though Wincanton managed to hold its holiday meeting for the first time since 1937. It would be more than six years before the last of the survivors, Uttoxeter, reopened and longer still before the final casualty list became clear, involving, as it did, disappointed hopes for such as Gatwick, Pershore and Tarporley and racing would never be quite the same as it had been. Nevertheless, at the end of 1945 it had emerged from six years of crisis with everything that really mattered remarkably intact.

CHAPTER 10

IN RETROSPECT (2008)

Looking back from well over sixty years later, a number of questions stand out that have never been answered in detail, perhaps because everyone was relieved at not having to do so and simply wanted to get on with post-war life. In particular, was racing preferentially treated compared with other sports, or was it discriminated against? Was it ever really in danger of being stopped? If so, who and what enabled it to continue? And then there are the What If questions: what would have happened if it actually had been stopped at some point; what would have happened if the Allies had not started to win the war when they did; what would have happened if Jockey Club Racecourses Limited had not been thwarted in its plans?

Opinions about how racing was treated need to be taken cautiously as they are rarely those of unprejudiced observers. According to the distinguished historian A.J.P.Taylor it was "treated gently". His view seems to derive from C.I.Savage, the official historian of wartime inland transport, who claims that "Horse racing must have been one of the few activities to escape through the now tightly-drawn net of war transport". Though the racing authorities got away with a lot before the net started to tighten in earnest, this seems a questionable analysis of the situation over the war as a whole. However, there were those inside racing who thought it had been well treated at least some of the time, notably the editor of Bloodstock Breeders Review, who lamented what he saw as the first break in the government's sympathetic attitude when jumping was eventually stopped in 1942. From a different angle, it is undeniable that racing was accommodated (unlike football, for example) by never being completely restricted to Saturdays and bank holidays, and that doing so was not even seriously contemplated until summer 1941.

One can also argue for the opposite view. The ban on rail transport applied only to horses travelling to race meetings and not for other reasons or to other equestrian sports. For example, in his autobiography John Betteridge describes taking horses by train from southern Derbyshire to Blackpool horse show in 1943. More significantly, other sports were allowed to take place simply because they provided entertainment and helped to keep up public morale, but NH racing, which met that criterion, was suspended. Flat racing was able to continue only because its importance to breeding enabled it to jump through the additional hoop of demonstrating that it was important to the economy and the empire. No other sport had to do that. By the end of the war the Home Office was under no illusions that racing had been given an easy time, hence the note by J.D.V. Hodge in early 1945 that "restrictions on racing have been stringent".

Of course, racing was different in character from almost all other sports, not least in facing a panoply of obsessives, bigots and opportunists (not to mention some sincere patriots) who wanted to stop it. On the other hand, other sports did not have participants who not only had no other purpose in life but also voraciously ate scarce foodstuffs, required an army of people to look after them and had to be transported long distances in large vehicles that could only carry two or three at a time. Nor did other sports generally rely on the entire crowd travelling to fixtures. The closest comparator was greyhound racing, but that involved smaller animals, locally trained, eating mainly things that humans would not, even in wartime, and providing entertainment for an overwhelmingly local crowd. Compare and contrast the football team that could fit into a small coach, played where the spectators lived and could perform military duties six days a week. Nevertheless, the Home Office fought consistently for parity of treatment between the three sports despite the opportunity to discriminate on grounds like these.

There is no doubt that racing several times came close to being stopped indefinitely. The first was the short, government-imposed suspension at Whitsun 1940. Had that not been inexplicably lifted a few days afterwards, trying to re-start later would have been even more controversial than the resumption in that September actually was. It was probably the most critical point of the war for racing as well as the country at large. As already mentioned, the proposal to resume was only acceptable because racing had been stopped not by the government but the Jockey Club. It succeeded because the timing was fortuitously right: had the Jockey Club approached the Home Office a week later and had the Germans started bombing urban areas a week earlier, the blitz would have started before a fixture list had been agreed and the government would almost certainly have backed away. That would have turned the absence of racing into the status quo and it is difficult to see any point before VE Day when it would have been politically feasible to relax the embargo: although it is true that NH racing emerged from suspension at Christmas 1944, that was only a thinkable option because ongoing flat racing made it so.

The next critical moment came in June 1941, around the time of the Derby furore, when the government briefly seemed to lose its nerve about what it was allowing and CDESC discussed the possibility of stopping racing. Their recommendation that there was no need to stop it altogether was agreed by War Cabinet, with Churchill making it clear that he would "strongly deprecate" any such proposal, but further cutbacks in the programme followed.

Finally, three years later, in the highly-charged atmosphere immediately after D-Day, the Parliamentary Secretaries again wondered about the need for suspension and the Home Office was sufficiently unsure about the rightness of their decision as to get War Cabinet to confirm that no action was required.

These incidents were only the pinnacles on the iceberg of threats to racing. Beneath the surface its case was constantly having to be argued against adverse press reports, hostile Commons questions, the lobbying of other interest groups and the conflicting priorities of government departments.

So who enabled racing to keep going? Racing writers have tended to credit the Jockey Club's astuteness and diplomacy in the face of a largely unsympathetic government, though Roger Mortimer gave some credit to the Joint Parliamentary Secretaries at the Ministry of Agriculture, Tom Williams and the Duke of Norfolk. In fact, the latter, though helpful at some key moments, were largely peripheral figures and their department spent much of the war pressing for reductions in racing so that they could look poultry and pig farmers in the face. The Jockey Club also had less control over events than might be imagined. Its position was not unlike that of Admiral Jellicoe in the First World War, who was criticised for his cautious strategy but was, as Winston Churchill pointed out, not only unable to do anything decisive to win the war but also the only man on either side who could lose it in an afternoon. Similarly, the Jockey Club could do nothing to guarantee the continuance of racing but had to be scrupulously careful to avoid overplaying its weak hand or scoring the kind of publicity own goals that might have turned the politicians decisively against racing. The stewards deserve full credit for achieving this, but their diplomacy was more to do with accommodating developments than managing them.

The prosaic fact is that racing survived because it was consistent government policy that it should do so like other sports. This sounds simple but was not: it is one thing to make public policy but quite

The Good News. The post-war boom brought in crowds like this one at York.

The Bad News. Except for the stands and enclosures, Newbury racecourse disappeared under miles of railway sidings and concrete roads. Restoration took six years to complete.

another to stick to it in the teeth of opposition and unpopularity. In the Great War racing had suffered from a wavering cabinet and an absence of coherent policy. This time there was a sympathetic prime minister, a clear policy and Home Secretaries brave enough to insist on it within government and defend it outside. Sir John Anderson and Herbert Morrison both faced down populist critics in the Commons when it would have been easier to cave in and agree to review policy, and Osbert Peake confronted Philip Noel Baker's attempts to harness Ministry of War Transport objectives to his personal distaste for racing. Just as important were the senior civil servants who analysed developments, weighed the options, advised ministers and wrote the papers for CDC and War Cabinet. The files on Restriction of Racing in the National Archives are a tribute to their professionalism in clarity of thought and expression, integrity of approach, intellectual honesty and speed of response - it was commonplace for letters to be answered within a day of arriving and for interested parties to be told about decisions on the same day that they were made. Faceless but not nameless, they were C.S.Petherham and J.D.V.Hodge, and their predecessors A.N.Rucker and F.C.Johnson.

Another bureaucrat whose role was crucial was Francis Weatherby, Secretary to the Jockey Club. He managed the Club and NHC secretariats single-handed throughout the war, remaining at the Cavendish Square offices during the blitz, and provided vital support for the stewards in dealing with ministers.

The answers to questions about what would have happened if events had taken a different turn are, of course, speculative, but it is possible to speculate intelligently on the basis of knowledge and similar experiences. So, if racing had failed to resume in autumn 1940 and remained suspended until summer 1945, what then?

Clearly, the breeding industry would have been severely reduced, because few commercial breeders could have carried on without buyers in sight or rations for thoroughbreds. Horses foaled between 1939 and 1941 would have been sold for whatever they could fetch in a buyers' market, mainly abroad, and particularly to the United States. Some stallions would also have followed Bahram and Mahmoud to America. Then most commercial breeders would, presumably, have pursued other interests, such as farming, to await better times but it is improbable that the large owner-breeders would have done the same. Having the resources and mindset to sit it out, it is likely they would have done so rather than disperse their bloodstock. Some, such as Jim Joel, were independent of official rations and able to supply their studs with produce from their own farms. The industry would, therefore, have been down but not out.

What about loss of the racecourse test, repeatedly stressed as vital by Lord Rosebery? A five-year hiatus would have prevented the 1939 to 1941 crops from racing in Britain at the ages of either two or three, but that might not have been long enough to cause major difficulty, particularly as breeding from unraced mares is not unknown. It is also conceivable that later in the war the government might have allowed some horses to be trained for racecourse trials behind closed doors, similar to the epreuves de selection allowed in France at times during the Great War.

Starting up again would have been more difficult. Breeders would have had to buy stock from abroad, this time in a sellers' market, the British industry would have found itself running third to France and America, the French would have dominated post-war Ascot and the Classics even more than they actually did, and the Jersey Act would have been discredited even sooner. Flat racing might have been unable to expand quickly enough at first because of a shortage of horses, though potential jumpers would doubtless have emerged much as they did in 1944-45, even after five years' interruption. As most of the racecourses that survived had been closed for a long time it is unlikely that complete suspension of racing would have caused more failures to re-open, but some valuable training grounds would have been lost under the plough or tank tracks because their preservation could not be easily defended while there was no racing.

Though 1943 was statistically the lowest point of wartime racing, with Sefton warning that the programme had reached an "irreducible minimum", the trough would probably have sunk even deeper had the Allies not gained the upper hand the previous winter. It is hard to imagine Ascot being allowed to reopen without a climate of dawning optimism and very easy to imagine that if there had been no light at the end of the tunnel by mid-1943 Noel Baker's demand for a cut to sixty days' racing (or, in those circumstances, perhaps even less) would have succeeded. That would have affected the size of the programme for the rest of the war because the expansion when better news eventually came would have been proportionate to the lower base.

And what if Jockey Club Racecourses Limited had been allowed to raise the capital to buy and run courses in 1945? The effect of taking over the three for which they were negotiating might have been little more than symbolic: buying the eight or nine originally suggested would have allowed them to set standards which the dividend-paying courses could not have ignored. In the event, the sinking of this flagship of the Ilchester Report heralded a retreat from implementing most of the other recommendations. Racing experienced a great boom from 1946 to 1950 and radical change began to look unnecessary as well as expensive. Unfortunately, nothing fundamental had changed and the boom in racing and other entertainments was a short-term result of post-war economic conditions: there was a lot of money in circulation but not much else to spend it on, with food and petrol rationed, consumer goods and luxuries scarce and exchange controls strangling foreign travel. The bubble burst in the early fifties, but by then racing and those who ran it had slithered quietly back into the mire of complacency. Nobody need have been surprised: a prophetic article in The Sporting Life in July 1945 had warned that precisely this might happen.

APPENDIX I

RACING DURING THE FIRST WORLD WAR

The way racing had fared in the First World War influenced expectations during the earlier part of the Second.

Racing was interrupted two days after the outbreak of war in August 1914 but resumed on the flat three weeks later and continued almost normally until the season ended in late November. Jumping resumed by mid-October and that, too, went on much as usual until the following May. In September 1914 the Jockey Club decided that "racing should be carried out where local conditions permit and the feeling of the locality is not averse to the meeting being held". This was understandable, because it was still widely assumed at the time that the war would end within months, so there was no point in retrenchment in response to temporary circumstances. It was a lot less understandable when the Club confirmed the decision in March 1915, with peace nowhere in sight and in a blaze of publicity that included a full page report in The Times. This was not what the country at large wanted to hear, but flat racing took place alongside the declining jumps season most days from late March. However, it did so against a background of adverse publicity and hostile Commons questions after (largely false) press allegations about particular incidents until, under heavy government pressure, the Jockey Club suddenly announced on 20th May that racing was to be confined to Newmarket with almost immediate effect. Owners and trainers were caught on the hop and when the next meeting took place there on 15ᵗʰ June after a three-week break, 214 runners turned out for the seven races, a record unlikely ever to be broken. The seventeen in the Derby was the smallest field.

From then onwards, racing took place in fits and starts for the rest of the war, largely dictated by knee-jerk reactions to immediate events. Flat racing for 1915 ended in late October, but a NH Committee delegation led by Col. Garratt persuaded Walter Runciman, President of the Board of Trade, to allow a couple of jumping meetings per week from January to early April 1916, using only Gatwick, Lingfield, Windsor, Hawthorn Hill and Colwall Park. This was achieved by emphasising the smallness and insignificance of the meetings and undertaking not to ask for extra trains, but it provided leverage for the Jockey Club when negotiating with Runciman for the 1916 flat programme. Although Newmarket, where both courses were available, remained the backbone with 38 days over eleven meetings, it was reinforced until mid-August by ten two-day meetings distributed between Gatwick, Lingfield, Windsor and Newbury. Not everyone was happy; there was anger in the north, where there had been no racing since May 1915, and courses without fixtures and, therefore, without income, were aggrieved at being expected to contribute to a fund to guarantee losses of those allowed to race. Alexandra Park and Sandown Park had already unsuccessfully sought compensation from the Defence of the Realm Losses Commission.

A NH programme on a similar scale as before was allowed from December 1916 to mid-April 1917, with Newbury added to the courses in use but, contrary to an earlier undertaking, the Board of Trade insisted that flat racing in 1917 should again be restricted to Newmarket. A programme of thirteen meetings and 44 days was agreed, starting on 17ᵗʰ April, but the anti-racing lobby launched their annual spring offensive in March with correspondence in The

Times and questions in Parliament. The climax came in late April after statements by junior ministers too unfortunate in their timing and content to have been accidental. The War Cabinet then decided, despite strong resistance by Lord Derby, to answer a forthcoming Commons question with an announcement that an order banning racing was to be made. Had that happened, there is little doubt that there would have been no further racing before the armistice, because an opportunity for a politically acceptable rescission of the order would never have arisen. Realising the danger, the Jockey Club asked to be allowed to suspend racing themselves. Such was the urgency that its announcement was made on a Sunday that all fixtures after 4th May were cancelled because the War Cabinet considered it undesirable that further racing should take place.

The racing world responded through the Thoroughbred Breeders Association and a series of meetings chaired by Horatio Bottomley, later exposed as a fraudster and charlatan but editor at that time of the populist and highly influential magazine, John Bull. The Jockey Club also issued a statement arguing racing's case and as they and the TBA started making headway in the propaganda battle, Lloyd George, the Prime Minister, decided to trim his sails. After a decent interval following a conciliatory meeting between Lloyd George and a Jockey Club delegation in late May, the cabinet decided to allow forty days racing between July and early November at Newmarket and any other courses agreed by the interested ministries, provided there were no extra trains and no use of cars or taxis. Rations would be allowed for 1,200 horses. Consequently, racing re-started on 17th July, followed two weeks afterwards by the latest ever runnings of the Derby and Oaks. Twelve days (almost all Saturdays) were shared between Windsor, Brighton, Manchester, Stockton and Ayr.

This emboldened the NHC to ask for fifty days on up to fifteen courses between late November and early April, but they were firmly rebuffed and only a very thin programme was allowed, starting in mid-January. Newbury, Hawthorn Hill and Colwall Park went out of the list and were replaced by Sandown Park and Manchester. The flat programme first agreed for 1918 was, by contrast, generosity itself. Besides the usual Newmarket meetings there were to be forty days, mostly Saturdays and bank holidays, on other courses, including Lewes, Gatwick, Windsor, Worcester, Warwick, Birmingham, Wolverhampton, Manchester, Haydock Park and Stockton. It was too good to last: the final German offensive in France changed everything and on 15th May the government told the Jockey Club for the third time in four years to confine racing to Newmarket. On 28th May the NHC was told there could be no jumping next winter, and as late as 8th October a request to reconsider this was refused. In June the Board of Trade even began at last to look at ways of stopping flapping, and produced a draft order a month later.

Racing finished on 1st November, ten days before the end of fighting. A week after the armistice, Sir John Norton-Griffiths asked the Prime Minister if he would now remove all restrictions on racing, but the answer was that it would have to be done gradually, and there was no more racing until New Year's Day 1919.

Though some of the First World War experiences were repeated in the Second, there were three significant differences.

First, racing remained controversial until almost the end of the Great War. As was to be the case from 1940 to 1942, whilst the war was going badly and defeat a possibility (albeit unspoken) there was a tendency to seek out and criticise anything appearing to be a waste of time, human resources or materials that might impede the national effort. Such things were thought to show that, in Sir Waldron Smithers' words "we are not sufficiently war minded". Unlike the Second World War, in which the Allies started getting the upper hand in late 1942 and such anxieties began to lose their urgency, the outcome of the First was uncertain until well into summer 1918. Therefore George Lambert and Duncan Millar, the

Great War counterparts of Smithers and Lyons, were still bombarding the government with questions about stopping racing until the end of May that year.

Secondly, the arguments were not exactly the same. Protection of the bloodstock industry was, as ever, the chief point in favour of racing, reinforced by warnings of a shortage of cavalry horses, as these were normally sired by thoroughbreds. However, the World War Two mantra about providing recreation for weary workers was never heard: on the contrary, there was much talk about racing causing absenteeism. This was said occasionally in the Second war (for example, concerning Nottingham in 1941), but in the First it was an obsession and those supporting racing had to demonstrate that they were discouraging the feckless lower orders from joining their betters at the races instead of working all the hours that God sent. Thus in early 1916 the Board of Trade ruled out any possibility of racing in the north in case it caused absenteeism among munitions workers, and the Minister of Munitions was later given statutory power to ban meetings for similar reasons. The government did reject a suggestion that it should impose a huge minimum admission charge, but the cheap rings remained closed at NH meetings "to discourage wage earners from putting in an appearance" as Bloodstock Breeders Review put it.

Beside the pragmatic objections, common to both wars, to racing as hindering the war effort, there was also a feeling that it was unpatriotic in a more general way and disrespectful of the sacrifice of those in the services. This was shared by the Duke of Portland, who fell out with other Jockey Club members when he made his views public in 1915. The counter argument was that maintaining racing was part of keeping the home fires burning for those away fighting, a point emphasised by the Earl of Durham, whose youngest brother had been killed in action in 1914 and who never himself went racing during the war despite his support for others doing so.

Finally, the government's approach was haphazard and

uncoordinated. Unlike World War Two, when a coherent policy towards sport was developed quite early and conscientiously adhered to, no over-arching strategy existed. Individual departments, particularly the Railways Division of the Board of Trade, made unilateral decisions based on the current situation in their own area of responsibility. There was no coordinating mechanism like the Parliamentary Secretaries' meetings and the cabinet bent with the wind of what it perceived to be current public opinion. Nor could the government be trusted to do as it said. Answering a question about the suspension of racing in April 1917, the Leader of the Commons insisted that it applied to all racing, yet it was over a year before flapping was tackled. Not long afterwards he assured another questioner that it was policy to treat all parts of the UK equally, but the very next day the government agreed to racing continuing in Ireland, which was still all within the UK.

APPENDIX 2

DIFFERENCES IN 1939

This summary of ways in which racing immediately before World War Two differed from the early 21ˢᵗ Century is not exhaustive but is intended to be sufficient to illustrate how different the sport then was and to help explain the context of wartime racing. It is mainly confined to quantifiable or factual differences, rather than ones to do with attitudes or culture.

Governance

The Jockey Club controlled only flat racing. Jumping was run by the National Hunt Committee, a completely separate organisation. Both of them were regulatory as well as administrative bodies. There was no overall racing authority.

Pony Turf Club racing was a full-scale sport in its own right, unlike the present events under Pony Racing Authority auspices, which are essentially a nursery for children and young teenagers.

The racing programme

There was far less racing. The number of flat fixtures was only about 35% of the present level and NH just under 50%, making 40% combined.

There was no winter flat racing. The break was typically from the fourth Saturday of November to the penultimate Monday of March.

There was no mid-summer jumping. The break was typically from Whit Tuesday to August Bank Holiday (the *first* Monday of August).

Courses chose dates of their meetings, subject to Jockey Club or NHC approval: they did not bid for fixtures.

There were more meetings of two or more days.

There was no evening racing (except under PTC rules), and none on Sundays.

The harder winters affected racing more. If a course was unfit on a day other than the last or only day of a meeting, that day's card was postponed and the *following* day's abandoned, though small NH courses could postpone meetings up to the end of the next week. Meetings were not transferred to other courses.

Racecourses

There were 92 courses, compared with 60 now.

There was no all-weather racing.

There was less watering and racing regularly took place on ground harder than would now be accepted.

There was less attention to safety: for example, rails were permanent and made of wood mounted on wooden, metal or concrete posts, not plastic.

Steeplechase fences were stiffer, often more intimidating in appearance and less carefully sited.

Courses had to be financially independent because there was no betting levy or other sources of external support.

There was little diversification into non-racing activities.

Races

There was little international competition, though French and Irish horses occasionally ran in major British races.

There was no grading of races and no system of pattern races

There was no rating of horses, and thus no races limited by reference to ratings, horses being handicapped race by race.

No races were sponsored. Instead of carrying sponsors' names or marketing slogans, most were named after local places.

Most big races were run between Tuesdays and Fridays: Mondays and Saturdays were regarded as down market days.

Most races were plates: that is, prize money was a fixed amount provided by the racecourse (which kept the entry fees) regardless of the number of entries.

There were more selling races, particularly under NH rules. Although any horse but the winner could be claimed out of a seller, there were no claiming races as such.

Rules about daily programmes ensured that there were at least two middle distance races and not more than two sprints for older horses on each flat card.

Prize money for two-year-old races before the Derby meeting was restricted.

Two-year-old races were limited to five furlongs until the Derby meeting and six furlongs until 1ˢᵗ September, when nursery handicaps also started.

Some of the most important two-year-old races were produce races.

There were fewer amateur flat races (though more than in the post war era).

The normal range of flat handicap weights before penalties or riding allowances was seven stone (lower in a few cases) to nine stone seven. For jumping it was ten stone (nine stone seven in most chases over extreme distances) to twelve stone seven. There was no long handicap, so no horses were allocated less than the minimum at any stage.

The percentage of chases on NH cards was higher.

The very few NH flat races were only for horses that had been placed in a chase, and ridden by amateurs who had been placed in at least three.

Three-year old hurdle races started on 1St September. The minimum distance was a mile and a half.

Conduct of racing

Entries for even the smallest races usually closed about a month before race day, with the last forfeit about a week before.

There were no overnight or 48-hour declarations: the actual runners only became known at final declaration, three quarters of an hour before the race.

The draw for flat races was made after final declarations.

There were no safety limits on field sizes, so no procedure such as balloting to restrict fields. Division of races was very rare.

Some courses had no automatic scales and still weighed jockeys using a balance bar with a seat hanging from one end and a tray of weights from the other.

There were no starting stalls. Flat races started from behind a multi-stranded, rising barrier.

There was no camera patrol or photo finish. The judge had to decide results and distances by naked eye.

Races were not electronically timed, except at Northolt Park PTC course.

Horses

The horse was not yet a purely recreational animal. Thousands still worked in agriculture or transport and were an everyday sight.

Most flat horses were British bred, because the "Jersey Act" was still in force, excluding from the General Stud Book those whose pedigree could not be traced back on both sides to ancestors in pre-1913 editions. This discriminated against foreign (particularly American) horses.

There was more emphasis on breeding middle-distance or staying horses, and less on sprinters or precocious types.

Although jumpers were becoming more highly bred, many steeplechasers were still of the traditional robust type. Many were Irish bred, but few came from other overseas sources.

The most common way of transporting horses over long distances, including travelling to race meetings, was by rail. Rail horseboxes had stalls for two or three horses and a bench seat and lavatory for the lad.

Jockeys

All jockeys and amateur riders were male.

There were no agents and jockeys arranged their own rides.

Apprentices could be indentured to a trainer at fourteen and usually signed on for five or seven years. Indentures could be transferred or sold to another trainer.

There were no apprentices' training colleges.

The weight allowance for apprentices in flat races was a uniform five pounds until they rode forty winners or became twenty-one. NH riders claimed five pounds until they rode fifteen winners.

Little protective clothing existed, although a basic form of skull cap was mandatory in NH races.

Whips were more severe. Whipping was more acceptable and some riders were notably hard on horses (it was suggested to the author that Midge Richardson, for example, "would not last a week" under present regulations).

Riding styles were different. Leathers were set longer and flat jockeys tended to crouch behind the horse's neck, rather than perch over its withers. NH riders (and Gordon Richards on the flat) adopted a more upright style.

Winning jockeys did not indulge in showboating.

There were no conditional jockeys under NH rules: riders were either amateur or professional. Having "ridden for hire", of which the definition was wider, made a rider irreversibly professional.

There were more licensed professional NH jockeys than the present total of conditional and full jockeys.

There were numerous amateurs under NH rules. It is difficult to know how many because they needed no permit until they had ridden ten winners.

Trainers

Trainers' licenses were not issued to women, even if in de facto control of a stable.

The Jockey Club's permission was required to train at Newmarket.

No formal training or induction was required or available for anyone becoming a trainer.

Leading trainers' strings were smaller. Few exceeded about fifty, and hardly any had more than eighty.

Discipline

With no camera patrol, riding offences were more difficult to spot or evaluate, so there was no routine intervention by local stewards over relatively minor offences.

Enquiries initiated by the stewards were less common and those arising from objections by other horses' riders more common.

There was less concern about misusing whips (see above).

There was no system of short suspensions of riders. To the extent that minor offences were punished, it was mainly by reprimands or fines. More serious offences might be punished by the Jockey Club or NH stewards withdrawing riding licences for a period of months or, particularly where corruption was involved, refusal of licence renewals or warning off. The inflexibility of this regime could lead to minor offences being more harshly punished than now.

Disqualified horses were placed last, regardless of the circumstances.

Trainers of doped horses were automatically warned off indefinitely, again regardless of the circumstances. However, there was no routine dope testing and no sophisticated procedures for collecting or analysing samples.

At the races

More racegoers went by public transport, particularly trains. Specials often ran from major centres to courses with good rail access.

Accompanied ladies might be admitted to Tattersalls ring at a discount.

Some courses deliberately made it difficult to obtain day club membership.

Racecards contained less information (e.g. nothing about riders, draw or form) and were small and cramped in layout. With no overnight declarations, they showed all horses left in at final forfeit stage and not the actual runners (which were unknown when the cards were produced).

Information about which horses were runners, their riders, overweights, and the results of races were shown on the number board, not announced by loudspeaker.

Except at Northolt Park PTC course, there were no race commentaries.

Although there was generally a luncheon room in the club enclosure, refreshment facilities elsewhere were unsophisticated (though the same was true of much eating out at the time) and often unattractive.

The media

Race cards in daily papers showed probable runners, omitting those still entered but unlikely to run. Some listed would, in the event, not run, but sometimes one not listed would run (and occasionally win).

The racing dailies were The Sporting Life and The Sporting Chronicle. There was no Racing Post yet.

There was a heavy bias towards flat racing, particularly in the ordinary dailies.

Reports of races tended to be rather unspecific and comments on running in the specialist dailies and form books were very sparse and unhelpful by present standards.

There was little investigative racing journalism and few published interviews with owners, trainers or jockeys. The discreet and rather deferential attitude of the journalists resulted in those that did appear being anodyne and rather dull.

There were radio commentaries on some big races, but TV was in its infancy and did not cover outdoor sport.

Betting

Betting on racing was very restricted by law but there were few other gambling opportunities.

Cash betting off course was illegal (though widely practised). Legal off course bets had to be placed through credit accounts by telephone or post.

There were no betting shops, and bookmakers' offices could open only outside racing hours for settling accounts.

Betting exchanges did not exist (not least because the technology did not exist either).

There was no levy on betting to support racing.

The Tote and pool betting was a relative novelty, but was starting to expand into the off-course market.

Ante-post markets were big, particularly on the spring and autumn doubles.

Public attitudes towards gambling generally were more censorious.

APPENDIX 3

FLAT RACE PRIZE MONEY 1938 TO 1945

TABLE OF COMPARISON

Season	Prize Money Per Horse		Median Win Prize Range	
	£ Cash	£ Real	£ Cash	£ Real
1938	190	196	***	***
1939	144	144	127-167	127-167
1940	80	68	166-168	145-158
1941	103	79	162-253	134-203
1942	100	71	167-272	124-200
1943	119	82	197-393	138-272
1944	128	85	283-375	192-254
*1945	***	***	252-305	166-200

* 1945 season to 1st September only

*** No details available

Prize Money Per Horse represents total win and place money for the relevant season divided by the total number of runners (Source: Sporting Life 12.3.45)

Median Win Prize Range represents the range of the median values for each month of winners' prize money during the relevant season.

Real values represent cash values for the relevant season adjusted to 1939 equivalents by applying the yearly values of £1 in House of Commons Research Paper 99/20 (Inflation: The Value of the Pound 1750-1998)

APPENDIX 4

THE ILCHESTER REPORT

The report was under six main headings - The Breeder, The Owner, The Public, The Racecourse Executive, The Racehorse, and Finance. This summary of the more significant recommendations is not under those headings, nor in exactly the same order. It is not exhaustive and does not try to cover the explanations given for the recommendations, but aims to give a brief overview of the committee's ideas.

The committee supported

- Allowing breeding companies to enter horses in races, but not to run them.
- Later closing dates for all races except produce, foal and yearling stakes and the Spring and Autumn Double races.
- Making all races stakes of not more than 0.5% of the added money to enter and 1% to run.
- Better prize money for placed horses.
- Allowances for at least part of horses' travel costs.
- Abolishing the rule allowing two-year-olds to run unnamed.
- Giving local stewards discretion to place disqualified horses immediately after the horse(s) they had impeded, instead of last.
- A bonus of 5% of win prize money for trainers and jockeys instead of informal presents from owners.

- Formalising and standardising arrangements for issuing free entry badges for race meetings.
- An annual meeting for owners to raise any matters they wished with the Jockey Club stewards.
- A specific area in each ring of racecourses to be railed of for betting purposes, preferably with over-head cover.
- Providing raised viewing areas in all rings.
- Improved "cloak room" facilities on racecourses, which should be subject to Jockey Club inspection.
- Major improvements in catering facilities, which were often "lamentably inadequate" and gave "bad and dirty service". These should also be inspected.
- Fair differentials between charges for enclosures (but without making grand stand charges so cheap as to attract "the noisy and undesirable elements who now confine themselves to the cheaper stands").
- Providing adequate press accommodation.
- Racecards meeting specified standards as to contents, layout and size.
- Saturday and bank holiday meetings confined to courses with large accommodation, and with improved prize money.
- Faster operation of number boards.
- Replacing manually operated scales with automatic ones.
- Improvement of stable lads' accommodation at racecourses.
- More scientific watering of courses, with watering to change the going only by permission of the Inspector of Courses.
- Maintenance of courses to come under a resident and licensed course manager instead of the Clerk of the Course.
- Announcement by loudspeaker of runners, riders and draw, and numbers, SPs and Tote dividends of the winner and placed horses.
- Increased powers and formal specification of the powers and duties of Stewards' Secretaries.

- Limiting selling races to one per day, imposing large penalties on winners and redistributing surpluses on sales between the placed horses and the racecourse.
- A sliding scale of apprentice allowances according to number of winners ridden.
- Various detailed changes to amateur riders' races.
- Retention of the prize money limit on early season two-year-old races.
- More valuable races for four-year-olds and upwards.
- Provision of races for the produce of low-fee stallions, particularly for fillies.
- Closure of certain (unspecified) courses perceived as redundant.
- The take-over, on fair terms, of a number of courses by the Jockey Club, to run them on a non-dividend basis.
- Provision of large amounts of extra finance by the Tote.

The committee opposed

- Adding breeders' bonuses to prize money.
- Concentrating meetings in particular areas at particular times.
- Compulsory car parking charges at racecourses.
- Overnight declarations.
- Loudspeaker commentaries on races.

The committee was open-minded on

- Evening racing
- Holding seven races a day as standard instead of six.

APPENDIX 5

THE RACECOURSES IN WARTIME

The following pages give brief details about every course racing under Jockey Club or National Hunt rules at the start of the war. Courses appear in the order in which racing was interrupted by wartime conditions, the date of interruption being regarded as that of the last meeting actually held. A second date shown in brackets is that of a later meeting (or the last of a number of such meetings) which was abandoned or transferred to another course. The date of resumption is that of the first meeting held after the interruption. In this case, a bracketed date refers to an earlier abandoned meeting, or the earliest of a number of abandonments. The Order column shows the order in which the individual resumption dates occurred.

The general suspensions of racing in autumn 1939 and summer 1940 have been ignored, as has the period of the emergency flat racing programme in October / November 1939. This is to keep things simple and reflect events that affected individual courses rather than racing in general. However, the suspension of NH racing from September 1942 to December 1944, being long and indefinite, has been taken into account.

The narrations are inevitably short, and sometimes fragmentary if information available is limited. It is important to note that military occupation was sometimes intermittent, with racing occasionally taking place alongside it. The forces often occupied only the buildings, particularly the tote, although they sometimes put up additional buildings. It was very unusual for the track itself to be damaged.

The following abbreviations have been used for different types of racing

JC Jockey Club flat racing

NH Racing under full National Hunt Rules

BF Bona fide hunt or military steeplechases

PP Point-to-point races

PT Racing under Pony Turf Club Rules.

Course	Rules	Interruption date	Resumption date	Order	Wartime history
Totnes & Bridgetown	NH	1.9.38	None		Used by Admiralty for boat-building. Damaged beyond repair. Racecourse company still extant 2008 and sponsoring annual hunter chase at Newton Abbot.
Perth Hunt	NH	29.9.38	23.4.47	64th	Probably used in connection with RAF Scone Park
Melton Hunt	NH	27.3.39	None		Course was on agricultural land
Warwick	NH JC	7.2.39 28.3.39	8.12.50 14.6.49	72nd	Requisitioned by the army in autumn 1939. Later became POW camp No 140.
Hawthorn Hill	NH BF PT	4.4.39 (19.10.40) 8.4.37 (5.4.39) None	None None 19.4.47		Known to have been potentially available for racing November 1943
West Norfolk Hunt (Fakenham)	NH	10.4.39	7.4.47	61st	Used for grazing.
Wincanton	NH	10.4.39	27.10.45	16th	In military use by early 1940. Used by US Army 1943-4. Derequisitioned early 1945 and sold by the former owners to a local syndicate.
Beaufort Hunt	NH	15.4.39	13.4.46	26th	Course was on agricultural land
Rothbury	NH BF	15.4.39 None	31.5.47 27.4.46	66th	Agricultural use. Resumed as bona fide before NH.
Tarporley	NH	26.4.39	None		POW Camp No 174
Cardiff	NH	27.4.39	None		Closed at outbreak of war because of uncertainty over the lease from the City Council. Occupied by the army as an air defence site by early 1940.
Pershore	NH	1.5.39	None		Requisitioned by the army in autumn 1939. Later used as an RAF training school.
United Border Hunt (Kelso)	NH	3.5.39	6.5.47 (22.3.47)	65th	Requisitioned as an army camp for British and Polish troops.
Chester	JC	4.5.39	7.5.46	36th	In army use from some time after mid-1940 until later than April 1945.
Glamorgan Hunt (Cowbridge)	NH PP	4.5.39 None	None 19.4.52		No information.
Hethersett	NH PP	4.5.39 None	None 30.4.53		RAF No 102 Gliding School from summer 1943.

Location	Type	Requisitioned	Derequisitioned	Rank	Notes
Wenlock Hunt	NH	5.5.39	None	73rd	No information
Uttoxeter	NH	9.5.39	12.4.52	70th	In use as an army camp by early 1940.
Sedgefield	NH	10.5.39	27.12.48	10th	Used for TA mobilisation September 1939.
Newmarket RM	JC	11.5.39	2.10.45	31st=	Operational airfield (RAF Newmarket Heath) from 2.9.39. Derequisitioned February 1945.
Market Rasen	NH	13.5.39	22.4.46	20th	In military occupation from late 1939.
Bridgnorth	NH	20.5.39	None	42nd	No information
Wye	NH	22.5.39	18.3.46		Course was on agricultural land. Weighing room was used as a hen house.
Colwall Park	NH / PT	25.5.39 / None	None / 9.5.49	45th=	Sold 1942 to machine assembly contractors Dowsett McKay, who promoted PTC racing for one season after the war.
Epsom	JC	26.5.39	4.6.46	43rd=	In military occupation from late 1939. Building Volunteers were billeted in the grandstand from August 1944. Also used as a reception centre for displaced Poles.
Bungay	NH / PP	29.5.39 / None	None / 23.4.53	28th=	Course was on common land
Cartmel	NH	29.5.39	10.6.46	58th	Racecourse company continued to pay rent throughout the war.
Hexham	NH	29.5.39	8.6.46	4th	Ammunition dump.
Towcester	NH	29.5.39	20.4.46	53rd	Army map storage depot.
Newport	NH	30.5.39	5.10.46	28th=	Top of the course was a public park. Lower part is believed to have been used as pasture.
Ascot	JC	16.6.39	15.5.43	34th	In army use by summer 1940, when it was also used as a transit camp for interned enemy aliens. The army retained some buildings after racing resumed.
Newcastle	JC	22.6.39	26.7.46	39th	Used for TA mobilisation September 1939. Buildings damaged by military occupation by late 1943.
Carlisle	NH / JC	10.4.39 / 29.6.39	20.4.46 / 10.5.46		In military use at various times, but no extra builings were put up.
Lingfield Park	NH / JC	1.5.39 / 8.7.39	19.12.47 / 26.4.46		Internment camp for enemy aliens from May 1940.
Ayr	JC	18.7.39	17.5.46		In army occupation from late 1939, at least partially as a transit camp.

Name	Type	Date 1	Date 2	Div	Description
Bogside	NH / JC	22.4.39 / 22.7.39	18.4.47 / 18.4.47	62nd	Air defence site protecting Ardeer explosives works and ROF Irvine.
Goodwood	JC	28.7.39	30.7.46	54th	Used by army and RAF from September 1939 until at least summer 1944.
Kempton Park	NH / JC	2.3.39 / 3.8.39	5.12.47 / 5.4.47	60th	Requisitioned by the army September 1939 and used by the Guards Division. Later became POW Camp No 9. Derequisitioned 1.9.46.
Yarmouth	JC	3.8.39	4.8.48	69th	Occupied by the army, initially as a forward defence site, September 1939 to August 1946.
Chepstow	NH / JC	8.4.39 / 7.8.39	27.3.48 / 28.6.47	67th	Requisitioned by the army 1.10.39. Extra buildings put up. Later used for parking aircraft and as an interrogation centre for suspected war criminals in 1945.
Sandown Park	NH / JC	18.3.39 / 7.8.39	28.10.46 / 29.3.47	59th	Used by the Guards Division throughout the war. Hit by a flying bomb in August 1944 but without significant damage
Derby	NH / JC	21.2.39 / 9.8.39	None / None		Requisitioned by the army as as an air defence site September 1939. Closed when Derby County Borough Council refused to renew the expiring lease in 1944.
Redcar	JC	14.8.39 (3.6.40)	11.8.45	8th	In intermittent military use from early 1940 until at least 1943.
Folkestone	NH / JC	4.5.39 / 15.8.39 (2.9.39)	9.9.46 / 24.7.46	52nd	Used as a landing ground in connection with RAF Westenhanger.
Pontefract	JC	19.8.39	25.4.41	1st	Partially taken over by the army in 1943 and huts erected beside the stands, though racing still went on. Also used as a training camp for mining conscripts (Bevin Boys).
York	JC	24.8.39	4.9.45	10th	Internment camp for enemy aliens from 1940 and later was POW camp No.11. Also some use for agriculture. Derequisitioned April 1945.
Buckfastleigh	NH	26.8.39 (13.5.40)	8.6.46	43rd=	Used by US Army before D-Day.
Hamilton Park	JC	26.8.39	25.5.46	40th	Occupied by the army and some extra buildings put up.
Brighton	JC	31.8.39	24.8.45	9th	Various agricultural, light industrial, vehicle and food storage and civil defence uses.
Devon & Exeter	NH	31.8.39	26.8.46	57th	Searchlight battery site.
Shirley Park	NH / PT	11.3.40 / None	None / 14.7.47		Public recreation, sports and entertainments.
Quorn Hunt (Loughborough)	NH	23.3.40	None		Became part of an airfield.
Hereford	NH	25.3.40	30.3.46	22nd=	Tented army camp September 1939 until at least late 1940. Later RAF No 50 Gliding School.

Location	Type	Requisition date	Release date	Rank	Notes
Huntingdon	NH	25.3.40	22.4.46	31st=	Course used as a Lammas meadow. Town centre offices let to local War Agriculture Committee.
Torquay	NH	25.3.40	None		The buildings were damaged beyond economic repair in an air raid 30.5.43.
Liverpool (Aintree)	NH JC	6.4.40 6.4.40	4.4.46 4.4.46	25th	In temporary military occupation September 1939 and June 1940. Occupied by US Army as a major depot from 1942 until 21.2.46. Also some agricultural use.
Bangor-on-Dee	NH	13.4.40	30.3.46	22nd=	Used as grazing by the landlord estate.
Doncaster	JC	13.4.40 (15.6.40)	28.6.46	48th	Requisitioned spring 1940 as RAVC headquarters. Also site of POW Camps 6 and 296A.
Alexandra Park	JC	20.4.40	7.7.47	68th	Used as a military depot
Fontwell Park	NH	24.4.40 (25.1.41)	25.10.45	15th	Potentially available for racing November 1943. Requisitioned at a later, unknown date but released in February 1945
Stratford-upon-Avon	NH	25.4.40 (16.5.40)	19.4.47	63rd	In military occupation, with extra buildings, by autumn 1943.
Oswestry and Llanymynech	NH	4.5.40	None		Used for agriculture and buildings demolished. Racecourse company liquidated September 1943.
Newton Abbot	NH	8.5.40	8.5.46	37th	No known temporary uses. Course was subject to flooding.
Woore	NH	9.5.40	16.5.46	38th	Course was on agricultural land.
Haydock Park	NH JC	9.3.40 25.5.40	29.11.46 14.8.46	56th	25 acres cultivated from 1940. Transit camp for French Navy summer 1940, but in army occupation by October. USAAF storage depot 17.3.44 to 10.5.45. Airstrip and extra buildings added.
Bath	JC	29.5.40	24.4.46	33rd	In army occupation May 1940 to November 1945. Toilet block was the only extra building.
Hurst Park	NH JC	11.3.39 1.6.40 (12.10.40)	30.12.49 20.4.46	28th	Used for TA mobilisation September/October 1939. Reoccupied by the army February 1942. USAAF Station No 508 from 5.6.43. Derequisitioned April 1945.
Lewes	JC	4.6.40	22.7.46	50th	Occupied by the army at some time between June 1940 and November 1942.
Beverley	JC	6.6.40	29.5.46	41st	Used for army night training exercises from June 1940 until at least March 1943.
Windsor	NH JC	16.3.40 8.6.40 (5.10.40)	10.2.45 (26.12.44) 23.5.42	3rd	Parts cultivated for cereal crops and sheep breeding. Some air raid damage to the NH course in December 1943.
Birmingham	NH JC	27.2.39 11.6.40	25.11.46 5.8.46	55th	Requisitioned by the army as an air defence site. Later used as a camp and storage depot. Damaged in air raids three times.

Racecourse					Notes
Gatwick	NH	28.3.40	None		Requisitioned by the Air Ministry September 1941 to enlarge the existing adjoining airfield which had been taken over in May 1940. Used for one post-war bona fide meeting but later bought by the
	JC	15.6.40	None		
	BF	None	21.4.48		Ministry of Civil Aviation to establish the civil airport.
Wolverhampton	NH	19.3.40	18.11.46	45th=	Air defence site, including rocket batteries.
	JC	18.6.40	10.6.46		
Leicester	NH	21.11.39 (13.2.40)	3.12.46 (2.12.46)	50th=	Probably requisitioned December 1940. US airborne units stationed there 16.2.44 to 23.9.44, with a
	JC	4.11.40	22.7.46		landing strip on the course. British artillery units were stationed there in August 1945.
Catterick Bridge	NH	4.3.39	10.2.45 (27.1.45)	6th	Commandeered lorries stored in summer 1940. In military occupation by mid-1942 with some extra
	JC	9.11.40	21.4.45		buildings by late 1943. Appears to have been released by October 1944.
Plumpton	NH	8.3.41	20.2.46 (25.1.46)	19th	Occupied by armoured units from April 1942 to June 1944. Released by October 1944.
	BF	19.4.39	None		
Taunton	NH	13.3.41	20.10.45	14th	Was never requisitioned. Probably used for agriculture.
Ludlow	NH	22.3.41	28.3.46	21st	In military occupation with extra buildings by November 1943. Used by US Army before D-Day.
Lincoln	JC	27.3.41	1.4.46	24th	No known use in WW2 (airfield in WW1). Round course was public open space.
Stockton	JC	12.4.41	2.5.42	2nd	Occupied by the army, apparently only temporarily, in May 1941.
Edinburgh (Musselburgh)	JC	13.9.41	15.4.46	27th	Used as a camping ground by the army. The Home Guard had a spigot mortar position at the Levenhall end of the course
Lanark	JC	20.9.41	24.9.45	11th	In army occupation 29.5.40 to October 1940. RAF use from 5.4.41 until at least 1.12.43
Newbury	NH	23.3.40	28.11.51	71st	In varying degrees of military occupation from late 1939. Still available for racing June 1942 but no
	JC	20.9.41	1.4.49		meetings were allowed. US Army depot from later in 1942 and covered by 35 miles of rail sidings.
Ripon	JC	27.9.41	10.7.46	49th	In varying degrees of military occupation from at least March 1940, but racing continued alongside it. Further meetings banned by government February 1942. Became POW Camp No 121.
Thirsk	JC	4.10.41	3.5.46	35th	In military occupation early 1940 and again from late 1942 / early 1943 until February 1945.
Manchester	NH	30.11.40 (1.1.41)	1.1.47	47th	Bombed 22.12.40. Potentially available for racing until after July 1942. Used for ammunition storage
	JC	16.11.41	13.6.46		and later by the US Army.
Southwell	NH	13.12.41 (24.1.42)	16.11.45	17th	Requisitioned by RAF in 1942. Used as a storage depot and ground interception station.
Nottingham	JC	11.10.41	22.4.46	18th	Army units were on the course from July 1940 to January 1941 but remained potentially available for
	NH	20.12.41 (28.2.42)	8.2.46		racing until July 1942. Still requisitioned in August 1945.

Worcester	JC NH	25.10.41 10.1.42 (7.3.42)	19.10.45 23.11.45	13th	Liable to flooding and never occupied by the military. Repossessed by the City Council in late 1943 after the racecourse company went into liquidation
Cheltenham	NH	21.3.42	6.1.45	5th	Some agricultural use. Brief military occupation July / August 1940.
Wetherby	NH	21.3.42	17.2.45 (26.12.44)	7th	Temporary military occupation in spring 1940.
Newmarket (July)	JC	None			Racing continued uninterrupted except in periods of general suspension.
Salisbury	JC	None			Racing continued uninterrupted except in periods of general suspension.

APPENDIX 6

COURSES AND MEETINGS AT NEWMARKET

The Newmarket racecourses are on the gently rolling grassland of the Heath. This is divided by The Ditch (not a ditch but a Dark Ages boundary bank), of which the July Course, the only one used during the war, is on the side further from the town.

This is L shaped, with both legs a mile long and the finish at the top of the "upright" one. From the "horizontal" leg, on which the longer races start and which is also used for some finishing on the Rowley Mile, the course turns ninety degrees right, onto the July Course proper, to run parallel with The Ditch without crossing it. The full length of this part is the Bunbury Mile, undulating at first but falling markedly into the dip just over a quarter of a mile from the end, only to rise sharply again for the final furlong.

There once were numerous winning posts on the various courses, dating from when most spectators were mounted, which allowed races with a variety of challenges to be devised, and at the time covered by this book there were two on the July Course. The main one was at the end of the Bunbury Mile, and the other a furlong short, in the bottom of the dip, catering for races with downhill finishes.

The individual courses finishing at the main winning post were the Summer Course (2 miles 24 yards) and the last 1 mile 6 furlongs 150 yards of it, which was used for the St. Leger; the Suffolk Stakes Course (a mile and a half), which was used for the Derby and Oaks, and the last mile and a quarter of it; the Bunbury Mile and races over the last seven, six and five furlongs of it (the last being known as the

Chesterfield Course). Wartime two and a quarter mile races were run by starting on an abandoned section of the course beyond the two-mile start.

The courses finishing in the dip were the Ellesmere Stakes Course (1 mile 3 furlongs, from the Suffolk Stakes start), and the last 1 mile 1 furlong of it (starting from the mile and a quarter post); the Beaufort Course (seven furlongs, from the Bunbury Mile start), the Exeter Course (six furlongs, from the seven furlong start), the New Two-Year-Old Course (5 furlongs 140 yards from a post used for no other races), and the last five furlongs of it (starting from the six furlong post).

Spring and autumn racing in peacetime has always been on the Rowley Mile Course, with only summer meetings on the July Course, where the going is easier in dry weather. Until the war there were three meetings (Craven, First and Second Spring) in April and May, the First and Second July meetings, and three between late September and early November (First and Second October and Houghton). Always beginning on Tuesdays, most were four days and the rest three.

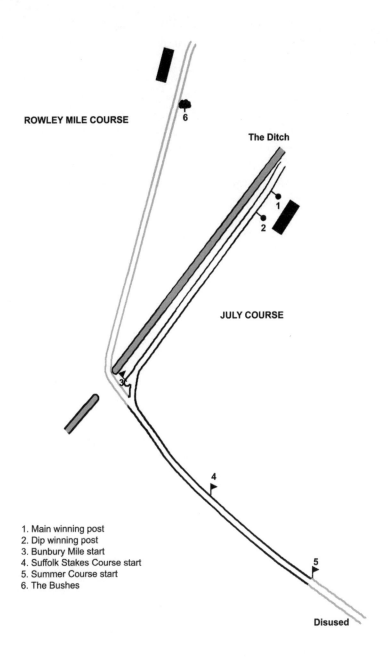

ROWLEY MILE COURSE

The Ditch

JULY COURSE

1. Main winning post
2. Dip winning post
3. Bunbury Mile start
4. Suffolk Stakes Course start
5. Summer Course start
6. The Bushes

Disused

BIBLIOGRAPHY

John Betteridge, *Born to Deal* (Matador 2005)
Philip Birtles, *World War 2 Airfields* (Ian Allan 1999)
Asa Briggs, *Go To It!* (Mitchell Beazley 2000)
Mike Brown, *Christmas on the Home Front* (Sutton 2004)
John Budden, *The Boss* (Mainstream 2000)
Dan Burglass, *Ken Oliver: The Benign Bishop* (Marlborough 1994)
Mark Connelly, *We Can Take It!* (Pearson Education 2004)
Grenville Davies, *A Touch of Colwick* (Pride of Place 1994)
Steve Donoghue, *Just My Story* (Hutchinson 1923)
Tim Fitzgeorge Parker, *The Ditch on the Hill* (Simon & Schuster 1991)
John Galsworthy, *The Man of Property* (Heinemann 1906)
John Galsworthy, *Swan Song* (Heinemann 1928)
Peter Gill, *Cheltenham's Racing Heroes* (Sutton 1998)
Juliet Gardiner, *Wartime Britain* (Headline 2004)
Edward Gillespie, [article in] *Kempton Park 1878-1978* (United
  Racecourses 1978)
Clive Graham, *Kempton Park* (Reid Hamilton 1950)
Reg Green, *The History of the Grand National*
(Hodder & Stoughton 1993)
John F.Hamlin, *The Royal Air Force at Newmarket 1939-1947* (1985)
David Hedges, *Mr Grand National* (Pelham 1969)
John Hislop, *Anything But A Soldier* (Michael Joseph 1965)
John Hislop, *Far From A Gentleman* (Michael Joseph 1960)
Mike Huggins, *Horseracing and the British* (2005)
Michael King, *The 1940s Revisited* (Finial 2002)
David Kynaston, *Austerity Britain 1945-51* (Bloomsbury 2007)
Pat Lucas, *Fifty Years of Racing at Chepstow* (H.G.Walters 1976)

The Hon.George Lambton, *Men and Horses I Have Known*
(J.A.Allen 1924)

Derrick Mercer (ed.), *Chronicle of the 20th Century* (Longman 1988)

Russell & Renate Miller, *Ten Days in May* (Michael Joseph 1995)

Naomi Mitchinson (ed. Dorothy Sherwin), *Among You Taking Notes*
(Victor Gollancz 1985)

Roger Mortimer, Richard Onslow & Peter Willett, *Biographical
Encyclopaedia of British Flat Racing* (Macdonald & James 1978)

Roger Mortimer & Peter Willett, *More Great Racehorses of the World*
(Michael Joseph 1972)

Roger Mortimer, *The Flat* (George Allen & Unwin 1979)

Roger Munting, *Hedges and Hurdles* (J.A.Allen 1987)

Donal Murray, *Great Southern Railways* (Ian Allen 2006)

Jeremy Paxman, *The Political Animal* (Michael Joseph 2002)

Chris Pitt & Chas Hammond, *When Birmingham Went Racing*
(CC Publishing 2005)

Chris Pitt, *A Long Time Gone* (Portway Press 1996)

Robert Rhodes James, *A Spirit Undaunted: The Political Role of George
VI* (Little, Brown & Co 1998)

Gordon Richards, *My Story* (Hodder & Stoughton 1955)

Eric Rickman, *On and off the Racecourse* (Routledge 1937)

Anton Rippon, *Gas Masks for Goal Posts* (Sutton 2005)

C.G.Roberts & B.L.Jackson, *Trams and Buses of Poole*
(Oakwood Press 2001)

C.I.Savage, *Inland Transport (History of the Second World War: UK Civil
Series)* (HMSO and Longman, Green & Co. 1957)

Michael Seth Smith, *The Head Waiter* (Michael Joseph 1984)

Michael Seth Smith, Peter Willett, Roger Mortimer & John
Lawrence, *The History of Steeplechasing* (Michael Joseph 1966)

Charlie Smirke, *Finishing Post* (Oldbourne 1960)

Doug Smith (with Peter Willett), *Five Times Champion* (Pelham 1968)

Michael Tanner & Gerry Cranham, *Great Jockeys of the Flat*
(Crowood Press 1989)

Michael Tanner, *The Champion Hurdle* (Pelham 1989)

A.J.P.Taylor, English History 1914-1945
(Oxford University Press 1965)

Patrick Taylor, *The West Clare Railway* (Plateway Press 1994)

John Tyrell, *Racecourses on the Flat* (Crowood Press 1989)

John Tyrell, *Running Racing* (Quiller 1997)

Peter Unwin, *The Narrow Sea* (Headline 2003)

John Welcome, *The Cheltenham Gold Cup* (Pelham 1984)

Peter Willett, *An Introduction to the Thoroughbred* (Stanley Paul 1966)

Peter Willett, *The Story of Tattersalls* (Stanley Paul 1987)

David Wragg, *The Southern Railway Handbook 1923-1947* (Sutton 2003)

David Wragg, *Wartime on the Railways* (Sutton 2006)

Kenneth Young, *Harry Lord Rosebery* (Hodder & Stoughton 1974)

Newspapers, periodicals and annuals

Bloodstock Breeders Review

Daily Express

Daily Herald

Daily Mail

Gloucestershire Echo

Manchester Guardian

Raceform

Racing Calendar Races Past

Racing Calendar Steeplechases Past

Racing Post

Sporting Chronicle Horses in Training

Sporting Chronicle Racing Up To Date

The Sporting Life

The Times

INDEX

Horses

255

257